SOCIAL SKILLS ACTIVITIES

for

Special Children

Darlene Mannix

Prentice
Hall

THE CENTER FOR APPLIED RESEARCH IN EDUCATION
West Nyack, New York 10994

Library of Congress Cataloging-in-Publication Data

Mannix, Darlene.
   Social skills activities for special children / Darlene Mannix:
illustrated by Tim Mannix.
      p.   cm.
   ISBN 0-87628-868-9
   1. Developmentally disabled children—United States—Life skills
guides.   2. Developmentally disabled children—Education
(Elementary)—United States.   3. Life skills—Studying and teaching
(Elementary)—United States.   4. Social skills—Study and teaching
I. Title.
   HV894.M37   1993   93-12222
   362.1'968—dc20   CIP

Printed in the United States of America

15   14

For my best friend,
Karen Iseminger

ISBN 0-87628-868-9

THE CENTER FOR APPLIED RESEARCH
IN EDUCATION
West Nyack, NY 10994

On the World Wide Web at http://www.phdirect.com

ABOUT THIS BOOK

Social Skills Activities for Special Children is a collection of lessons, activities, and ideas designed to help elementary children with special needs become aware of acceptable social behavior and to help them develop proficiency in acquiring basic social skills.

For special children, the social component of school is as important as the academic aspect. Skills such as getting along with others, making friends, and developing a pleasant personality are life-long endeavors for many students. Some students have a lot of difficulty following rules, remembering rules, and even being aware that rules exist in certain situations. Yet these are all part of fitting into society—for all people, not just special students. While most children may breeze through social situations with a minimum of instruction, special children typically lack some of these social skills. They are often the target of children who are intolerant, who tease, and who demonstrate poor social manners, training in appropriate school behavior, and compliance with expectations, but special children in particular may need the special, directed teaching to become aware of social skills and how to be a good member of society.

As with academics, teaching social skills subjects itself to using methods that will work in a teacher's classroom. Social skills training is becoming popular enough and important enough that classroom time is devoted regularly in many classrooms to the training and practice of these skills. School itself is the major focus of social life for many students, and it is there that students hopefully will learn to get along with other students; follow the directions of a teacher; solve problems in logical, peaceful ways; and develop friendships. It is also at school that students learn to fight, to tease others, and to manipulate situations to get their way. It would seem, then, that school is a good place to work on the development of social skills, both personally and for cooperation within a group.

The purpose of *Social Skills Activities for Special Children* is two-fold. First of all, it is a tool for you to use to guide your students in thinking about social skills and why they are important. Through questions and discussion, you can involve the students in evaluating the necessity of each social skill. Second, it provides a hands-on activity for students to work through, think about, discuss, and practice in or outside of the classroom. What works in one classroom may not work in another; one group of students may respond entirely different than another. But through the expression of ideas and listening to others' ideas (social skills in themselves!), students are exposed to models of ideal or appropriate social skills. Ultimately, the choice of behavior is up to the student, but creating an *awareness* of the skill and opportunity to *practice* the skill are both steps towards the likelihood of the student *using* the skill appropriately.

The activities are targeted for elementary special children, although any elementary classroom teacher or counselor may find something useful among the lessons. Several portions are directed to parents for teaching or reinforcing skills at home. The lessons can be adapted, expanded, or combined to suit many types of situations.

Contents

The book is divided into three major sections with a total of 142 individual lessons. Each lesson contains (1) an objective that can be modified to fit specific classroom needs, (2) a rationale of why the skill is important or needed, (3) several thinking questions that the students are to discuss to help direct thoughts towards problem solving and draw upon past experiences, (4) an activity page for hands-on working through of problem situations, and (5) ideas for follow-up after completing the activity.

Special Features: Eleven *parent letters* are included to precede the use of the main parts of the book. These can be reproduced to send home to parents to increase their awareness of what will be discussed in school. These letters contain ideas for helping to reinforce the ideas at home.

Classroom ideas for each section are listed with references to corresponding skills in the workbook. These can be worked on in the classroom to extend experience with the skill taught.

Finally, three original *stories* featuring characters who are in the process of developing appropriate social skills are available for you to read aloud to the class. Children love to be read to! Students who may be fighting and arguing one minute in the classroom somehow manage to quiet down to hear a story and look at the pictures while the teacher is reading.

The Sections

... Section I is about *Accepting Rules and Authority at School.* The 52 lessons in Section I deal with the student as a member of a school group, particularly having to interact with teachers and other adults within the school and following school rules that affect their behavior. The story is *Mrs. Tryit's Ideas,* about a teacher who becomes very frustrated with her class's inability to walk down the hall correctly, so she devises some unusual training techniques.

- Part I—"Understanding the Teacher's Role." This part has lessons that help the student understand the teacher as a classroom leader and as a person who deserves respect and obedience.

- Part II—"Classroom Rules and Responsibilities." This covers skills that are typical of most classrooms, such as paying attention to the task, sitting appropriately, and complying with rules that are conducive to learning.

- Part III—"Other Authority Figures." Adults other than teachers are part of the school structure and also deserve respect and polite behavior from students. This includes the principal, substitute, guests, and the bus driver.

- Part IV—"When You Have Problems." There are reasons why students have problems getting along with authority figures. This part helps students seek alternative methods of coping with difficult situations at school. Lessons include getting yourself organized, accepting the blame for problems, and asking for help appropriately.

... Section II is entitled *Relating to Peers*. The 30 lessons in Section II focus on the student as a member of a peer group, at school, home, or in the community. Here the student is considered as part of a larger group, as someone who must relate to others and their needs. The corresponding story is *Ralph and His Purple Face,* about a boy who learns to ignore the teasing of his classmates and eventually displays some desirable qualities.

- Part I—"Learning and Working with Others." This part examines the student's role in relationship to other students in the classroom. Lessons stress being a cooperative member of a group as well as refraining from bothering other classroom members.

- Part II—"Making Friends." These lessons show students ways to make themselves inviting to others without being overbearing. Skills such as helping others, being a good listener, and learning to say nice things about others are included.

- Part III—"Keeping Friends." More friendship skills are examined in this part, including keeping promises, sharing a friend with other people, and recognizing that a true friend is not someone who would try to get you in trouble.

... Section III focuses on *Developing Positive Social Skills*. These 60 lessons deal with the student as a positive force, taking control of his or her actions to successfully cope with daily situations and learning to recognize social situations as such and to make good choices for what to do in these situations. The story for this section, *The Accident,* is about two girls (one very assertive, the other overly passive) who collide on the swings at school and exchange personalities for a few days.

- Part I—"Understanding Social Situations Correctly." These lessons help students with skills such as determining the moods of others; deciding on the appropriateness of the time, place, and people involved before acting; and reading facial features of others as clues to the person's behavior.

- Part II—"Positive Personality Attributes." The development of a nice, pleasing personality is the ultimate goal of these lessons that discuss patience, being a leader, complimenting others, being organized, and other useful skills.

- Part III—"Getting Along with Others at Home." There are similarities between accepting a parent as an authority figure and accepting a teacher as such; likewise, peers and siblings both can cause friction and the need for compromise in getting through daily tasks. These lessons allow the student to think through and express feelings about getting along with people who are part of life, but not necessarily at school.

- Part IV—"Everyday Etiquette." Good manners and simply knowing the "proper" things to do in everyday social situations are life-long skills that set people apart from the crowd. Being well-mannered and socially adept by demonstrating skills such as having good table manners, refraining from gossiping, and being considerate of others in public places are characteristics of the kind of student we all wish we had in class!

Darlene Mannix

ABOUT THE AUTHOR

DARLENE MANNIX has taught emotionally handicapped, language disordered, learning disabled, and multiply handicapped students.

Ms. Mannix received her Bachelor of Science degree from Taylor University and her Master's degree in Learning Disabilities from Indiana University. She is a member of the Council for Exceptional Children and has addressed CEC conventions in Virginia and Illinois.

She is the author of *Oral Language Activities for Special Children* (The Center, 1987), *Be a Better Student: Lessons and Worksheets for Teaching Behavior Management in Grades 4-9* (The Center, 1989), and *Life Skills Activities for Special Children* (The Center, 1991), as well as *I Can Behave: A Classroom Self-management Curriculum for Elementary Students* (ASIEP Education Company of Portland, Oregon, 1986) and *Sight Word Stories and Seatwork Activities* (Remedia Publications, 1988).

CONTENTS

I

Accepting Rules

and Authority

at School

Every one of us has to follow rules and submit to some sort of authority figure. We pay our taxes (maybe not cheerfully ...), meet with the boss, drive our cars close to the speed limit, and probably feel a little nervous when we go past a police officer. Rules are a necessary part of life (think of the alternative!), and people to enforce and make rules are needed to make sure that changes make sense.

We, as adults, are always role-models for our children. We are making impressions on them as we comment, "Our mayor/congressman/president doesn't know what he's talking about," or "Hey, I got out of paying that fine!" But probably one of the most difficult situations is when students hear one set of rules at school and another at home, putting them in a difficult situation when it comes to knowing what to do. Mutual respect for teachers and parents is crucial for a child. The more supportive home and school systems can be of each other, the better for the child who lives in both. It is hard when a child tells his or her teacher that Dad says the assignment is stupid, or Mom thinks the school is unfair. Teachers, too, need to be careful of criticizing the home environment, especially in front of a child.

Section I is about the need for rules and structure in a classroom or school setting, and establishing a relationship of trust and obedience to the authority figures there. The story for this section is *Mrs. Tryit's Ideas,* about a frustrated, but creative teacher whose pupils have difficulty following the simple rules of walking down the hall in a line. Mrs. Tryit just keeps plugging away, making more and more ridiculous steps to help the students walk down the hall until the students are tired of all the trappings required to complete this simple request and finally just do it. The students were capable; they just needed to accept the rule and comply. It was harder to misbehave than to behave.

As teachers, we are not trying to form unthinking, boring little beings who never have a divergent thought; but we do need to channel the energy, the creativity, and the motivation of our students into more meaningful behaviors than looking for lost pencils, finding new excuses for lost homework, and hanging on the teacher while whining about who is doing what to whom. Hopefully, this section will give you some ideas for controlling classroom behavior and give students some insights into how to have a happier school life!

In Section I, "Accepting Rules and Authority at School," you will find:

- Parent Letters 1 through 4

- Classroom Ideas

- "Mrs. Tryit's Ideas" *(story)*

- Part I: Understanding the Teacher's Role *(activities)*

- Part II: Classroom Rules and Responsibilities *(activities)*

- Part III: Other Authority Figures *(activities)*

- Part IV: When You Have Problems *(activities)*

PARENT LETTER #1

**RE: Accepting Rules and Authority
at School—Understanding the Teacher's Role**

Dear Parents,

We will be starting a course of study about learning social skills. The first section deals with lessons involving rules and authority at school.

The first set of lessons involves understanding the teacher's role. The teacher is more than just a person who engineers the learning of a lot of content and skills; he or she cares about the needs and interests of each student. Though your child may encounter teachers through the school years who are more or less to his or her liking, the teacher is a very important individual. These lessons try to acquaint the student with some of the aspects of being a teacher.

Here are some ways that you can help reinforce these ideas at home:

- Ask your child to tell you about the rules at school. Why are they necessary?

- Talk about the teacher—in a positive way! What are his or her interests? Can you help make the teacher a human being for your child?

- Handle conflicts with the teacher in an upfront, positive manner—not in front of your child. Remember that there are two sides to every story. Before you become upset, call the school and find out what's going on if you are concerned. Information can be misrepresented. Find out the facts.

- Reinforce respect for the teacher. Our lessons will focus on treating the teacher politely, being trustworthy, and allowing the teacher to do his or her job as smoothly as possible.

Sincerely,

_____

Teacher

**RE: Accepting Rules and Authority
at School—Classroom Rules and Responsibilities**

Dear Parents,

Our next unit of study for social skills involves following classroom rules and taking seriously the responsibility of being a student—and all that that implies—while at school. Rules are a necessary part of life for efficient functioning. Hopefully, the rules will make sense and contribute to a good learning environment.

Some of the lessons in this part include working independently, entering and leaving the classroom quietly and mannerly, following instructions, being a good listener, bringing homework to school, and completing assignments.

You can help your child with these skills by:

- Discussing specific classroom rules. What is important in your child's classroom? Does the child KNOW the rules?

- Watching out for homework or other assignments that come home each day. Is your child prepared to finish them independently? If you don't dig through the backpack or pockets, would the homework be shown to you?

- Request that your child enter and leave the rooms of your house in a quiet, mannerly way. Although the house is a different building and environment than the classroom at school, it is similar to that running, pushing, or destroying things are not appropriate behaviors at either place.

Sincerely,

_____

Teacher

RE: Accepting Rules and Authority at School—Other Authority Figures

Dear Parents,

Besides the classroom teacher, other individuals are at school to help your child learn and help keep school a safe place to be. Other people who will be (or are) authority figures at school include: the principal, other teachers, the bus driver, the counselor, and substitute teachers. We hope that our children will be respectful to these adults as well.

Here are some ideas to keep in mind:

- When you know there will be a substitute teacher in class, go over your expectations for good behavior with your child. This is not the time to write off the day as babysitting. Inform your child to be as cooperative and helpful as possible.

- If you are upset with the principal or other administrators, discuss your concerns with them—not your children.

- You may not agree with the decisions made for your children by the adults in school, but first try to understand. You can negotiate better by understanding the position of the other side.

- The bus driver does not have an easy job. He or she must have control to ensure a safe ride for the children. If your child becomes unruly or uncooperative on the bus, discuss the consequences with him or her.

- Be a good role-model yourself. Show respect for people who have authority over you. Your boss, city officials, the police department— your attitude towards them conveys your respect.

Sincerely,

_____

Teacher

PARENT LETTER #4

RE: Accepting Rules and Authority at School—When You Have Problems

Dear Parents,

Everyone experiences difficulties at some time. One of the coping strategies we want our children to understand is that there are resources and techniques available to them to help them get through their difficulties.

The lessons in this series include defining the problem, asking for help, looking harder at the problem, avoiding excuses, using a peer-tutor, keeping an assignment notebook, doing homework, and seeking out adults or friends who can help.

YOU are a resource for your child when he or she is facing a problem. Keep in mind:

- Talk to your child every day. Find out what's bugging him or her. What happened at school? Are things going okay? Keep in touch.

- Let your child know that you care about him or her. Spend time together, even if it is just by washing the dishes together or waxing the car.

- Listen. Can you let your child talk for one entire minute without interrupting?

- Encourage your child to talk to the school counselor, his or her teacher, a respected adult, or an older student whom you trust. It may be difficult for a child to open up to you, but it might be easier after bouncing some ideas off other people. Maybe you are too close to the problem. Don't shut off other avenues for your child to get some help.

Sincerely,

_____

Teacher

CLASSROOM IDEAS FOR SECTION I
Accepting Rules and Authority at School

Part I. Understanding the Teacher's Role

- For a writing assignment, give students these titles: If I Were the Teacher for a Day ... , School Rules I Could Live Without, or When I Become a Parent, I'm Going to ... **(I-1, 2)**

- Allow volunteer students to teach a fairly easy task or short lesson to the class. Afterwards, discuss how it was hard/easy/fun and how you would evaluate learning. **(I-3)**

- Have students write instructions for making or doing something (but don't give the answer). Just by reading the instructions out loud, can you figure out what the task is? **(I-6)**

- Leave the room periodically, allowing students a chance to control their own behavior. Have students take turns being "in charge" to handle questions, visitors, etc. Sometimes the most disruptive child does a complete turnaround when he or she is empowered to be the one with the responsibility. **(I-7, 8)**

- Have students role-play ways to get the teacher's attention. **(I-9)**

- For constant complainers/arguers, pretend to put on "ear muffs." Take them "off" when the student is ready to discuss the matter calmly. **(I-10, 11)**

- Have a signal for the class to know when you need them to listen. It may be tapping something with a pencil, clearing your throat, or simply saying, "Time to listen." Be consistent with your cue. No one can be in a state of perpetual listening—let them know *when* you need their undivided attention. **(I-12)**

Part II. Classroom Rules and Responsibilities

- Allow the students time to talk. Perhaps you can sandwich these "breaks" in between quiet activities or before they go outside for recess. Knowing that they can expect five minutes at a certain time each day might help them store up those conversations that they desire for the right time. **(II-2)**

- Some students work better with complete quiet. Others function better with noise, music, or movement. Allow students (as far as possible) to work in the way they work best. If it doesn't bother you or other students, permit them sometimes to work with the lights dimmed, the window open, sitting on the floor, etc. **(II-8)**

- Some students who crave attention may benefit from being applauded by the class. Select one student each day who, when he or she enters the room, gets a standing ovation. **(II-10)**

- For students who have to leave in the middle of class (for special classes or whatever), develop a quiet signal acknowledging that he or she has permission to leave. If possible, let that student have a seat close to the door so leaving is convenient. **(II-11)**

- Change line leaders periodically so everyone has a turn and everyone knows his or her turn will come. Avoid fighting over who gets to go first. **(II-13)**

- If your line spreads out and you have stragglers, designate certain "stopping points" throughout your journey. The line leader must stop at the point and wait for everyone to catch up before continuing. **(II-13)**

- Display students' best papers, tests, and projects prominently in the classroom. Explain the difference between a "first draft" or "rough planning" and the final product. **(II-15)**

- Reward students who have been faithful at bringing in homework by a special night in which ONLY they do not have any homework. Or, assign a silly homework assignment for that night, such as eating an ice cream cone or watching a television show. **(II-16)**

- Allow students breaks to rest their minds, let them daydream. Sometimes just resting their heads on the desk, walking around the room, or shutting down for a few minutes can give them a fresh start. **(II-18)**

- Have lunch in the classroom and class in the cafeteria one day. Does it really matter what is done in each room when it comes to appropriate behavior? **(II-20)**

Part III. Other Authority Figures

- Have a special box, game, or surprise for the students, that only the substitute is allowed to distribute. Make sure students know that at a certain time during the day, if their behavior has been appropriate, they will have a surprise. **(III-1)**

- When it is your assistant's birthday, arrange to have a surprise party. The students will enjoy planning and carrying out the event. Make sure all students sign a card, perhaps including nice comments or funny remarks. **(III-2)**

- Get to know your principal! Invite him or her in for a special activity, or if time allows, have him or her listen to your students read a story. Some classes enjoy having lunch with the principal (either in the cafeteria or a "feast" in the classroom). **(III-3)**

- Invite the school secretary in as a special guest speaker and have him or her share with your class some anecdotes about what it's REALLY like to work in the office. What are the funniest excuses he or she has heard? What were the wildest moments? **(III-4)**

- Make a bulletin board featuring other teachers in your school. Include a display showing their interests, hobbies, awards, other jobs, etc. Have some leading questions on the board, such as: Which teacher tried skydiving? Who has four dogs? **(III-5)**

- Plan to have guest speakers periodically to visit your class. This will give your class practice in asking questions, listening to speakers, and material for students to write about afterwards. Have students come up with a list of ten questions that they would like to ask the speaker. (This will also give the guest speaker some idea of the interests of your class.) **(III-7)**

- Before going on a field trip, go over the DO's and DO NOT's of what to expect from the field trip helpers. For example, DO NOT beg for money; DO NOT wander off alone; DO stay where you can see your leader at all times, etc. Field trips can be fun, or they can be a real hassle. If you're lucky enough to have volunteer helpers, make sure that students realize how important they are to ensure future trips! **(III-9)**

- Invite your school counselor (if you have one—the principal may do double-duty) to visit your class and explain what "services" are available for students. Some schools have little groups that meet to discuss divorce, homework help, peer-tutoring, how to improve grades, etc. **(III-10)**

Part IV. When You Have Problems

- Use magazine pictures of faces showing various emotions. What problem might each person be thinking about? Have students make cartoons showing what the person could be thinking. **(IV-1)**

- Make posters emphasizing the techniques discussed for help with problem solving. Let students work in groups—one does the art work, one can do the lettering, etc. Display the posters around the room or in the hallway. **(IV-3, 4)**

- Give peer-tutoring a try. If you can find a few older-grade students who can work with minimal supervision, have a half-hour set aside for the students to mix and work on fairly straightforward tasks, such as drilling on math flash cards, playing "fish" with word cards, working together on writing and illustrating a story, etc. Problems to watch for: students who try to take advantage of their tutors (have them sit out the next session), not being clear on task directions for the tutors (write out specifically what the task is), or having too lengthy of a session (limit it to 20-30 minutes). **(IV-6)**

- When you give an assignment that extends over a day or routinely assign homework, write it succinctly in a certain place on the board each day. That way, the students will look for it, will copy it the same way, and will have no excuse for not knowing what the task was. **(IV-7, 8)**

- There are many helpful people in a child's life. Have each student compile a small book containing pictures of friends, family members, helpful adults at school, etc., with several paragraphs written by the student telling about the person. **(IV-9)**

Mrs. Tryit's Ideas

Mrs. Tryit's class just could not walk down the hall in a line.

Oh, they started out pretty well, but soon the students had all kinds of problems.

No matter how often they started out looking like this. . .

. . .it was only a matter of minutes until the line looked like this.

Sometimes somebody would walk a little too fast and would step on the heels of the person in front of him or her.

Or somebody would walk too slowly and everyone behind would pile up like a traffic jam.

One or two people always got out of line and had to fight to get back in.

And little Sheldon Shufflesnout just could not stop looking in every classroom that they passed along the way and give a friendly wave to the people inside.

The teacher, Mrs. Tryit, always had an idea or two to try.

First, she went to the supply room, got some black paint and a brush, and painted footsteps all the way down the hall for the students to follow. This way, she thought, they wouldn't walk all over the hall, but would go exactly where they were supposed to go.

So, five minutes before they had to go down the hall, the students had to take off their shoes so they wouldn't scrape the paint off the floor.

But there were still problems. The students kept switching places while they were walking. No one could remember where they were supposed to be.

But Mrs. Tryit had an idea.

Mrs. Tryit gave every child a number that was to be taped on his or her back as the students left the room.

"No changing places," she said. "You have to stay in this order."

So 10 minutes before it was time to go down the hall, the class took off their shoes and got their number cards.

But there were still problems. Some people in the class walked too fast and were always bumping into other people.

But Mrs. Tryit had an idea.

She went to a used car lot on her lunch break and got some old tires. Each student wore one so that if someone behind him or her walked too fast, the jolt would not be too hard.

So, 15 minutes before it was time to go down the hall, the class took off their shoes, got their number cards, and put on their tires.

But there were still problems. Some people walked too slowly and couldn't keep up with the others.

But Mrs. Tryit had an idea.

She had a friend who used to work in a circus, training elephants. She borrowed the leg chains that they used to keep the elephants together. When all of the chains were in place, the students could stay together.

So, 20 minutes before it was time to go down the hall, the students took off their shoes, got their number cards, put on their tires, and waited for Mrs. Tryit to attach the leg chains.

But there was one more problem. As the class walked down the hall, they kept looking into classrooms, restrooms, and any kind of can, box, or desk that they passed.

But Mrs. Tryit had an idea.

She lived next door to Farmer Fred who had some draft horses that pulled a big cart at the county fair. He put big black blinders on the horses' heads so they could only look straight ahead - not to the right or to the left. Mrs. Tryit asked if she could borrow some.

So 25 minutes before it was time to go down the hall, the students took off their shoes, got their number cards, put on their tires, waited for Mrs. Tryit to attach the leg chains, and put on their blinders.

Now, finally, the class was able to walk down the hall with no problems.

Did I say no problems?

It took the class so long to get ready to go anywhere, that by the time they got to where they were going, they had to turn right around and go back.

Some days they had to eat lunch while they were still walking in the hall.

And the day of the fire drill it took them so long to get their things together that Mrs. Tryit just told them to jump out of the window and not tell anyone.

Finally, the students had had enough. They looked at Mrs. Tryit, got down on their knees, and begged: "Mrs. Tryit - this is all just too much trouble! We'll walk right from now on! Give us a chance!"

Mrs. Tryit smiled. "I think we're all ready to give it a try," she said. "Open the back closet and let's toss everything in."

Now the class has no problems at all walking down the hall anymore. No one has missed lunch in a long time and fire drills are back to normal. In fact, once someone commented that Mrs. Tryit's class was the fastest and quietest down the hall!

If the class ever forgets and starts to push or shove or walk a little too fast or too slowly, all Mrs. Tryit has to do is go to the back closet and start to stir up the black paint a little bit.

I-1 AN INTERVIEW WITH A TEACHER

Objective:

The student will identify at least three characteristics (behavioral, physical, and nature) of a favorite teacher.

Rationale:

There are as many different "kinds" of teachers as there are teachers! You can't put them into a mold, because each is an individual with different strengths, interests, and personalities. By interviewing a teacher, the student will become aware of the differing characteristics of teachers.

Thinking Questions:

1. Are all teachers exactly alike? *(no)*
2. How are they different? *(some are mean, some are men, some are lots of fun, etc.)*
3. Why do you think people want to become teachers? *(they like kids, they enjoy helping others, they like summers off!)*
4. Can you think of ways to describe your favorite teacher? *(fun, helpful, etc.)*
5. Would you like to become a teacher someday? Why/why not?

Activity:

Directions: Have students select a teacher who would be willing to be interviewed. Help students arrange a time and place for the interview. You may want to add questions or have the student think of additional points that would be interesting to find out about the teacher.

Follow-up: Have students share their findings with the class. Did they find any teachers who disliked children? What did they discover that was interesting about a particular teacher? What did most of the teachers like/dislike about teaching?

I-1

An Interview with a Teacher

Teacher: _____ Subject or Class: _____

Questions

1. Why did you go into teaching? _____

   _____

2. What do you like best about teaching? _____

   _____

3. What don't you like about teaching? _____

   _____

4. How would you describe yourself as a person? _____

   _____

5. What are some things that you do in your spare time? _____

   _____

6. Do you have a family/children/pets? _____

   _____

7. _____

8. _____

9. _____

10. _____

Section I

I-2 HOME RULES VS. SCHOOL RULES

Objective:

The student will differentiate between rules that are applicable at school, at home, or applicable to either place.

Rationale:

Students often operate under different sets of rules—home rules and school rules, for example. It is important for a student to realize that some rules are appropriate for both settings, and other rules may only apply to a specific situation. The child needs to have a means to understand what he or she is expected to do in each situation, if the rules are not the same. For example, if a child's parents have told him or her that fighting is all right to settle differences, but fighting is against the rules at school, the child must understand that school rules prevail while at school.

Thinking Questions:

1. What are some rules that you have to follow at home?
2. What are some school rules? *(no running in the hall, do your work, etc.)*
3. Are there any rules that are the same for both places? *(don't argue, clean up your mess, etc.)*
4. Can you think of some rules that might be different? *(rules that apply to bedtime, personal activities, etc.)*
5. Why do you think there are so many rules? *(to help keep things running smoothly, so everyone does things the same way, etc.)*

Activity:

Directions: Have students complete the worksheet about home and school rules. Tell students not to "stretch" each situation to make both answers fit (e.g., "Don't tease your baby brother" would be a home rule, because a baby would probably not be at school in a typical situation), but to think about the most typical situation.

Answers:	1. H	3. S	5. H,S	7. S	9. S
	2. S	4. H,S	6. H	8. H	10. H,S

Follow-up: Discuss why the example rules may have been necessary. Why are some rules good for almost all occasions? *(They refer to treating people with respect.)* Focus on why teachers may have different rules to enforce than parents.

Home Rules vs. School Rules

Write 'H' if this sounds like a Home rule; write 'S' if this sounds like a School rule. Some rules might be both 'H' and 'S', so think carefully!

1. Make your bed!! _____

2. Put your name at the top of your paper. _____

3. Raise your hand to talk. _____

4. Don't interrupt when someone else is talking.

   _____

5. Take off your coat and hang it up when you come in.

   _____

6. Ask before you invite your friends to play.

   _____

7. Keep your feet under your desk. _____

8. Don't tease your little baby brother. _____

9. Don't take pencils off the teacher's desk.

   _____

10. Don't throw food at other people.

    _____

I-3 EVERYONE LEARNS IN DIFFERENT WAYS

Objective:

The student will identify several different learning styles exemplified by characters.

Rationale:

Although students will often find themselves lumped together in a group or class, they should realize that students (like teachers) are individuals and have individual needs. The purpose of this lesson is to create an awareness of individual differences in learning. This is something that a teacher must deal with, and it is helpful for a student to have that awareness.

Thinking Questions:

1. What is something that you learned how to do in the past few weeks? *(answers will vary)*

2. How did you learn to do it? *(someone taught them, they read a book, etc.)*

3. Do you think everyone learns to do things the same way? *(no)*

4. Why do you think it is harder for some people to learn? *(not physically able to do something, need more practice, etc.)*

5. If someone wanted to teach you how to draw a horse, what are some ways he or she might go about doing that? *(get a real horse to watch, trace a picture, work on drawing one part, etc.)*

Activity:

Directions: Read the directions to students from the worksheet. They are to figure out which of the four students who are making cakes match the style of learning stated at the top.

   Answers: 1. Dana   2. John   3. Max   4. Carol

Follow-up: The example on the worksheet involved making a cake, but what are other examples of tasks that can be completed in a variety of ways? *(learning to read, memorizing spelling words, etc.)* What are some ways to help learn something that students can use or have used? Why is it helpful for a student to know what strategies are helpful for him- or herself?

Everyone Learns in Different Ways

Each of these students is trying to learn how to make a cake, but they are learning in different ways. See if you can match the name of each student with the picture by using the clues given below.

JOHN is learning to make a cake by reading a recipe.

CAROL is learning by listening to a friend tell her what to do.

MIGUEL already knows how to bake a cake, so he is using his memory.

DANA is watching a friend make a cake and is doing what the friend does.

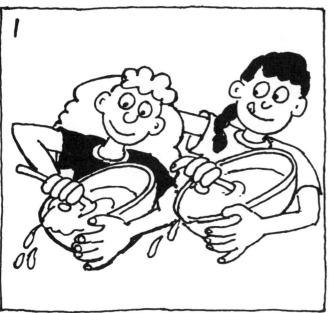

I-4 THE TEACHER BELONGS TO EVERYONE

Objective:

The student will identify ways that a teacher can pay attention to many students in a class.

Rationale:

Some students are extremely possessive of the teacher, demanding attention for every step taken towards a task, wanting constant praise, and even refusing to attempt a task unless the teacher is watching. This lesson is directed at students who need to learn to "share" the teacher with others.

Thinking Questions:

1. How many students are usually in a class? *(10-30)*
2. How many teachers are usually in a class *(1 or maybe 2)*
3. What would happen if everyone in the class needed help at the same time? *(some people would have to wait)*
4. How do teachers show attention to students in the class? *(look at them, listen to them, nod head, etc.)*
5. How would you feel if there were 25 kids in a class but the teacher only paid attention to one or two kids? *(left out, angry, etc.)*

Activity:

Directions: Have students read (or listen to) the cartoon on the worksheet. The teacher pays attention to the students in several different ways. Students are to count how many students received some sort of teacher attention.

   Answer: 8

   Follow-up: What are some ways that the teacher noticed students in the class? *(talked to them, patted on the back, waved finger to indicate he would be right there, etc.)* Just because a teacher is helping one student, does that mean he or she won't help anyone else? Does it mean the teacher doesn't like a student if the teacher is talking to someone else?*(no)* What are some other ways that a teacher can let you know he or she hasn't forgotten you, but will get to you soon? *(brief comment, wink, eye contact, a smile, etc.)*

The Teacher Belongs to Everyone

Read the cartoon about Mr. Teech and his class. Count how many different students he pays attention to and write the number at the bottom.

I-5 WHAT IS RESPECT?

Objective:

The student will state that *respect* means treating someone as a valuable person.

Rationale:

Everyone wants to be treated with respect. Often, however, students unthinkingly make comments that are disrespectful about teachers because they are angry, want to show off, or simply are rude. This lesson demonstrates ways to treat the teacher with respect, while still letting your feelings out.

Thinking Questions:

1. How would you feel if I slammed the door in your face? *(mad, upset)*
2. How would you feel if I knew that you were in a hurry at the store and I let you go through the line first? *(pleased)*
3. Which of those examples shows having respect for someone else? *(second)*
4. What does respect mean? *(treating someone as a valuable person)*
5. What are some ways that students show respect for their teacher? *(being polite, being quiet, saying kind things, etc.)*
6. How do you think a teacher feels when the students show respect? *(good, proud)*

Activity:

Directions: Have students consider the responses or actions of the students on the worksheet. They are to circle the students who are showing respect to the teacher and X the ones who are not.

Answers:	1. circle	4. circle	7. X
	2. X	5. circle	8. X
	3. circle	6. X	9. circle

Follow-up: Go through the cartoons and discuss why the student was or was not showing respect. What could the X'd students have done differently to express their frustration or anger without being disrespectful? *(explain why they were mad at the teacher, ask the teacher to move politely, discuss anger calmly with a friend, etc.)*

What Is Respect?

Some of these students are showing respect for their teacher. Some are not. Circle the respectful students. Put an X on those who are not showing respect.

I-6 GIVING INSTRUCTIONS

Objective:

The student will give examples of instructions that a teacher may give.

Rationale:

Part of the teacher's job is to explain how to do something or provide instructions for the student to enable him or her to work through a task in order to learn something. The purpose of this lesson is to show students the importance of the teacher's instructions.

Thinking Questions:

1. How do teachers help you learn something? *(tell you, show you, etc.)*

2. Why do teachers give instructions? *(so you'll know what to do)*

3. Why can't you just figure things out by yourself? *(sometimes it's easier if someone tells you how to do it, there may be a special procedure, etc.)*

4. What might happen if you don't follow instructions? *(make mistakes, take longer)*

5. What instructions might a reading teacher give to students? *(how to sound out words, how to separate compound words, etc.)*

Activity:

Directions: Students are to complete instructions for four fictitious teachers. Explain to students that they are to think about what content might be taught in music, science, math, or P.E. and to pretend to give instructions for doing a task that would be appropriate for that class.

Answers: (examples) **Music**—how to play an instrument, how to sing a specific song, etc. **Science**—how to make a rock collection, how to grow some plants, etc. **Math**—how to count by 2's, how to make a number line, etc. **P.E.**—how to do push-ups, how to play volleyball, etc.

Follow-up: Discuss the importance of listening to the teacher's instructions. What might happen in these four situations if the student didn't listen? *(Use student's examples of instructions for discussion).* Help students make a list of five or six instructions for tasks that they have learned or worked on in the past day.

Giving Instructions

Here are some teachers from a nearby school. What are some instructions that each might give to their students? Pay attention to what each teacher teaches! Write your instructions next to each teacher.

**Mr. Bluenote
Music Teacher**

I will teach you how to. . .

**Miss Landform
Science Teacher**

I want you to. . .

I want you to learn . .

Listen carefully, kids, I will now demonstrate. . .

**Mrs. Counter
Math Teacher**

**Mr. Whammo
Physical
Education Teacher**

I-7 BEING TRUSTWORTHY

Objective:

The student will state that someone is trustworthy if he or she does what he or she promises to do or is expected to do.

Rationale:

What happens when you send a student on an errand? Will you ever see him or her again? At times we must trust the student to behave or to do the right thing without being told explicitly what to do. This lesson is about students whose behavior may or may not make someone else want to trust them.

Thinking Questions

1. What does "trust" mean? *(you believe what someone else says)*

2. If I say that a person is "trustworthy," what does that mean? *(you can count on him or her)*

3. What is supposed to happen if someone tells me that they want to run an errand or to work alone in the hallway? *(the person should do it)*

4. Why is it hard sometimes to take longer or fool around when you're not being watched? *(lose track of time, get distracted)*

5. Do you think it is important for a person to get a reputation for being trustworthy? Why? *(yes, get to do more things)*

Activity:

Directions: Students are to read several sentences about characters on the worksheet and then to decide whether or not the person could be trusted to perform the task.

> *Answers:*   1. yes
>   2. no
>   3. no
>   4. no

Follow-up: Discuss with students what problems came up with the characters on the worksheet. Did they do things that were really wrong or just at the wrong time? How would their teacher feel about what they did?

Being Trustworthy

Do you think these students are trustworthy? Read about them and circle your answer.

1. Albert was sent to the office with the absentee list. He went right there and came right back.

   YES   NO

2. David said he had to go to the bathroom. On the way, he went out to the playground and played baseball with another class.

   YES   NO

3. Sally wanted to do her math in study hall. She drew pictures of horses all over her paper and the desk she was sitting at.

   YES   NO

4. Ed wanted to go to the library to return his book. He went to the library and put the book on the table. On the way back, he went to the bathroom, got a drink, talked to a friend, went to the office, and went outside to pick a flower for his mother.

   YES   NO

Section I

I-8 WHEN THE TEACHER LEAVES THE ROOM

Objective:

The student will identify appropriate and inappropriate behaviors for students when the teacher is not in the room.

Rationale:

There's nothing more embarrassing than walking down the hall towards your room, hearing an awful commotion, and finding out that it's coming from YOUR room! Students need to learn that even when an authority figure is not physically in the room, good behavior is still expected.

Thinking Questions:

1. What would happen if the teacher left this room for a few minutes? *(students would continue working, some would play)*

2. What do you think students *should* do when their teacher is gone for a little while? *(continue doing what they were told to do)*

3. Before your teacher leaves the room, what does he or she tell you or ask you to do? *(continue working, sit quietly, etc.)*

4. Why do you think it's important for things not to get out of control while the teacher is gone? *(someone might get hurt, it wastes time, etc.)*

Activity:

Directions: Students are to observe the classroom of characters who are alone in the classroom. They are to circle or X the children according to their behavior. Make sure that students understand what the children on the worksheet are doing if it is not clear.

> *Answers:*   **Circle**—Mike, Kathy, Dave, John, Kevin, Ellen
> **X**—Pete, Chou, Sue, Dick, Sandy, Jane

Follow-up: Discuss why the X'd students were not following directions while the teacher was gone. What are some possible consequences of their behavior? *(get behind on work, disturb other students, etc.)*

Name _____ Date _____

When the Teacher Leaves the Room

Mrs. O'Brien got an emergency phone call in the office and had to leave. She said:

Circle the children whom she could trust to behave in the room. X those whom she could not.

You all have work to finish. Stay in your seat and work quietly until I get back. No noises!

I-9 GETTING THE TEACHER'S ATTENTION

Objective:

The student will identify several appropriate ways to get the teacher's attention.

Rationale:

Students will need the attention of their teacher from time to time, to clarify things, to get some extra help, or maybe just to tell the teacher something. They will need to know how to make that contact with the teacher. Do you want to be interrupted while you're working with someone else? How can a student reach you? This lesson offers items for discussion about how to get the teacher's attention in an appropriate way.

Thinking Questions:

1. What do you think the teacher thinks when you raise your hand? *(you know the answer, you want something)*

2. Why is raising your hand a good signal for the teacher to let him or her know you want some attention? *(it's quiet, easy, fairly noticeable in class, etc.)*

3. What are some other good ways to let the teacher know you need some attention? *(go up to the desk, call his or her name quietly, put a question mark card on your desk, etc.)*

4. What are some ways that don't work very well in a classroom? *(making noises, yelling out, etc.)*

5. What system works well in your classroom? *(classrooms may vary as to their method of connecting teacher with student—ask students for their experiences in other classrooms)*

Activity:

Directions: Students are to think about the ten suggestions for getting the teacher's attention and to put a check mark next to the best ones.

Answers: Check marks by 3, 6, 7, 9.

Follow-up: Discuss why the unchecked answers were inappropriate. Although some may result in getting the teacher's attention *(throwing a book at him or her)*, what kind of attention would it get? *(probably a reprimand!)*

Getting the Teacher's Attention

Which of these are good ways to get the teacher's attention? Put a ✔ next to each good answer.

1. Yelling as loudly as you can: "Hey, you!"   _____

2. Throwing a book at him or her.   _____

3. Raising your hand.   _____

4. Pulling on the teacher's sleeve while she is working with a
   small group in the back of the room.   _____

5. Standing on your chair.   _____

6. Going up to his desk and waiting quietly.   _____

7. Looking at the teacher's face.   _____

8. Telling your friend to go get the teacher and make him come
   over to your desk.   _____

9. Using the teacher's name to call him over.   _____

10. Yelling the teacher's name as loudly as you can.   _____

Part I   Understanding the Teacher's Role

I-10 COMPLAINING ABOUT WORK

Objective:

The student will identify characters who are making noncomplaining remarks about work.

Rationale:

Complaining leads to arguing and noncompliance. Although it would be nice if all students enjoyed doing their assigned work, many do not—and are quick to voice it. This lesson compares complaining statements with noncomplaining statements and puts the student in the position of having to decide which he or she would rather listen to.

Thinking Questions:

1. How do you feel when you're given an assignment you don't really want to do? *(in a bad mood, frustrated, tired, etc.)*

2. What are some comments that students might make about doing something they don't want to do? *("Do we have to?" "I don't like this." etc.)*

3. Do you think that complaining about work changes things? *(probably not; might aggravate the teacher)*

4. What are most of the complaints that you hear about? *(work is too hard/long/boring, etc.)*

5. If complaints don't get you anywhere, what could you do instead? *(just do it, talk to the teacher about legitimate reasons why you're having trouble, commiserate with your friends after class, etc.)*

Activity:

Directions: A teacher has given a class some work to do. There are two characters shown for each assignment. The student is to circle the one from each pair who is not complaining.

> *Answers:*   1. second   3. second
>   2. first   4. second

Follow-up: Discuss ways that students can voice their frustration or problems with work. Is it a problem of not wanting to do the work or simply wanting to complain about it? Is the first character in #3 really in pain or making a big deal about nothing? What does it feel like to hear constant complaining?

Complaining About Work

Which of these students would you rather listen to? Circle the student in each pair who is *not* complaining.

1. **I want you to finish all of page 12 in your workbook.** — **What? That's so much! It's too much to do. It takes too long.** — **I'd better get started!**

2. **Before we go to gym, clean off your desks.** — **Why do we have to do that now? Can't we do it later?** — **Wow, this is a mess!**

3. **Write your stories in your journal.** — **My hand hurts. I don't like to write. I think I have to see the nurse!** — **I'll write about camping.**

4. **If your handwriting isn't readable, you'll have to do it over.** — **I don't want to do this. I want to read a book. I'm tired. I don't want to write anything.** — **I'll have to be very careful the first time.**

I-11 ARGUING WITH THE TEACHER

Objective:

The student will state comments that are argumentative and then give reasons why the comments are impolite, unhelpful, or unnecessary.

Rationale:

The step after complaining seems to be all-out arguing. Some students feel that they have to find something negative about every situation, no matter how neutral that situation may be. This lesson gives the student a chance to think of argumentative comments, and then to decide whether or not the arguing is helpful or unnecessary.

Thinking Questions:

1. What does it mean to argue with someone? *(try to tell your point of view which is probably different from the other person's)*

2. What are some bad things that come from arguing? *(hurt feelings, loud voices, nothing solved)*

3. Can good things come from arguing? *(possibly—if one side really listens to the other)*

4. Can you change someone's mind in another way other than arguing with them? How? *(be logical, be polite when talking about how you feel, etc.)*

5. If you disagree with your teacher about something, is arguing about it going to help? What would help? *(arguing probably wouldn't help; ideas from question 4 might)*

Activity:

Directions: This time, students get to be arguers! They are to fill in the balloon with words that the arguing student might say to the teacher. Remind students not to go overboard (using bad language or gestures!), but to think like an arguer!

Answers: (examples)

1. It is not.
2. They lined up first yesterday! It's not their turn!
3. I don't want to use a pencil.
4. I don't want to read it out loud.
5. That's too much work! I don't want to!
6. Ten pages are too much! Why can't we do one? I don't like that assignment.

Follow-up: Have students volunteer their answers and talk about similarities between Arthur's arguments. How many times do the words *don't, won't,* and *not* appear? Students may want to role play the situations and keep the argument going back and forth a few times. Have them think about the bottom line: did anything change because Arthur argued? If you were Arthur's friend, what would you advise him to do? How could Arthur change his words to get his point across with (a) complaining and (b) arguing?

Arguing with the Teacher

Meet Arthur Q. Arguer. He likes to argue with teachers about everything and anything. Write what you think Arthur might be saying in each situation below.

1. "Your handwriting is very hard to read, Arthur."

2. "It's the girls' turn to line up first."

3. "Don't do your math in markers - use a pencil."

4. "Today we're going to read our story out loud."

5. "Everyone must help clean up the room because we're having visitors this afternoon."

6. "Your assignment is to read 10 pages in this book."

Part I   Understanding the Teacher's Role

I-12 WHEN THE TEACHER IS TALKING ...

Objective:

The student will state the rule: when the teacher is talking, be quiet and listen.

Rationale:

When the teacher is addressing the class, students need to (a) be quiet and (b) listen. Not only is this respectful to the teacher, but it also enables the students to hear what is being said and reminds them to pay attention.

Thinking Questions:

1. Are there times when the teacher is talking that you don't need to listen? *(if the teacher is talking to an individual, etc.)*

2. How do you know when you are supposed to be listening to what the teacher says? *(when it's in class, when he or she is giving a lesson, etc.)*

3. What are some distractions to hearing the teacher's words? *(noises in the classroom, other conversations, something going on outside, etc.)*

4. If the teacher is saying something really important, what do you think students should do? *(listen, be quiet)*

5. How does this show respect for the teacher? *(shows that you value the teacher's words and actions)*

Activity:

Directions: The characters on this worksheet have a word below them. Students are to find the characters who are quiet when the teacher is talking and write the word that goes with him or her *in order* on the lines below the drawing.

Answer: Be quiet and listen.

Follow-up: Discuss why the rude students are not listening to the teacher while he is talking. What are they doing instead? *(talking, yelling for help, whistling, etc.)* Why is it important not only to follow the rule but to show manners and respect by being quiet?

When the Teacher Is Talking. . .

See if you can finish the rule. Underneath each student who is listening to the teacher is a word. Put the words together *in order* to finish the rule.

be   good   loud   quiet

to   from   and   bad

hear   see   listen   help

Part II   Classroom Rules and Responsibilities

II-1 Paying Attention to the Task

Objective:

The student will identify characters who are paying attention to a given task.

Rationale:

Part of the responsibility of being a good student is to be able to pay attention to the task at hand. Paying attention might involve eye contact, taking notes, or tuning out other distractions and really listening. The purpose of this lesson is for students to focus on thinking about what paying attention to a task involves.

Thinking Questions:

1. What does it mean when someone tells you to "pay attention"? *(listen, be quiet, etc.)*

2. How could you tell just by looking if someone is paying attention? *(the person might be quiet, look interested, etc.)*

3. Why is it easier to pay attention to some tasks than others? *(might be more interesting, easier to understand, etc.)*

4. Why do you think it is important to pay attention to whatever job you are supposed to be working on? *(do a better job, get better grade, won't have to do over, etc.)*

5. If you're working on a task you don't like, could paying attention to what you're doing make it any easier? *(possibly—understanding it better might make it easier to perform)*

Activity:

Directions: On this worksheet, students are to select the student in each pair who is paying attention to the task. Students are to circle the correct student. Make sure students understand each task.

Answers:	1. first student	4. second student
	2. second student	5. second student
	3. first student	

Follow-up: Discuss the tasks on the worksheet with students. When a teacher accuses someone of "not paying attention," what might the teacher be seeing? *(a student doing something else, not doing anything at all, etc.)* How can a student look and act like he or she is paying attention?

Paying Attention to the Task

These students are supposed to be working on different tasks at school. Circle the student in each pair who is paying attention to the job.

1. Writing spelling words on a piece of paper:

2. Making a cat out of modeling clay:

3. Copying the sentence off the board:

4. Reading the story in the book:

5. Cleaning out the desk:

Part II   Classroom Rules and Responsibilities

II-2 Talking to Your Neighbor

Objective:

The student will identify appropriate and inappropriate times to talk with nearby students in class.

Rationale:

Some students just love to talk! This is particularly annoying when the teacher is trying to give instructions and a student is not listening and is preventing another student from hearing as well. Students have a responsibility to refrain from talking under certain circumstances.

Thinking Questions:

1. Why do you think there are rules like "No talking in class"? *(so people can hear the teacher, keep room quiet, etc.)*

2. What if you sat right next to your best friend and had something important to tell him or her? Should you talk then? *(depends—what is the teacher doing? Can you say it quickly? etc.)*

3. Why might it bother other people if you were talking? *(they couldn't hear)*

4. What are some times during the school day when you could talk to your friends? *(lunch, recess, in the bathroom, etc.)*

Activity:

Directions: Students are to decide whether each situation is a good time for talking to friends or not. After thinking about each situation, they are to write YES or NO on the line next to each problem.

Answers: 1. no   4. no
            2. yes   5. no
            3. no   6. yes (quietly)

Follow-up: Discuss the problems that accompany inappropriate talking in each of the "no" situations. If you already know how to do something, why wouldn't it be okay to talk? *(disturb others)* Discuss what times are acceptable for talking in your classroom.

Name _____ Date _____

II-2

Talking to Your Neighbor

Is this a good time to talk to your neighbor? Write YES or NO on the line next to each situation.

1. The bell just rang and you want to tell your friend all about the birthday presents you got over the weekend. _____

2. It's lunch and you are sitting by your best friend. He or she wants to talk about what you'll do when you spend the weekend together. _____

3. You are in P.E. class and the teacher is explaining how to play kickball. You already know how to play kickball, so you want to tell the boy next to you about what was on T.V. last night. _____

4. The teacher is telling the answers to your math worksheet. You got a lot of them wrong, so you ask your neighbor to show you how to do them correctly. _____

5. RING! It's a fire drill!! While you are lining up, you want to tell your friend about the time you rode in a fire truck. _____

6. All of your work for the day is done, so the teacher lets you go to the back table and work on an art project with a friend. You have a great idea for a poster and want to ask your partner what he or she thinks. _____

Part II   Classroom Rules and Responsibilities

II-3 Oops, Wrong Assignment

Objective:

The student will identify whether or not an assignment shown on the worksheet is the one assigned by the teacher.

Rationale:

How many times have you looked at papers that were laboriously completed—but the assignment was the wrong one? A student needs to be sure that he or she understands what the assignment is and does it according to the directions! This lesson gives the student practice in identifying whether or not the assignments were the specified ones.

Thinking Questions:

1. How do you know what assignments you are supposed to do? *(teacher says something, written on boards, etc.)*

2. What might happen if you weren't listening when the teacher gave the assignment? *(might do the wrong one)*

3. How could you make sure that you are doing what the teacher asked you to do? *(listen, write it down, check with a friend, etc.)*

4. What happens in some classes if you do the wrong assignment? *(might have to do it over, etc.)*

5. Why do you think the teacher chooses certain assignments for you to do? *(they practice what you've been doing in class, the teacher knows you are able to do them, etc.)*

Activity:

Directions: Students are to look at the assignments given to characters by a teacher and then to decide whether or not the student did the given assignment. Students must use picture cues to determine what the characters did. Tell students not to make assumptions (e.g., the girl did more math problems on the *back* of the paper), but just to use what's obvious from the picture.

Answers:

1. no (she only did 4)
2. yes
3. yes
4. no
5. no (the book is open to page 24, so we assume that the student didn't even see the sentences on page 26)

Follow-up: Discuss with students why some of the characters did the wrong assignment and what could have been done so that they would not have made the mistakes they did. Have students tell about experiences in which they may have done the wrong assignment and what happened because of it.

Oops, Wrong Assignment

Here are some assignments given to the class by the teacher. But not all of the students did the correct assignment! Check each student carefully to decide whether or not the assignment is the right one. Then write YES or NO on the line.

1. Do math problems 1 through 10. _____

2. Do the reading game on the computer. Use the disk that is on the right side of the computer. _____

3. Run to the far side of the field, touch the tree, and run back. _____

4. Cut out 5 pictures of things that begin with the letter "M." _____

5. Copy all of the sentences in the spelling book on page 26. _____

Section I

II-4 Did You Say "Listen"?

Objective:

The student will state or draw pictures of possible consequences of not listening to the teacher's comments.

Rationale:

Sometimes students miss out on an opportunity to find a shortcut, learn something the first time, or participate in something special just because they aren't listening. This lesson gives the student a chance to express ideas of what could happen to people who don't listen to the teacher.

Thinking Questions:

1. What are you supposed to do when the teacher asks you to "listen"? *(try to hear and understand what he or she is telling you)*

2. What do you think are some consequences or problems that might come up by not listening? *(do something wrong, do wrong assignment)*

3. Is listening more than just being quiet? *(yes—it's concentrating)*

4. Have you ever missed out on something because you weren't listening at the right time?

Activity:

Directions: Students are to draw pictures of possible consequences of not listening to the teacher. Students should be encouraged to be creative and humorous, as long as they are following the instructions. You may want to have students select only two or three of the situations if they have difficulty drawing.

   Answers: (examples)

1. the student may do the wrong assignment
2. one student doesn't line up
3. the student asks what the word means
4. the student gets hit on the head with a ball
5. the student doesn't get ice cream
6. the student makes the letter incorrectly

Follow-up: Discuss with students reasons why not listening would make it difficult to complete the tasks correctly. Have students share their drawings with the group.

Did You Say "Listen"?

Draw a picture showing what could happen to a student if he or she didn't listen to the teacher while . . .

1. . . .the teacher explains a new math assignment.

2. . . .the teacher tells the students to line up to see a movie.

3. . . .the teacher explains what a word in your reading book means.

4. . . .the P.E. teacher tells the class how to play Dodgeball.

5. . . .the teacher asks everyone who wants ice cream to raise his or her hand.

6. . . .the teacher shows the class how to make an "l" in cursive.

II-5 Complying with Instructions Right Away

Objective:

The student will identify examples of characters who are complying with teacher directions right away.

Rationale:

When a student is given a task to do, even something as simple as "sit down" or "come over here," we expect him or her to comply right away. There are many students, however, who comply at their leisure (if at all), as if their slowness to respond might cause the teacher to forget the command! This lesson focuses on students identifying characters who respond right away.

Thinking Questions:

1. When a teacher (or parent) asks you to do something, what do you usually do *(do it)*

2. How long does it take before you actually get started doing something that you may not want to do?

3. Does it make the job any easier to put if off? *(usually no)*

4. Why do you think people put things off or procrastinate? *(hope it will go away)*

5. What do you think a teacher expects when he or she asks you to do something? *(to do it right away)*

Activity:

Directions: This activity involves having students read about characters who have been asked to do something. They must decide whether or not the character complies quickly or not.

Answers: 1. no   3. yes   5. no
             2. no   4. no   6. yes

Follow-up: Discuss the character's responses to the teachers' requests. What do students think that the characters might say to defend their actions? *("I was going to do it … ")* Is there anything wrong with looking out the window or cleaning out a desk? *(No, but wrong timing)*

Complying with Instructions Right Away

Is the student doing what the teacher asked him or her to do right away?
Circle YES or NO.

1. Mrs. Brown asked Tommy to come up to her desk. Tommy walked over to the window. YES   NO

2. Mrs. Smith asked Susan to put away her math book. Susan did four more math problems. YES   NO

3. Mrs. Green asked Mike to hang up his coat. Mike got up and hung it up. YES   NO

4. Mr. Peters asked the class to line up for lunch. George started to clean out his desk. YES   NO

5. Mr. James asked Joan to put her pencil down. Joan put it in her ear. YES   NO

6. Miss Clark asked Mark to take a note to the office. Mark said, "Who does it go to?" Miss Clark said, "It goes to Mrs. Jones." Mark took the note and went to the office. YES   NO

II-6 Being Prepared to Work

Objective:

The student will state necessary items for completion of a given task.

Rationale:

A common complaint among teachers is that students are not prepared to begin working. Before the actual task can be started, the student needs to identify what materials will be needed for the task. This lesson provides the student with several situations to consider.

Thinking Questions:

1. What are some common materials or tools that students use to do their work? *(pencil, paper, computer, etc.)*
2. Why is it important to have everything you need together before you start a job? *(save time, don't have to run and get things, etc.)*
3. What might happen if you didn't have something you needed? *(you'd have to stop and go get it)*
4. What things might you need if you were working on math/reading/English/etc.? *(books, pencils, word cards, etc.)*
5. What are some ways that you might be able to help yourself remember everything you need to get? *(organize your desk, keep things for each subject together, make a checklist, etc.)*

Activity:

Directions: Each of the characters on this worksheet is given an assignment. Students must draw a picture of what materials are needed before completing the task. (Do not penalize students for poor artwork. Oral explanations of their pictures are good for discussions!)

Answers: (examples)

1. paper, pencil, colored pencils (for pictures)
2. watercolor paper, brushes, cup of water
3. computer, disk, calculator (?)
4. bat, ball, glove, bases

Follow-up: Discuss other classroom tasks that require preparation. What about coming to class with *ideas* to contribute? What frustrations would the characters on the worksheet run into if they were missing something? How would it affect other students in the class? *(David's class might not be pleased if he forgot the ball!)*

Being Prepared to Work

These students are getting ready to start working on their various assignments. Draw pictures of what you think each student will need to be prepared.

1. Martha's assignment is to write a story about taking a trip to the zoo.

2. Jake's job is to make a water-color picture of a scene from the park.

3. Jennifer is about to use the computer to practice solving math problems.

4. David is supposed to gather things that the class will need to play softball.

II-7 Knowing When to Quiet Down

Objective:

The student will identify situations in which the class climate should be very quiet.

Rationale:

The noise level varies between teachers and classes; however, most teachers agree that certain situations call for silence and attention. This lesson describes situations and tasks that should prompt students to quiet down.

Thinking Questions:

1. What would it sound like in a room if everyone talked at once? *(loud, distracting)*

2. Are there some things that you do at school that should be done with everyone being quiet? What? *(taking a test, working on something that requires concentration, etc.)*

3. What are some things that you can do without being especially quiet? *(recess, working in groups, playing in the gym, etc.)*

4. What are some clues that you may see that let you know it is time to go from being loud to being quiet? *(teacher flicking the lights off and on, finger to lips, "shhhhhh," etc.)*

5. What are some problems or bothersome things that might occur if someone didn't quiet down? *(would be hard for others to hear, they might miss what's being instructed, etc.)*

Activity:

Directions: Students are to read the situations and decide whether or not it would be a good time for students to be quiet. You may want to discuss what "quiet" and "very quiet" mean in your classroom. Do you expect silence? Do you tolerate low voices? Make sure students understand *your* expectations in situations.

Answers: 1. yes
2. yes
3. (depends on your class)
4. yes
5. no
6. yes
7. (probably some noise will be tolerated)
8. yes
9. no
10. yes

Follow-up: Discuss what degree of noise is acceptable in your classroom for each of the situations on the worksheet and add other times when your students need to be quiet. What cues do you use to let students know that the noise level is getting too high?

Knowing When to Quiet Down

Put a ✔ next to each situation if you think it would be a good time for the class to be very quiet.

1. A guest walks into the room. _____

2. The bell for the fire drill just went off. _____

3. The teacher said to get into your small groups to discuss plans for the Christmas party. _____

4. The teacher is getting ready to teach the class how to run a new computer program. _____

5. Everyone is outside for recess. _____

6. If everyone finishes his or her work quickly, the whole class can go to the gym for free time. _____

7. The art teacher wants everyone to get up and get their materials from the front table for working with clay. _____

8. The art teacher is explaining how to make the clay soft. _____

9. The bell rang and everyone is going out the door to go home. _____

10. The teacher is reading off the answers to the test that the class took the day before while students are correcting their own papers. _____

Part II   Classroom Rules and Responsibilities

II-8 Working Alone

Objective:

The student will identify characters in a classroom who are working on a task independently.

Rationale:

When students are given a task that they are well-prepared to handle, we as teachers expect them to work on it with a minimal amount of help. Assuming that they have been properly instructed, students should be able and willing to undertake tasks independently and to complete them without constantly badgering others, asking irrelevant questions, and completely giving up!

Thinking Questions:

1. What are some things you do at school in groups? *(games, cooperative learning tasks, partner reading, etc.)*

2. What are some things that you do all by yourself? *(worksheets, silent reading, etc.)*

3. Why do you think you are supposed to work by yourself sometimes? *(it's something you need to know how to do without another person, it's quieter, you can work at your own rate, etc.)*

4. When you're working on something alone, how does it make you feel to know that you did it without any help? *(smart, fast, proud of self)*

5. If you like to work with other people, what are some activities you could do with a partner or small group in reading/spelling/math/etc.? *(call words to each other, take turns working on problems, read stories by alternating sentences, etc.)*

Activity:

Directions: Students are to read all of the thoughts and statements on the worksheet and write the names of the characters who are working alone on their assignment. Note that Pete is not working on the task. Assume that characters who *look* like they are working alone are.

Answers: Pam, Frank, Tom

Follow-up: Discuss the problems that the others in the class had. What was Mike's problem? *(he said he couldn't figure it out)* How did that bother Angela? What was Matt's alternative to working? *(looking out the window)* What consequences might he feel? *(not getting the assignment done, being yelled at for being out of his seat)* How might Sheila's behavior bother others? *(her yelling is disturbing to others)* Discuss with your students how *their* independent behavior makes it nicer for others. Be aware that some students just cannot sit still for long periods of times. What adaptations can you or do you make for those students?

Working Alone

Which of these students is working on a task without needing help? Write their names at the bottom.

Angela, help me! I can't figure this out!

Amy, all you have to do is read the directions! It's easy!

Mike

Pete

Amy

Let's see . . . I add these numbers together, then write the answer on the line.

Frank

I give up. I'll just look out the window until someone notices me.

Pam

Teacher!! Teacher!! Help me! Help me! Teacher!!!!

Matt

Tom

Independent workers:

_____

_____

Sheila

II-9 Sitting Appropriately

Objective:

The student will state, demonstrate, or identify proper sitting posture.

Rationale:

Some students have creative ways of positioning their bodies in a chair, on the carpet, or other items of furniture which are intended for housing a student. If students are given a clear definition of "sitting appropriately," it is easier to enforce the teacher request to "sit down" or "sit still." For purposes of this lesson, "sitting appropriately" is defined as having one's bottom down on the chair or floor with arms and legs kept to oneself.

Thinking Questions:

1. How many ways can you sit on a chair? *(forward, backward, sideways, etc.)*

2. Why do you think your teachers care how you sit? *(looks more orderly to all sit facing forward, if you stretch out too much you're in someone else's way, you might hurt yourself if you fall, etc.)*

3. Where are some other places around school that you might have to sit? *(auditorium, cafeteria, bleachers, etc.)*

4. Why do you think it's important to "sit still" sometimes? *(so you don't touch others, so you don't disturb others with wiggling, etc.)*

5. What would be a good definition for sitting appropriately? *(bottom down, arms and legs to yourself, etc.)*

Activity:

Directions: Students are to circle the characters on the worksheet who are sitting appropriately. They are to X the ones who are not. Be sure students understand your expectations for sitting appropriately. (#11 might fit the definition, but if sitting backwards bothers you, this would be an X'd person.)

Answers: Circle 2, 5, 7, 9, 12.

Follow-up: Discuss why the other students received an X. What were they doing that did not satisfy the definition? *(#1 wasn't in his seat at all, #6 had his knees on the seat, etc.)* Discuss proper sitting positions for other areas of the school. How should they sit at the computer lab? The art room? On the floor in the gym?

Sitting Appropriately

Look at this class of students. Circle the ones who are sitting appropriately. Put an X on the ones who are not.

II-10 Entering the Classroom

Objective:

The student will state or demonstrate appropriate ways to enter a classroom.

Rationale:

It is very disturbing to have a lesson interrupted by a noisy entrant or to lose the attention of the class to students who bring outside aggravations, arguments, or moods into the class. It is an important classroom skill for students to walk into a classroom (ongoing or not) in a quiet, mannerly fashion.

Thinking Questions:

1. When you walk down a hallway, what is usually going on in the classrooms you pass? *(teachers teaching, students working, perhaps singing or talking, etc.)*

2. Do people come into your room from time to time? Who and what is their purpose? *(guests, parents, other teachers, school nurse, etc., to pick up students, to talk to the teacher, etc.)*

3. When you have interruptions, what usually happens in class? *(students stop what they're doing to watch)*

4. When you have to walk into a class that has already started, what are some ways you could go in without interrupting too much? *(tiptoe in quietly, go to the back of the room, etc.)*

5. How could the whole class enter a classroom peacefully? *(go in a few at a time, go in quietly, lower voices, stop talking about what went on in the hall, etc.)*

Activity:

Directions: The worksheet shows examples of students entering a classroom in various, loud ways. Students are to write at least one way the student(s) could improve this aspect of their behavior.

Answers: (examples)

1. Ellen could stop tattling about what went on during the bus ride.
2. John should leave the paper airplane in the restroom.
3. Andy and Frank should finish their lunches in the cafeteria.
4. Sandy should talk to Dottie about her dress later.

Follow-up: Have students pay attention to what kinds of conversations go on as students enter the classroom. Do students bring outside problems (fights, arguments, bad moods) into the class? You may want to have students role-play alternatives to coming into the classroom noisily and seeking attention.

Name _____   Date _____

II-10

Entering the Classroom

These students are entering the classroom, but they are not coming in quietly. What could each student do to improve his or her behavior?

1. Ellen is coming in first thing in the morning.

> Hey, I want to tell you what Fred and Pete were doing on the bus! Boy, were they going to get in trouble!

Ellen could _____

2. John is coming into the room after going to the restroom.

> Look out, here it comes!

John could _____

3. Andy and Frank are coming into the room after lunch.

> No way!!

> Give me some of that.

The boys could _____

4. Sandy is coming into the room while the teacher is leading a discussion in the front.

> Hi Dottie! What do you think of this dress? Come here and look at this!

Sandy could _____

Section I

II-11 Leaving the Classroom

Objective:

The student will state or demonstrate appropriate ways to leave a classroom.

Rationale:

As with entering a room, leaving a room is a time in which some students enjoy "grandstanding" or making noises or long farewells with friends. Students should be taught to leave the room quietly, quickly, and without fanfare.

Thinking Questions:

1. What are some reasons that you might have to leave the classroom while the rest of the class stayed? *(special reading, go to the bathroom, go to the office, run an errand, etc.)*

2. Why might it bother other people if someone left loudly? *(they might be trying to finish their work)*

3. How could it be a problem if someone wanted to touch and pat people on their way out the door? *(it's like "tag"—the touched person will want to touch back, patting is invading someone's space, etc.)*

4. What are ways that people shut the door that are bothersome? *(slamming the door, making the door creak, taking a long time to go out the door, etc.)*

5. What is a good way for people to leave the classroom when they have to go out? *(go quietly and quickly without trying to get attention)*

Activity:

Directions: Students are to consider several examples of characters leaving a classroom and write YES or NO in the box next to each example to indicate if the character is leaving appropriately.

   Answers: 1. no   2. yes   3. yes   4. no   5. no

Follow-up: Discuss why the characters who got a "no" were not leaving appropriately. *(#1—did lots of talking, interrupting; #4—slammed the door; #5—touched people on his way out)* Discuss what method the teacher wants to use for people who want to leave to use the restroom. Should they raise their hands? Interrupt the teacher during reading groups? Convey your preferences to students so they will know at what times they are allowed to disturb you to go out.

Leaving the Classroom

These students need to leave the classroom. Do you think they are leaving appropriately? Write YES or NO in each box.

1. *Mrs. Santinini, I'll hurry - I promise! I'll go right to the restroom and then come right back! Good-bye everybody!!*

2.

3. *George, it's time for you to go to speech.*

OK.

4. SLAM

5.

II-12 Moving Around in Class

Objective:

The student will identify characters who are moving about the classroom in an acceptable way.

Rationale:

Students need to be able to move around the class, not only to gather materials and go to different groups, but to change their positions and remain active learners. It is important for students to move around the class without bothering others or wasting time. It is also important to realize that students need to move around!

Thinking Questions:

1. Do you have to sit in your seat all day or can you move around? *(move around to get things, change groups, go outside, catch the bus, sharpen pencil, etc.)*
2. What is the shortest path to the pencil sharpener/closet/window/etc.? *(answers will vary)*
3. If the shortest way to get somewhere takes you past someone who wants you to stop and talk or across a table in the middle of the room, why should you think twice before going that way? *(might get in trouble for talking, shouldn't walk on a table)*
4. What are some good things to keep in mind when moving around the class so you don't bother others? *(be quiet, don't stop and talk, etc.)*
5. If you feel like you need to get up and move around, what are some things you can do or areas of the room you can go to? *(varies—might stretch, stroll by the window, look at the aquarium, etc.)*

Activity:

Directions: Students are to read short paragraphs about students who have to move around the class and to pick the one in each pair who is moving appropriately. They are to write the name of the student on the line.

   Answers: 1. Denny   2. Sally   3. Doug

   Follow-up: Discuss why Rick, Maria, and Ben were not the best movers. *(Rick—jumping on the desk; Maria—disturbing others, wasting time; Ben—making four trips instead of one)* What could they do differently? What is the best time or place to jump, show people new watches? How could Ben plan his project better? *(organize himself first, then make one trip)*

Moving Around in Class

These students need to move around in the classroom. One is doing a better job than the other. Write the name of the student who is moving around the classroom appropriately.

1. Rick and Denny need to sharpen their pencils on the other side of the room.

   Rick jumps across the desks to get to the other side quickly.

   Denny walks quietly around the back of the room and doesn't touch anyone.

   _____

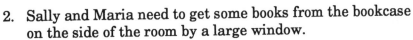

2. Sally and Maria need to get some books from the bookcase on the side of the room by a large window.

   Sally walks quietly over to the bookcase and takes the books she needs.

   Maria stops to show everyone her new watch on the way to the bookcase.

   _____

3. Ben and Doug are supposed to work on a science poster at the table in the back.

   Ben takes his pencils back, then has to return to his desk to get a ruler. Then he goes back again to get some glue. Now he needs to get his science book and get some ideas.

   Doug thinks about what he needs, then gathers everything up and makes one trip.

   _____

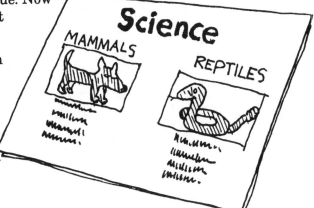

Part II   Classroom Rules and Responsibilities

II-13 Moving as a Group

Objective:

The student will indicate characters who are moving in a line without running, touching each other, talking, or otherwise stopping the progress of the group.

Rationale:

Movement between classrooms is often a monumental task in itself. It's hard to watch everyone, and it's a time when students are close together and may want to talk or goof around. Teaching students how you want them to move from place to place is a skill that requires practice and clear directions. In this lesson, students are instructed to stay together, not change places, be quiet, and not touch each other.

Thinking Questions:

1. What are some times or places where the entire class has to move together to get somewhere else? *(lunchtime, P.E. time, going to the buses, etc.)*

2. Why would it cause problems if everyone wanted to be first in line? *(only one person can be first, others might shove, be angry, etc.)*

3. What would happen if people wanted to keep changing places while the class was moving down the hall? *(would make others behind stop, might be noisy, others would want to change places too, etc.)*

4. Why would this be a bad time to stop and tie your shoe, wave to a friend in another class, or play tag? *(it would stop the whole group)*

5. What are some good rules to remember about walking as a group? *(stay together, don't change places, be quiet, don't touch)*

Activity:

Directions: Students are to read (or listen to) the story about students walking to the library. Using the clues, they are to label each character in the story and count how many children were moving as a group correctly.

Answers: 1. Richard 3. Ellen   5. Steve   7. Tom
            2. Ron   4. Ben   6. Mike   8. Susan
            Four students were walking correctly.

Follow-up: Discuss the problems that each character had and made for others. Discuss which part of the rule was violated.

Moving as a Group

Read the story below and use the clues to write the name of each student in the boxes.

Mrs. Jones' class was on its way to the library. On the way, Steve and Mike were throwing a softball back and forth. This made it hard for Tom and Maria to keep walking in line, but they did. Ron was walking behind Richard, who was walking at a good rate. Ben was upset, however, that Ellen was walking too slowly, so he decided to give her a push.

How many students were walking correctly? _____

II-14 Thinking About Consequences

Objective:

The student will identify at least one possible consequence for a given situation.

Rationale:

Wouldn't it be nice if students thought through what might happen before they did something? This lesson provides students with a few situations to consider and to identify one consequence (or "thing that might happen") if they didn't stop and think first.

Thinking Questions:

1. What might happen if you stayed up all night and then remembered you were supposed to study for a test the next day at school? *(might be frantic with worry, might give up on the test, try to cram, etc.)*

2. What could avoid a problem like that? *(planning ahead, thinking)*

3. What do we mean by "consequences"? *(something that happens because of something you do)*

4. What would be a possible consequence of studying hard for a test? *(do well)*

5. Think about some things that you do at school. Can you give examples of good consequences and then bad consequences? (**good:** *getting a good grade for working hard, getting recess because you finished your work;* **bad:** *having to stay in because you aren't done, not being invited to a party because you teased someone at school, etc.)*

Activity:

Directions: Students are to draw a possible consequence for each situation on the worksheet. Make sure students understand that not all consequences are bad, but that these students were in situations where they didn't think it through first and ended up with a possible bad situation.

Answers: (examples)
1. may do poorly on test
2. might get beat up
3. might forget to do it
4. might give Sharon something that won't be returned

Follow-up: Discuss how each character on the worksheet could end up with a totally different consequence by changing their own behavior to a more positive action.

Thinking About Consequences

What might happen as a consequence if you didn't think through a situation? Draw or write a possible consequence for each student's situation below.

1.

I think I'll skip my homework tonight and go to a movie with my friends instead.

2.

I know that kid is a lot bigger than I am, but I'm going to tell him that he's fat and ugly.

3.

That list of vocabulary words is so long - I think I'll just copy it tomorrow instead of today.

4.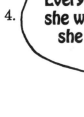

Every time Sharon comes up to me, she wants to borrow something and she never gives it back. Oh, oh - here she comes!

II-15 *Doing It Right the First Time*

Objective:

The student will identify consequences of not doing a task properly the first time around.

Rationale:

Just because a student says that he or she is finished, it doesn't mean that it was done correctly. Students also need to be aware that the task isn't done until it is done correctly. This lesson gives students examples of jobs that are "done," but not "done correctly."

Thinking Questions:

1. What would happen if you did the wrong assignment in a class, but everything you did was right? *(might still have to do it over)*

2. Do you think it is more important to be the first one done with a job or to do it correctly? Why? *(to do it correctly, because even if you're done first, it wouldn't matter)*

3. What about people who take a long time to get things done? Should they try to speed up to get finished or stay slow and get it done right? *(eventually a balance would be nice, but probably most teachers would strive for accuracy first)*

4. Why do you think it's important or better to do things right the first time? *(don't have to do it over, faster in the long run, etc.)*

5. What are some ways that you can help yourself remember to do something right the first time? *(slow down at first, make sure you understand the directions, check your work over before turning it in, etc.)*

Activity:

Directions: Students are going to read about characters who turned in work, but did not do it right. They are to write suggestions for how the character could have avoided the problem.

Answers: (examples)

1. slow down, write clearly
2. take time to understand the directions
3. read the directions
4. make sure you have the right assignment; write down the assignment at the top of the page
5. listen to all of the directions, ask if you don't understand

Follow-up: Everyone makes mistakes, but some mistakes can be avoided by listening and thinking. Have students tell about some mistakes that they may have made in class and how they learned to do it right. Be sure to display examples of good student work in your room or in the hallway!

Doing It Right the First Time

Here are some students who are ready to turn in some work, but there are some problems because they didn't do it right the first time. How could these students have done it right the first time?

1. John was the first one done, but no one can read his work because he wrote so fast.

_____

_____

2. Mary finally finished her math worksheet. All of the answers are wrong because she just put down any number to make it look like she was done.

_____

_____

3. Larry finished his reading assignment, but he didn't read the directions. He wrote the *opposites* for each word instead of words that mean the *same*.

_____

_____

4. Martha did page 35 instead of page 36.

_____

_____

5. Ben wrote a nice long story on the computer, but he wasn't listening when the teacher told the class how to SAVE their work. He just turned off the computer.

_____

_____

Part II   Classroom Rules and Responsibilities

II-16 Doing Homework

Objective:

The student will identify characters who are or are not completing a specified homework task.

Rationale:

What good is it to send home homework if it doesn't get done? This lesson focuses on identifying whether or not someone is actually doing the homework. Most teachers use homework as extra practice or for unfinished classroom assignments, so students should not have too many excuses for not getting it done.

Thinking Questions:

1. What are some kinds of homework assignments that you have had? *(finish something, read a story, bring in something, etc.)*

2. Why do you think students have homework sometimes? *(extra practice, punishment—someone will say it!)*

3. Sometimes people try to avoid doing something they don't really want to do. What are some ways students might try to avoid doing homework? *(play with friends, lose their papers, forget to bring books home)*

4. Are there any good consequences for *not* doing homework? *(probably not)*

5. What are some good ways to help you get homework done? *(do it right away, do it correctly, have a friend help you study, put it where you will remember to do it, etc.)*

Activity:

Directions: Students are to select the one character from each pair who is doing the assigned homework and to write the name on the line.

Answers: 1. Maria   2. Bob   3. David   4. Sarah   5. Beth

Follow-up: There are lots of excuses for not doing homework. What excuses will Ann, Mark, Pedro, Martha, and Randy give at school the next day? Discuss with students that there is a proper time to play in leaves, watch television, or do other things—and that time, in most cases, is probably after the homework is done!

Doing Homework

Mrs. Wright gave all of her students homework. Write the name of each student from the pair who is doing his or her homework.

1. Find five different kinds of leaves.

Ann   Maria

_____

2. Have someone call your spelling words to you at home for practice.

Bob   Mark

_____

3. Read a story by yourself.

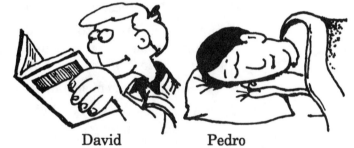

David   Pedro

_____

4. Finish your art collage.

Martha   Sarah

_____

5. Answer all of the questions on the science worksheet.

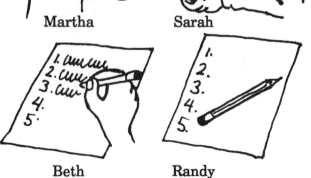

Beth   Randy

_____

Part II   Classroom Rules and Responsibilities

II-17 Bringing Homework to School

Objective:

The student will give at least two reasons why it is important to bring homework to school.

Rationale:

How many times have you heard, "I did my homework! I just left it at home!" Even the most conscientious student will, at times, forget to bring something in. But the habitual offender is the one who loses out because the homework never shows up. This results in sorting through an even bigger mess. Should he or she re-do it? Call Mom to bring it in? It would be so much easier on everyone if students would accept the responsibility to finish the homework task by bringing it in!

Thinking Questions:

1. Have you ever forgotten to bring something to school? What? *(homework, note, treats, extra pencils, etc.)*

2. Why is it hard to remember to bring things in sometimes? *(lots on your mind, busy evening, put it off until the morning, forget to write it down, etc.)*

3. Everyone forgets sometimes. Why is it so important to remember to bring in your homework? *(so you'll get points or a grade, so you won't have to remember it for the next day, so you'll be caught up on assignments, etc.)*

4. Whose responsibility is it for bringing in homework? Is it your teacher's job? Parent's job? *(THE STUDENT'S)*

5. What are some ways that you could help yourself remember to bring your homework to school? *(put it in your backpack the night before, put it on the table, etc.)*

Activity:

Directions: Students are peeking into Fred's room—a real mess!—to locate his homework. They are to circle the items among the mess.

Follow-up: Discuss why Fred probably has trouble bringing things to school. Would it help Fred if his mother cleaned his room? *(He might not know where things are anymore.)* How could Fred be more organized?

Bringing Homework to School

Poor Fred! He did his homework - but forgot to bring it to school. Find and circle the following items in Fred's room:

science book	ruler	poster of a truck
colored pencils	math sheet	note to Mom from teacher

Part II   Classroom Rules and Responsibilities

II-18 But I'm Having Such a Good Dream ...

Objective:

The student will identify characters who are daydreaming, given cartoon clues.

Rationale:

We cannot always tell where a student's mind is. Though he or she may appear to be concentrating on our every word, in actuality, the student may be a hundred miles away, on a sunny beach, sipping a root beer float ... Yet students need to understand that when we accuse them of daydreaming, it is only because we *need* for them to listen or pay close attention. This lesson gives students an opportunity to identify characters who are daydreaming, with the intent that it will provide a basis for discussion of how it affects learning in the classroom.

Thinking Questions:

1. What is your favorite daydream?

2. Are people able to concentrate on more than one thing at a time? Could you daydream and still give your full attention to something else? *(some students will insist that they can, but most will agree that it's harder to shift back and forth)*

3. Is it easy to tell if someone is daydreaming? Are there any clues? *(it's not always easy; clues may include loss of eye contact, staring out the window, having to repeat instructions, etc.)*

4. If the teacher was trying to show you how to do something that you didn't already know how to do, how would daydreaming get in the way? *(wouldn't really understand what was going on, wouldn't hear all of the directions)*

5. Is there a good time to let yourself relax and have some good daydreams? When is your favorite time? *(while talking to friends, right before falling asleep, during free time, etc.)*

Activity:

Directions: Explain that the teacher on the worksheet is teaching the students a task that is new for them (paper folding), so they need to pay attention. Students are to look at the characters on the worksheet and write the names of the students whose minds are on the teacher's directions.

Answers: Tim, Sam

Follow-up: Discuss what was on the minds of the other students in the class. When would be a better time for the students to think about those things? *(Jenny—outside; Max—get a good night's sleep; Jane—during lunch; Allen—watching television; Joe—he is in love and probably won't be able to think for awhile; Donna—after the lesson)*

But I'm Having Such a Good Dream. . .

The teacher is showing the students how to do origami - Japanese paper folding! Some of the students are daydreaming instead of listening. Write the names of the students who have their minds on the teacher.

II-19 Finishing the Job

Objective:

The student will assist cartoon characters in completion of a given task.

Rationale:

One of the most aggravating conditions teachers deal with is unfinished work. How can we evaluate a paper if it's only half done? What if the half is not enough to tell us whether or not the student understands the concept of the lesson? Students may come up with lots of excuses for not finishing *(I didn't understand; it was too long; I couldn't think of anything),* but for most appropriate tasks that have been well-taught and serve some purpose, the excuses are not good enough. This is one skill that will follow them all of their adult lives—finish the job!!

Thinking Questions:

1. Why is it important to finish what you start? *(otherwise it doesn't count, it looks better to have something all the way done, etc.)*

2. What are some things that you have to finish in order to win something or to get a prize? *(a race, a contest, papers at school for a sticker, etc.)*

3. What would happen if you only painted a room halfway? Or the bus driver wanted to stop in the middle of the route? Or your chicken dinner was only cooked a little bit? *(answers will vary, but you'd have a mess)*

4. Can you think of other jobs that are important to complete all the way? *(vacuuming a room, building a swing set, reading a book, etc.)*

5. What happens if a job needs to be done and the person who is supposed to do it doesn't finish? *(someone else may have to complete it, won't get full credit for the job, etc.)*

Activity:

Directions: Students are to examine the "assignments" of the characters on the worksheet and to complete the task. Assume that the characters either had excuses for not finishing or just did not want to finish. Provide whatever materials are necessary for your students to complete the job (markers, crayons, rules for letter-writing, etc.).

Answers: (examples)

1. draw another Indian and a horse or two
2. finish coloring in the numbers
3. match the rest of the words with the pictures
4. add a few lines such as: —you? I'm fine. I'm playing baseball these days. Write back. Your friend, Tim.

Follow-up: If your students interviewed the characters from the worksheet, what excuses might they hear? *(I can't draw, I was tired, I don't like to write, etc.)* How hard were the tasks for them to finish? *(not hard)* Discuss ways in which jobs that aren't as fun to do could be done to make them easier. *(don't stop until you're finished, work with a friend, think about it first, etc.)*

Finishing the Job

Help these students finish their assignments.

1. Carrie is supposed to draw a picture of Indians and horses.

2. George is coloring a math worksheet.

I'm done.

3. Phyllis is matching words and pictures.

Zzzz

1. cat
2. dog
3. house
4. man
5. rabbit

4. Tim is writing a letter to his pen-pal.

Dear Bob,
How are _____

© 1993 by The Center for Applied Research in Education

Part II   Classroom Rules and Responsibilities

II-20 This Is the Cafeteria, Not the Classroom

Objective:

The student will state rules that are appropriate for any typical school situation, not a specific room or time.

Rationale:

Some students seem to demand an explicit list of rules for every situation instead of generalizing. For example, a student who shows that he knows how to sit at a desk may think that sitting in the auditorium is a completely different skill. This lesson explains that some rules are based on common sense; just because a room is not the classroom in which the rules are taught doesn't mean that the rules do not apply.

Thinking Questions:

1. What are some classroom rules that we have been learning about? *(pay attention, comply with instructions, quiet down, sit appropriately, don't make noise entering or leaving room, etc.)*

2. Do you think that any other classrooms have these rules? *(probably all of them)*

3. Why are some rules the same no matter what room you are in or what school you go to? *(they are good rules, the situations are the same no matter what school you go to, etc.)*

4. Do you think some rules are good for teachers and students both? What? *(treat each other with respect, be polite to each other, give your best, etc.)*

5. Why do you think students who behave in one place might have trouble in another room? *(don't think about the rules, don't know the rules, don't like the teacher, etc.)*

Activity:

Directions: The students are looking at a scene from a school cafeteria. Although the characters know about school rules and responsibilities in their classrooms, it seems as though they have forgotten everything once they entered the cafeteria. Students are to make a list of classroom rules that would still apply to the cafeteria.

Answers: (examples) pay attention to the task *(the girl is daydreaming and didn't finish her lunch);* sit appropriately *(the boy has his feet on the table);* enter the cafeteria quietly *(the boy is yelling for attention);* know when to quiet down *(one student is yelling while the other is patting him);* move around the room without bothering others *(two characters don't have their hands to themselves);* etc. Students will probably think of other good rules!

Follow-up: Discuss what problem situations might surface in rooms such as the music room, hallway, restrooms, locker room, or other rooms that are not specifically a classroom. What rules would be necessary? Why is the *intent* of the rules more important than what room you happen to be in? What are some rules that are necessary in one place that would be silly in another? *(wash your hands before you leave the room / restroom; put your bat and ball away / gymnasium; etc.)* Can students identify the room based on the rules given?

This Is the Cafeteria, Not the Classroom

These students are in the cafeteria. What classroom rules should still apply here?

Rules to Remember:

_____

_____

_____

_____

_____

III-1 It's a Substitute!

Objective:

The student will identify appropriate behaviors for when a substitute teacher is in charge of the classroom.

Rationale:

When the regular teacher is gone, some students feel that they can take advantage of the substitute. Often, the classroom teacher is horrified to find out how the class behaved in his or her absence! This lesson focuses on how a student should behave for a substitute.

Thinking Questions:

1. Has your regular teacher ever missed a day of teaching? Why? *(probably— conferences, illness, personal days, etc.)*

2. Who usually fills in when the regular teacher is gone? *(a substitute, another classroom teacher, sometimes the principal)*

3. What do you think the job of a substitute teacher is like? What situations might he or she run into during the day? *(job might be confusing at first; knowing who everyone is, how the class routine is conducted, unusual situations, bad behavior of the class clowns, etc.)*

4. How does your regular teacher expect you to behave with a substitute? *(the same, or some expect **better** behavior)*

5. Why do you think some students show their worst behavior when there is a substitute? *(the substitute might be meek, students might think they won't be punished for anything they do that day, etc.)*

6. How should students act when a substitute is in charge of the room? *(follow the instructions as if he or she were the regular teacher)*

Activity:

Directions: Students are to consider the list of behaviors on the worksheet and put a check mark next to the ones that are respectful to a substitute teacher.

> *Answers:* 2 (if it is a sincere greeting), 4 (if the substitute seems to need help), 5, 8, 9

Follow-up: Discuss your expectations for the class in your absence. Explain that you will deal with discipline problems, that you expect the students' best behavior, and that you will be in contact with the substitute about the day's events. Perhaps you could offer a special reward or incentive for "good helpers." Don't overload the substitute with complicated instructions for managing the day!

It's a Substitute!

There is a substitute in your classroom today. Put a ✔ next to each thing that shows respect for the substitute.

1. Switch seats so she doesn't know who anyone is. _____

2. Say "hello" when you walk into the room. _____

3. Pretend that you are sick and have to go to the nurse. _____

4. Show her where the reading workbooks are kept. _____

5. Follow all of her instructions right away. _____

6. Tell her that you aren't supposed to have any homework, even if you really do. _____

7. Walk into class late. _____

8. Raise your hand to answer questions. _____

9. Be quiet when she is talking to the class. _____

10. Argue about who goes to lunch first. _____

III-2 The Classroom Assistant

Objective:

The student will identify at least ten common activities that the classroom assistant helps the teacher or class with each day.

Rationale:

The classroom assistant (if you are lucky enough to even have one) works alongside the teacher by helping, reinforcing, reteaching, cutting, pasting, drilling, caring, and working hard in the classroom. Students sometimes treat an assistant differently in the classroom, acting as though he or she is "not the real teacher." This lesson strives to create an awareness of the many tasks an assistant helps out with in the classroom.

Thinking Questions:

1. Why do some classrooms have assistants? *(many children, younger children, need extra help)*

2. Is an assistant the same as a teacher? What is the difference? *(some assistants do have degrees in education; however, the role in the classroom is for the assistant to help carry out the teacher's plans and instructions)*

3. What are some activities that the assistant helps out with? *(listening to students read, running off worksheets, etc.)*

4. How do you think a classroom assistant should be treated? *(with respect, just like any other adult)*

5. What would happen if you didn't like the assistant? *(still be cooperative, try to follow the directions, respect him or her as you would the teacher)*

Activity:

Directions: Students are to list ten different tasks or responsibilities of an assistant with whom they are familiar. These could be daily tasks or tasks that occur occasionally (helping with a fun fair, helping with a birthday party, etc.).

Answers: Will vary, but may include hands out stickers, helps check papers, watches in the lunchroom, calls spelling words, etc.

Follow-up: Discuss how important an assistant is to you—allowing you as the teacher to get more accomplished in class. By conveying your appreciation towards the assistant in front of the class, you will provide a good example to follow.

The Classroom Assistant

Your classroom assistant does many things. Make a list of at least ten different activities that the assistant helps your class with during the day.

1. _____

_____

2. _____

_____

3. _____

_____

4. _____

_____

5. _____

_____

6. _____

_____

7. _____

_____

8. _____

_____

9. _____

_____

10. _____

_____

III-3 The Principal

Objective:

The student will identify ways that the principal of the school could be shown respect.

Rationale:

The principal is the leader of the school, but hopefully has time to get to know many of the students on a personal level. The principal is only a menacing threat to students who do not choose to follow the school's rules. It is wonderful to see students who seek out the school's leader to share a special moment or to seek a compliment. The principal is not a police officer, but should be shown absolute respect as one who has to enforce policy.

Thinking Questions:

1. What do you think a principal does all day? *(you'll probably get all kinds of surprising answers!)*

2. Do you think the principal has the power to do away with or make any rules he or she wants to? *(realistically, no)*

3. What are some school rules that the principal has to enforce or make sure that everyone does? *(no fighting at school, don't skip out, take notes home to your parents, etc.)*

4. How do those school rules help everybody at school? *(for protection, to give students a chance to learn at school by being at school, to communicate with parents)*

5. What are some nice things or fun things that your principal has done? *(maybe helped with a field trip, sat in a "dunk" booth at the fair, gave prizes for good readers, etc.)*

Activity:

Directions: Students are pretending that they are the school's principal and see six faces outside their office. They are to circle the students who are being respectful.

Answers: 3, 4, 6

Follow-up: Although the principal may see lots of students like numbers 1, 2, and 5, why are those situations unpleasant to the principal? *(show defiance, apathy)* Discuss how students can convey their problems in a respectful manner.

Name _____ Date _____

III-3

The Principal

You are the principal! Which of these students would you like to have in your office? Circle the students who are being respectful and pleasant to the principal.

1. Hey! My teacher sent me here because I forgot my homework. I'm not doing it, either!

2. I was fighting on the bus. But I won!

3. Mr. Collins, will you eat lunch with us in the cafeteria today?

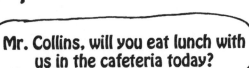

4. I wanted to show you the "A" I got on my test!

5. I don't have to do what you say. My uncle is a lawyer and we'll sue you.

6. Thank you for helping me get into the right art class when I was mixed up.

III-4 The School Secretary

Objective:

The student will write polite or respectful requests for something needed from the school secretary.

Rationale:

At many schools, the secretary is the "catch-all" person—handling everything from minor emergencies on the playground to screening problems for the principal, not to mention shuffling daily paperwork, counts, and other records. Though this is a very important position, students may view the secretary as their own personal servant. ("Call my mom." "I need that book." "Run this off for me.") Students should be respectful to this very important person—who also may run off their report cards on the computer!

Thinking Questions:

1. What are some of the responsibilities of a school secretary? *(keep attendance records, type, answer the phone, schedule meetings, etc.)*

2. Do you think the secretary knows a lot about what's going on at the school? Why? *(probably—she's in the center of activity, probably is near the principal's office, sees kids coming and going)*

3. What might be hard about being a secretary? What might be fun? (**hard:** *handling many problems at once, answering to mad parents, etc.;* **fun:** *talking to all the kids, answering the phone, etc.)*

4. What kinds of things do you think people ask the secretary to do for them? *(run off materials, find certain things, make phone calls)*

5. What are some ways that you could show respect to the secretary if you needed something? *(ask politely, be sure to thank her, be patient when waiting your turn, etc.)*

Activity:

Directions: Students are to help the characters on the worksheet ask for something from the school secretary in a polite manner. They are to write what the character might say.

Answers: (examples)

1. May I please use the telephone?

2. I would like some supplies, please.

3. Mrs. George sent me for the menu.

4. Hello, this is for you. I have to leave early.

5. Could I wait here for my parents, please?

Follow-up: The secretary may be a liaison between the principal and the parent, the teacher and the parent, the principal and the teacher, etc. Explain that when someone is in the middle, as this job may put someone, extra patience is required while both sides connect through her. Ask students to think about what parties are connected through the secretary in these examples. *(#1—student and parent; #2—student and supplies; #3—teacher and cafeteria; #4—parent/dentist and school; and #5—teacher and parent)*

The School Secretary

Each of these students is talking to the school secretary. Write something that each might say to the secretary that is respectful.

1. Molly needs to use the telephone to call home.

_____

_____

_____

2. Luis wants to buy a pad of paper and two pencils.

_____

_____

_____

3. Benjamin's teacher sent him to the office to pick up lunch menus for the month.

_____

_____

_____

4. Jennifer is supposed to give the secretary a note telling that she has to go to the dentist and must leave early.

_____

_____

_____

5. Randy got in trouble at recess and is supposed to ask if he can wait in the office for his parents to come and get him.

_____

_____

_____

Part III   Other Authority Figures

III-5 You're Not My Classroom Teacher!

Objective:

The student will identify instances in which a person who is not the classroom teacher should be obeyed.

Rationale:

Though students may be obedient and have won the respect of their classroom teacher, those same students may not feel that they have to listen to any other teachers or other adults in the school. This lesson gives the student opportunities to think through situations in which any teacher is his or her teacher.

Thinking Questions:

1. How many teachers have you had since you started school? *(numbers will vary)*

2. When you went on to the next grade, was the teacher you had before still your teacher? *(in a way since there was a relationship, but not directly anymore)*

3. Would you still be expected to do what those teachers asked you to do if you were in their classroom? *(yes)*

4. Would you be expected to follow their instructions if you weren't in their classroom? *(yes—there would be a reason for whatever instruction was given)*

5. What about teachers on the playground, in art and music, or teachers walking down the hall—are they teachers *for* your school even though they may not be your teacher *in* school? *(yes—should still be respected)*

6. Who are some teachers at school who give instructions to you even though they aren't your teacher? Why do they give you instructions? *(teachers of other grades, music and art teachers, lunchroom supervisors/give instructions because they were needed in the situation)*

Activity:

Directions: This worksheet follows "Pete" through part of his day at school and his encounters with several teachers who each give Pete something to do or an order to follow. Students are to circle the examples of teachers giving Pete instructions.

Answers: 1, 2, 4, 6, 7, 8, 9

Follow-up: Discuss why the teachers on the worksheet were or were not giving Pete instructions. Why were the instructions given important? *(#1—the floor was slippery and it could have caused an accident; #2—probably other people wanted to use the restroom too, etc.)*

You're Not My Classroom Teacher!

Circle every example you can find in this picture of someone who is NOT Pete's classroom teacher, but who is giving him instructions. How many can you find?

1.
"Watch out - the floor is slippery. Don't walk over there."

2.
"Get in line to use the restroom."
BOYS

3.
"Good morning, Pete."

4.
"Hey - slow down, Pete. No running in the hall."

5.
"Hi."

6.
"Would you drop this off in the office as you go past? Thanks."

7.
"Everyone get a ball and mitt. Put the jump ropes away now."
COACH

8.
"We're having class - please don't peep in the door."

9.
"Buses aren't here yet. Wait inside the door."

Part III   Other Authority Figures

III-6 The Bus Driver

Objective:

The student will identify situations regarding the bus and bus driver that require student compliance.

Rationale:

The bus driver is an authority figure who is an extension of the school. Without him or her, parents would have more work to do getting their children to school. Thus, it is extremely important for students to get along on the bus, especially so that they do not contribute to the driver's need for concentration. Everyone will be safer with the bus driver able to concentrate on driving, not disciplining.

Thinking Questions:

1. How do students get to and from school each day? *(enumerate ways: walking, parents, carpooling, bus)*

2. How does a bus driver help make getting to school easier—or even possible—for some students? *(parents can get to work on time, saves a long walk for some, etc.)*

3. What do you think a bus driver has to think about when he or she is operating the bus? *(other cars, remembering to stop at the right places, watching out for children who are walking, etc.)*

4. What are some problems that a bus driver might have if the students on the bus weren't cooperative? *(lack of concentration, might have an accident, longer bus ride, etc.)*

5. What are some good rules for riding the bus safely? *(sit down, be quiet, don't change seats, don't throw things, etc.)*

Activity:

Directions: Students are to evaluate four situations to decide whether or not the characters are being respectful to the bus driver by following his or her instructions. They are to write *yes* or *no* on the lines.

    Answers: 1. no   2. yes   3. no   4. yes

    Follow-up: Discuss how the students in #1 and #3 could resolve their problems without involving the bus driver. What are safe, quiet activities that could be done on the bus?

The Bus Driver

Write YES if the students are being respectful to the bus driver; write NO if they are not.

1.

2.

3.

4.

Part III   Other Authority Figures

III-7 Guest Speakers

Objective:

The student will identify several inappropriate behaviors that show discourtesy to a guest speaker and state appropriate behaviors.

Rationale:

We always hope that students will exhibit their best behavior when there is a guest in the room, especially one who stays for awhile or is doing a favor by talking to the class. Students need to be taught that a guest speaker deserves even more courtesy because of the time and effort that he or she has given to visiting the class. Appropriate behaviors might include asking relevant questions, paying close attention, not getting the guest speaker sidetracked, and showing special courtesy to the speaker by being quiet and letting others listen.

Thinking Questions:

1. Who are some guest speakers that you have heard in your class? *(community leaders, parents of other students, etc.)*

2. What do guest speakers tell about that your teacher might not be able to tell you as well? *(court procedures, trips to foreign countries, things about a specific career, etc.)*

3. Do most guest speakers want to be paid? Why or why not? *(they visit as a service or as a favor to the school or class)*

4. How could you show that you are interested in what a guest speaker is talking about? *(act like you are listening, ask questions, tell about an experience you had that relates, etc.)*

5. What are some ways that some students are silly or don't show good behavior when there is a guest? *(might try to act like they are dumb to get attention, might take the opportunity when the teacher is busy to act up, etc.)*

6. What are some ways the class could prepare for a guest speaker to make sure he or she feels welcome and that the class is prepared to listen? *(talk about the subject before the guest comes, prepare a list of questions to ask, figure out where everyone is going to sit, etc.)*

Activity:

Directions: Students are to evaluate four situations in which a student (or two) is not being courteous to the guest speaker. They are to write the inappropriate behavior on the lines next to each picture.

Answers:

1. student is sleeping
2. student is making fun of the picture
3. student is being silly
4. students are not paying attention

Follow-up: Discuss ways that the characters on the worksheet could show appropriate behavior to the guest speaker. *(e.g., sit up, keep silly comments to yourself, answer questions appropriately, pay attention)*

Name _____   Date _____

III-7

Guest Speakers

What are each of these students doing that is discourteous to the guest speaker? Write your answer on the lines next to the picture.

1.

2.

3.

4.

III-8 The Custodian

Objective:

The student will identify several jobs that the school custodian is responsible for.

Rationale:

Many students have no idea what a school custodian does. This is the person who single-handedly can make your life easier, as he or she often helps with the little things that you need to make your class run more smoothly. Getting a bigger desk, an extra desk, fixing a broken window, moving a television and VCR are all "small" things, but important. The jobs are all important, and the custodian is a valued member of the school staff. Convey this to your students!

Thinking Questions:

1. What happens if there is a burned-out lightbulb in the room? *(custodian fixes it)*

2. What are some of the jobs that a custodian does? *(fixes things, finds things, cleans things, etc.)*

3. Why are these jobs important? *(someone needs to know where everything is kept, how to keep things running properly, make the school property look nice, etc.)*

4. Why is it important for the school building to look nice? *(we want to work in a nice environment, shows pride in the school)*

5. How does the custodian help make the teacher's job easier? *(teacher doesn't have to take class time to find materials, keeps things working properly so the teacher can use them in class, etc.)*

Activity:

Directions: Students are to circle all of the jobs on the worksheet that a school custodian is probably responsible for. Discuss the activities that *your* custodian does for your school. You may have somewhat different job descriptions.

Answers: (possible answers—depends on the individual school) 1, 2, 3, 5, 7, 9, 10, 12, 14

Follow-up: Discuss who might be responsible for the activities that were not selected (4, 6, 8, 11, 13). Are there other jobs that you could add to the custodian's list?

The Custodian

Circle all of the jobs that a school custodian might do in your school.

1. | Bring another desk to your classroom. |

2. | Fix a broken window. |

3. | Clean the floor in the restroom. |

4. | Drive the principal to school. |

5. | Put in a new blackboard. |

6. | Cook the lunch in the cafeteria. |

7. | Repair a broken record player. |

8. | Help students with their homework. |

9. | Empty the trash after lunch. |

10. | Cut the lawn in front of the school. |

11. | Coach the track team. |

12. | Paint parking lines in the teachers' parking lot. |

13. | Type a letter for the principal. |

14. | Polish the floors in the hallway. |

III-9 Field Trip Helpers

Objective:

The student will identify ways that he or she can help a field trip helper during a field trip with the class.

Rationale:

Field trips can either be a lot of fun or a nightmare! When there are helpers to go along, they can make things run more smoothly for the class, allowing everyone to enjoy the tip. Prepare children for field trips by going over expectations before, during, and after the field trip. Name tags, emergency procedures, objectives for the trip, and restroom/lunch procedures should all be covered with the helpers so everyone knows what to do. Then enjoy the trip!

Thinking Questions:

1. What are some field trips that you have taken through school? *(museums, zoos, picnics, special events, etc.)*

2. Who goes along on the trips to help out? *(parents, bus driver, older siblings, other teachers, etc.)*

3. What are some things that could go wrong on a field trip if it wasn't planned carefully? *(leave someone behind, not have enough lunches, forget medication, etc.)*

4. How do field trip helpers make a field trip easier and more fun? *(let you have smaller groups, get around easier, some parents are really fun, don't have to wait as long, etc.)*

5. What are some ways that you or our class could help a field trip helper have an easier time? *(wear name tags, go over the class rules, make sure they have maps, money, special instructions, etc.)*

Activity:

Directions: Students are to match each picture with the description of how the student is being helpful to the field trip helper.

Answers: 1. d   2. a   3. e   4. b   5. c

Follow-up: Make a class list of field trip procedures. What could go wrong? What will the emergency procedures consist of? What are good rules to have in effect for field trip safety?

Field Trip Helpers

How are these students being helpful to the field trip helpers? Match each student with the answer on the right.

1. Wait here until we're ready to move on!

2.

3.

4. Let's go!

5. Everyone - go to the restroom now!

a. wearing a name tag

b. staying with the group

c. following instructions to go to the restroom

d. obeying the helper's request to wait

e. sitting quietly through the movie

III-10 School Counselors

Objective:

The student will identify several reasons why he or she could visit the school counselor.

Rationale:

Depending on your school, the counselor (if you are lucky enough to have one!) may be responsible for scheduling, handling discipline, some teaching, and even counseling needy students! This is a wonderful resource for *all* students. Make sure that your students know that this person is available to *all* of them.

Thinking Questions:

1. Who could you go to if you were having problems with schoolwork? *(teacher, principal)*

2. Who could help if you had problems that were bigger, like problems getting along with other kids or problems at home? *(school counselor, teachers)*

3. Counselors are people who are specially trained to help students get through school as well as possible. What might a counselor do that a teacher doesn't? *(work with small groups instead of large class, be able to talk about personal things, doesn't give homework)*

4. What are some reasons that someone might go see the counselor? *(problems at home, problems at school, just want someone to talk to, scheduling, excused from school, etc.)*

5. Do you have to have a problem to see the counselor? *(hopefully not; ideally a counselor should interact with all of the students on some level—teaching study skills, problem-solving skills, etc.)*

Activity:

Directions: Students are to read about the seven students on the worksheet and decide whether or not that student could go to see the counselor.

Answers: Any of them should be able to see the counselor.

Follow-up: Discuss how a counselor could fit into your classroom needs. What activities is he or she responsible for in your classroom?

School Counselors

Which of these students below would be welcome to see the school counselor? Circle each student that you choose.

1. MARY is very worried because her parents are getting a divorce. She wishes she had someone to talk to about this.

2. GEORGE got an A on his science project and wants to let someone know.

3. JUANITA has been getting bad grades in math. She doesn't know how to study very well.

4. ALEX is new in the school and doesn't have many friends. He feels scared and lonely.

5. SANDRA wants to know if she can take an art class for free choice period instead of going to volleyball.

6. ANDY can't get his locker open.

7. DOROTHY has a note that says she has to leave school early to go to the doctor. She will miss three days of school.

Part IV   When You Have Problems

IV-1 Having a Problem

Objective:

The student will identify common problems that one might experience in school or at home.

Rationale:

The first step in problem solving is identifying what the problem is—the nature of what we are dealing with. Everyone has problems at some time, and solving those problems can be a challenge as well as a chore. This lesson centers around deciding what the basic problem is in several situations.

Thinking Questions:

1. When you think of problems that you may have at home or school, what do you think of? *(getting along with the teacher or students, keep up with work, remembering things, etc.)*

2. What are some problems that may come up on the playground or after school? *(fighting over equipment, chasing others, trying to fight when the teacher isn't around, etc.)*

3. What are some problems that most kids have to deal with in the classroom? *(doing work, understanding the work, finishing the work, remembering homework, etc.)*

4. What are some ways that people try to blame others for the problem? *(saying that it's someone else's responsibility, giving up and letting someone else finish, etc.)*

5. Do you think there is an answer or solution for every problem? *(answers may vary—hopefully they will decide that there are solutions out there that can be sought after!)*

Activity:

Directions: Students are to decide what the problem is in each of the situations on the worksheet and then to write their answer on the lines.

    Answers: (examples)

1. boy can't tie his shoe	4. boy is having trouble reading
2. girl needs a new pen	5. boy can't reach something
3. boy is bothered by the other boy	

    Follow-up: Have students discuss what each character might try in order to begin solving their problem. Discuss the seriousness of each situation. Is each problem worth getting upset about? Which are not as crucial or important?

Having a Problem?

Each of these students is having some difficulty. What is the problem that each student below is bothered by? Write your answer on the lines next to each student.

1. I can't get this stupid shoe tied! I'm going to trip and fall!

_____
_____
_____

2. This pen isn't working! How can I get my story finished?

_____
_____
_____

3. If you give me that look one more time, I'm going to POUND you!

_____
_____
_____

4. I just can't figure this out. It doesn't make any sense!

_____
_____
_____

5. I - - - can't - - - quite - - - reach - - - this - - -

_____
_____
_____

IV-2 Asking for Help Politely

Objective:

The student will identify polite ways to request help from others.

Rationale:

Simply asking for help on something may get a response, but asking *politely* will get a better response. Most requests can be delivered in a clear, appropriate manner and still get results. Students should focus on requesting, rather than demanding.

Thinking Questions:

1. When you want something from someone, what do you do? *(ask them for it)*

2. Do you think it makes a difference in *how* you ask someone for something? *(most people prefer to be asked nicely)*

3. What are some things you would ask for help on at school? *(questions about schoolwork, the teacher's time, etc.)*

4. What are some things you might ask for help on at home? *(homework, chores, running errands, etc.)*

5. Do you think there is a way to ask for help politely, rather than demanding help? *(yes)*

6. What could you do to make a request for help sound more polite and pleasant? *(add "please," be patient with request, don't be pushy, etc.)*

Activity:

Directions: Students are to circle the students on the worksheet who are asking for help politely. They are to X those who are not.

Answers: **Circle**—2, 3, 5; **X**—1, 4, 6

Follow-up: Discuss how the X'd students could have asked for help politely. Discuss why "You!" and "Hey!" are impolite. Explain that *asking for help* is not a bad thing; in fact, it is necessary for lots of problem-solving situations. But adding that polite touch will make a difference in how others respond to you.

Name _____ Date _____

IV-2

Asking for Help Politely

Which of these students are asking for help in a polite way? Circle the students. Put an X on those who are not being polite or respectful.

1.  You!!! HELP!! Right now!

2.  Jackie - could I borrow your pen when you're done? Sure.

3.  Mrs. Klaus, do you have time to show me how to print my story on the computer?

4.  Hey! Pass the salt!

5. I don't understand the directions. Could you help me?

6.  Check my work right now so I can go to recess.

IV-3 Taking Another Look

Objective:

The student will identify ways to solve problems by looking at the situation carefully.

Rationale:

Some problems can be solved simply by taking a good look at the situation at hand. Minor things can be overlooked such as the location of materials, glancing at a page without really "seeing" it, or assuming that something is in place when it actually isn't. Teach students to carefully assess the problem situation before getting upset about it.

Thinking Questions:

1. Have you ever looked all over for something and eventually found it—right under your nose? *(probably someone will have an anecdote!)*

2. Why do you think people make mistakes like that? *(in a hurry, looking in the wrong spot, etc.)*

3.. Have you ever made mistakes in school where you just didn't look hard enough at something? *(ask for anecdotes)*

4. What's a way to help get out of that problem of just not seeing something? *(double-check your work, slow down, etc.)*

5. How can another person help you take another look? *(ask a friend to check it over for you or with you, different perspective!)*

Activity:

Directions: Students are to go through Tom's day, finding clues that Tom overlooked—resulting in his having a very bad day. They are to circle the clues that Tom should have noticed.

> *Answers:*
>
> 1. math book in desk
> 2. problem was 2 + 3
> 3. directions asked for complete sentences
> 4. no name on paper
> 5. the clock shows that it's past 10 o'clock—the class is at recess
> 6. the door was shut, but came open again

Follow-up: Discuss with your class the idea of saying, "Take another look," if you notice a problem that the student should be able to solve simply by looking again at the situation.

Taking Another Look

Tom is having a very bad day. Nothing is going right for him. Help him get through his problems by *taking another look* at the situation. Circle something that Tom should look at carefully in each picture below.

1. *I can't find my math book. How can anyone expect me to get my work done if I can't find my book?*

MATH

2. *That answer is not wrong! 2 + 2 is 4! It's always been 4! Why is this marked wrong?*

$$\begin{array}{r} 2 \\ + 3 \\ \hline 4 \end{array}$$

3. *I answered the questions! It said to answer the questions! What's wrong with this?*

Answer in Complete Sentences
1. Yes
2. No

4. *Don't forget to put your name on your paper, Tom.*

I did.

Name _____

5. *I don't understand why everyone is gone. Where is everybody?*

10:00
RECESS

6. *Did you close the door?*

Yes.

IV-4 Thinking Harder

Objective:

The student will identify multiple solutions to problems by spending time thinking about alternatives.

Rationale:

We train our students to spit forth quick answers to many problems or situations, rather than allowing them to mull things over for awhile before answering. Allowing students—no, requiring students!—to think through possible solutions before giving an answer is a good skill for thinking (on the part of the student) and waiting (on the part of the teacher).

Thinking Questions:

1. When someone asks you a question, how soon do they want the answer? *(usually right away)*

2. When you stop and think about something for awhile, do you sometimes change your mind about how you feel about it or what you think of it? *(ask for anecdotes)*

3. If you had a problem situation, why might it be important to think about it for awhile rather than just do something quickly? *(you might not know the whole situation, time might change things somewhat)*

4. When someone tells you to "stop and think about it," is it hard to do? Why or why not? *(probably—we're used to quick answers)*

5. Do you think there are several answers to some problems? Why? *(yes, especially when many factors are involved)*

Activity:

Directions: Students are to generate several possible (plausible, too) solutions for the situations given. Encourage them to "stop and think" before putting down only one answer.

Answers: (examples)

1. invite them both over to your house; go to one's on one day, one the next day; ask if you could all play

2. borrow from a friend; call a neighbor; go home at lunch; etc.

3. ask if they could hold the book for you; borrow from a good friend; ask if the book will be at the library later

4. ask Tony to help you clean your room (a true friend would do that!); ask Tony to wait; ask your mother if you could clean both your room and the kitchen if she lets you play now

Follow-up: Discuss the concept of "brainstorming" with your students: first, generate lots and lots of ideas, even silly ones, then think through the best choices and begin to eliminate the ones that are not as good. Explain that when there is no clear-cut right answer, a lot of good thinking will help narrow down your choices to several possibilities.

Thinking Harder

Sometimes problems can be solved by thinking them over for awhile. What are at least three possible solutions for each of the following problems? Think before you answer. . .

1. Both Mary and Elizabeth invited you over after school to come to their houses. You like both of them, but you can't be in two places at one time. What could you do?

   a. _____

   b. _____

   c. _____

2. It's the day of the big volleyball game at lunch. Oh, no! You left your gym shoes at home and your mother has already gone off to work. What will you do?

   a. _____

   b. _____

   c. _____

3. There is a book sale in the library. You really want to buy the book about papier-mâché projects, but it costs $1 more than you have. It's the last day of the sale. What might you do?

   a. _____

   b. _____

   c. _____

4. Your mother wants you to clean your room before company comes over. It's a mess (as usual). Your friend Tony wants you to play ball with him before it gets dark. You only have about an hour. What will you do?

   a. _____

   b. _____

   c. _____

© 1993 by The Center for Applied Research in Education

IV-5 Excuses, Excuses

Objective:

The student will identify given excuses as legitimate or not acceptable, considering the circumstances.

Rationale:

We often hear excuses for why homework wasn't turned in, why someone is late for class, or why it isn't necessary for someone to do the entire assignment. As teachers, we don't always know the entire circumstances surrounding the problem; however, we do know the students who are habitual in providing us with excuse after excuse. We should help students differentiate between giving a good *reason* for the problem happening and giving an *excuse* as a substitute for having a good reason. Without playing word games, help students realize that mistakes can happen to anyone, but if circumstances could be controlled and should have been controlled, an excuse is often not good enough to make up for not having something done.

Thinking Questions:

1. What are some of the excuses you hear for not having something done? *(I lost it, I was too tired, I was busy, etc.)*

2. What would be considered a "good" excuse for not having your homework done? *(if you were in an accident, if the teacher forgot to pass out the homework, etc.)*

3. If someone gives excuses all the time, what might you begin to think about that person? *(doesn't really want to work, doesn't care, not responsible)*

4. When is an excuse good enough to get you out of something? When you couldn't control the situation or if you didn't want to change a situation? *(physical pain is usually a good excuse, poor planning is not)*

5. Are you responsible for your dog if he destroys a school book? *(you are responsible for the damage)*

6. If you are not careful with where you put things or what you do yourself, could accidents happen? *(yes)*

7. If accidents happen because you were careless, is that excuse acceptable? *(not if it is habitual—if you don't learn from the mistakes)*

8. Do you think most people would understand something going wrong for you if they knew the circumstances? *(hopefully)*

9. Why do some people get "excused" from school early or "excused" from doing extra work? *(depends on the circumstances: going to the dentist might be an emergency, that person's situation might be entirely different than yours)*

Activity:

Directions: Students are to read the set of excuses and decide whether or not each excuse is acceptable to the point that no punishment should occur for missing or late work. Encourage students to think hard about the situations—is the student trying to get out of work or is he or she really explaining about a problem situation? If not enough information is given to make an informed decision, have students ask questions that they would need to know to make a judgment.

> *Answers:*
> 1. probably no (what was it doing sticking out of the car window?)
> 2. no (you are responsible for the dog's behavior—could have found another pencil)
> 3. no (you could control how late you were up)
> 4. yes (going to the dentist is usually acceptable)
> 5. no (trying to blame Joe's mom is not good enough)
> 6. probably yes (a promise was made to the brother and mother, so that would come first)

Follow-up: Impress upon students the importance of planning ahead to avoid common household situations that turn into problems. Don't blame the dog, the wind, the television—direct the focus of whose responsibility it is to where it belongs.

Excuses, Excuses

These students have many different excuses for not having something done or done right. Do you think each is a good excuse? Write YES or NO on the line next to each situation.

1. I don't have my homework because it flew out of the car window last night when I was holding it out.

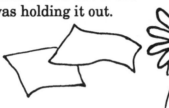

_____

2. My dog ate my pencil so I couldn't finish my worksheet.

_____

3. I was up too late last night watching the horror movies and I overslept and couldn't finish my reading.

_____

4. I'm late because I had to go to the dentist to get a filling in my tooth.

_____

5. I'm late because I stopped to have breakfast at Joe's house and his mom cooks slowly.

_____

6. I can't come over after school to help you with your bike because I promised my little brother I'd take him to the store for my mom.

_____

Section I

IV-6 Having a Peer-Tutor

Objective:

The student will identify several ways that a peer-tutor can assist a student in school.

Rationale:

Sometimes students learn best from other students. Having a slightly older student work with a younger student is not only fun for them both, but both can benefit in different ways. The older student has the status of being a role-model, and the younger student may feel more comfortable receiving help from someone who is close to him or her in age, ideas, and experiences. Some special students "bond" well with their special tutor and may exhibit exceptional behavior in anticipation of spending time with their helper.

Thinking Questions:

1. If you are having trouble with something, who in the class would you go to for help? *(name several responsible students)*

2. Do you think that students can learn from other students? Why or why not? *(yes—if they will listen to each other, accept help, etc; some may think no—students won't respect other students)*

3. If you wanted some help on your math, for example, what skills would you want a student helper to be good at? *(math!)*

4. Why would it be hard to learn something from a student who just wanted to goof around? *(they wouldn't be taking it seriously)*

5. If you wanted a student helper to help you with something, what would be important to look for? *(a person who knew something about the problem, good explainer, maybe someone older who had already been through the book, etc.)*

6. What would be fun about having a peer-tutor if you were having problems with something? *(get to talk to another student, etc.)*

Activity:

Directions: The worksheet lists ten different activities for a peer-tutor. The student is to put a check mark next to the ones that would be likely or appropriate for a peer-tutor to do with a student.

Answers: Check marks for 1, 2, 4, 5, 6, 7, 8, 10.

Follow-up: If you have tried peer-tutoring, discuss with students how it could work in your classroom. What was successful? What was a problem? What qualifications are the most important for a peer-tutor? What students might be able to benefit from such a helper?

Having a Peer-Tutor

What are some ways that a peer-tutor could help someone out? Put a ✔ next to each possible way.

1. He could help you read the questions on a worksheet.   _____

2. She could quiz you over your spelling words.   _____

3. He could do your work for you so you'll get a good grade.   _____

4. She could explain what a word means if you don't understand it.   _____

5. He could show you ways to think about a story problem.   _____

6. She could show you how to use a calculator to check your work.   _____

7. He could listen to you read out loud.   _____

8. She could play a game with you when you're finished with your work.   _____

9. He could help you make spitballs.   _____

10. She could show you how to run the computer and play a game on it.   _____

IV-7 Assignment Notebook

Objective:

The student will demonstrate ability to write down an assignment (given orally or taken from writing) on a piece of paper or notebook.

Rationale:

As students become older, they will probably work more with assignment sheets and coding homework assignments in notebooks. This is one way to help students remember their homework, become more organized, and hopefully to begin using notebooks to keep track of specific tasks. As a teacher, however, you must be careful to teach your students how you want them to code the assignments in the notebook. (List the date? subject? pages? check when finished? etc.)

Thinking Questions:

1. If you had ten assignments to take home to do tonight, how might you remember to do them all? *(write them down, take all your books home, call a friend to help remember, etc.)*

2. How could you use an assignment notebook to help you remember what to do? *(write things down that you need to remember)*

3. What kind of information should be kept in the notebook? *(the subject, actual pages or materials needed, date that it's due, etc.)*

4. What could you put in your notebook to show that you finished the assignment? *(cross it out, put a * or check mark, etc.)*

5. Why would a notebook be better than little scraps of paper? *(less likely to lose it, can check back on old assignments, etc.)*

Activity:

Directions: A sample portion of an assignment notebook is drawn on the right of the worksheet, with the teacher giving the assignment on the left. Students are to write down what they could put in their assignment notebooks that would help them remember what to do.

Answers: (examples)

1. Spelling words—3 times
2. Reading—Magic Violin
3. Art—bring old clothes
4. Bring cookies for tomorrow
5. Take box home, put hat inside

Follow-up: Have students share their responses. Decide on a good system for writing down assignments. What shortcuts worked well?

Name _____   Date _____

IV-7

Assignment Notebook

What would you write down in your assignment notebook for each situation below?

1. You have a review test tomorrow. Copy your spelling words three times.

2. Get the green books. Read the story, "The Magic Violin."

3. Bring some old clothes to school tomorrow because we'll be doing some messy painting.

4. John, will you bring in cookies for the party tomorrow?

5. Put something in the box that begins with the letter "H."

IV-8 Homework

Objective:

The student will state at least two reasons why homework might be beneficial in school situations.

Rationale:

Homework is sometimes viewed as punishment rather than as an extra opportunity to learn. However, homework may not only serve to reinforce a concept, it can also serve to show parents what is going on in the classroom, give a student extra time to work on an assignment, and allow students to pursue related interests that can count for class credit. This lesson requests that students think about the positive aspects of taking work home.

Thinking Questions:

1. What is homework? *(work that you do at home)*

2. Why do students have homework? *(don't finish work at school, need to look things up at home, so parents know what you're working on, etc.)*

3. If you were having trouble reading something out loud, how would extra practice at home make it easier if you had to read a story out loud at school the next day? *(could prepare, could make sure you know all the words, aren't as nervous)*

4. What about having a test? What kind of homework might be helpful the night before a test? *(a review sheet, going through words in the book, studying with a partner or family member at home, etc.)*

5. How would having homework help your parents know what was going on with you at school? *(they can see your answers, see what you're having trouble with, might be able to help you out with ideas for a project, etc.)*

Activity:

Directions: Ellen is a student who has a lot of homework! After the teacher gives her a homework assignment, Ellen realizes that she can benefit from the work. Students are to circle A or B to indicate how Ellen will benefit.

Answers: 1. b   2. a   3. a   4. b

Follow-up: Have students talk about how often they work on homework, where they work, how much parental involvement is usual at their homes, and how long it takes. Can they think of ways to make the homework more fun? *(do it with a friend, have a parent make a game out of it, etc.)*

IV-8

Homework

How can the following homework assignments help Ellen do better in school? Circle a or b.

Study your social studies for 30 minutes before we have a test.

1. **a.** Ellen will enjoy looking at the pictures.

   b. It will help Ellen remember things that she has read and studied.

Solve 20 subtraction problems on the worksheet.

2. **a.** It will give Ellen extra practice in subtracting.

   b. It will stop Ellen from watching television at night.

Finish answering the science questions that you didn't get done in class.

3. **a.** Ellen can use the extra time to answer the questions.

   b. Ellen can rush through the questions quickly in class so she won't have to do any at home.

Draw a floor plan of your bedroom.

4. **a.** Ellen can take a nap in her bedroom before she works on her homework.

   b. Ellen can work on the assignment while she is in her bedroom.

IV-9 People Who Can Help

Objective:

The student will identify several people who would be able to help them if they had a problem.

Rationale:

There are many human resources available to students if they are aware of them and willing to ask for help. This lesson requests students to think about some possible people who could be used as resources and ways that he or she might be helpful to the student if a problem came up.

Thinking Questions:

1. If you had a problem, what person or persons might you be most likely to talk to? *(answers will vary—friend, teacher, family member)*

2. Did everyone have the same answer? Why? *(probably not—everyone has their own circle of resourceful people)*

3. How can family members help you with school problems? *(mother might talk to the principal, help you with homework; older sibling might help you out with a bully; a neighbor might help with driving or providing you with materials, etc.)*

4. How might school people help you with home problems? *(have some ideas for talking to your parents, a classmate might have had a similar problem, etc.)*

5. Do you think most people are willing to help other people? *(probably yes—ask students how they feel when someone asks them for help!)*

6. Did you ever have an experience when you felt bad and someone who you least expected turned out to be a good listener or problem solver? Tell about it. *(answers will vary—it might turn out to be a teacher!)*

Activity:

Directions: Students are to list ways that the individuals on the worksheet might be able to help students with their problems. "Problems" is undefined and can be interpreted according to the students' own situations. The idea is to generally indicate how a person in that role (parent, sibling, neighbor) could be a resource in times of trouble.

Answers: (examples) the person might be a good listener, really like working with kids, be especially understanding, or be protective of the student.

Follow-up: Allow students to volunteer their responses, if desired. If someone has an abusive father, it is unlikely that he or she would see that person as a resource since he *is* a problem. Perhaps the students could go to the father, however, if help was needed on building something, cooking something, or going somewhere. Allow students to personalize their responses, if this is easier for them.

People Who Can Help

If you have a problem, how could each of these people help you out?

1. A parent. . .

2. Your older sister. . .

_____

_____

3. The school counselor. . .

4. A favorite teacher. . .

_____

_____

5. The principal. . .

6. Your best friend. . .

_____

_____

7. A good neighbor. . .

_____

_____

Part IV   When You Have Problems

IV-10 Problem Solvers

Objective:

The student will match students with problems to a likely solution or method of working out the problem.

Rationale:

This is a review lesson, combining several types of problems and possible solutions. When a problem is encountered, there are multiple ways to search for and reach resolution. This lesson shows several techniques.

Thinking Questions:

1. If you were having nightmares, would you work harder on your spelling words to take care of it? *(if your nightmares were about spelling tests, but probably not)*

2. If you were being bullied by a kid in another class, could you help solve the problem by asking your teacher politely for the glue? *(probably not—solution doesn't fit the problem)*

3. What are sensible ways to solve these problems? *(think about the circumstances, what's causing the problem)*

4. What are some ways that we have talked about solving some problems? *(ask for help, take another look at the problem, think harder, avoid excuses, get help from a tutor, use an assignment notebook, do homework, use other people)*

5. If one solution doesn't take care of the problem, what should you do? Give up? *(keep trying—find another way to work on the problem, try another resource, etc.)*

Activity:

Directions: Students are to match the characters on the left (who have a specific problem) with the solution on the right (that is specific as well).

Answers:	1. d	3. f	5. b	7. g
	2. c	4. e	6. a	

Follow-up: Have students discuss their responses. Ask for additional problem-solving ideas for each of the situations. Though only one matches on the worksheet, are there other solutions that could work for each situation? What?

Problem Solvers

Match each student with a problem to the way that he or she worked on solving that problem. Write the letter next to each student.

1. Jorge was getting bad grades on his spelling tests.

   _____

2. Marta couldn't read a lot of the words in her reading book.

   _____

3. Pete kept getting the wrong answers on his math.

   _____

4. Cindy kept forgetting to bring her art materials to school.

   _____

5. Art was bothered by the boy who sat behind him in class.

   _____

6. Jeannine was worried that she was going to be late to school.

   _____

7. Fred got in trouble for yelling at the teacher when he couldn't find his pencil.

   _____

a. Her mother bought her an alarm clock so she could wake up on time.

b. He asked his teacher if he could move to another seat.

c. Her teacher found another student who was a good reader to help her with the words.

d. He took his spelling words home and studied them at home at night.

e. She wrote down things to remember in a little notebook.

f. He checked the numbers over very carefully and looked over his work.

g. He worked on politely asking the teacher if she would help him find his pencil, please.

section

II

Relating

to Peers

We are seldom entirely alone. Throughout each day, people have to deal with other people on the bus, at the store, walking down the street, at sporting events, and at parties. While companionship at its best is fulfilling and fun, there are many circumstances involving other people that are not pleasant. It is not too hard to come up with examples of people who are irritating, mean, or whiney. And although we like to think we can pick our friends, we do not have a lot of choice as to our co-workers, family members, neighbors, and classmates.

In a classroom full of students, it is a dream to think that everyone would get along with each other. There are many different backgrounds, ideas, personalities, and habits in one confined area! Special students, in particular, are often cited for poor interpersonal skills. It is not easy for many of them to make friends, keep friends, or even to make it through a typical school day without experiencing some sort of difficulty involving other people.

Section II is about getting along with other people, specifically in a school environment, but more generally with peers across many settings. The story for this section is *Ralph and His Purple Face*. Ralph is a boy with a short fuse who is constantly teased by classmates, triggering a response of a purple face and red

137

smoke pouring out of his ears. Ralph, with the support of his teacher, learns to ignore the bad behavior of his unkind classmates and finally allows them to see that he is a nice person.

In Section II, "Relating to Peers," you will find:

- Parent Letters 5, 6, and 7
- Classroom Ideas
- "Ralph and His Purple Face" *(story)*
- Part I: Learning and Working with Others *(activities)*
- Part II: Making Friends *(activities)*
- Part III: Keeping Friends *(activities)*

PARENT LETTER #5

RE: Relating to Peers—Learning and Working with Others

Dear Parents,

Our next series of lessons involves getting along with other people, particularly classmates at school. As you can probably imagine, putting many children together and expecting complete cooperation is sometimes quite difficult. School is an excellent place, however, for learning to get along with others. This is a lifelong skill that will follow children into the workplace as adults.

Some of the lessons in this section involve being a good leader, being a good follower, doing your share of the work, accepting the blame for mistakes, not creating a classroom disturbance and yet ignoring those who do.

Although you may not have a household of 20 or 30 children all the same age, you may feel that sense of chaos and disharmony all the same! Here are some ideas to help reinforce these concepts at home:

- A family requires getting along with each other just as a classroom does. Assign chores on a rotating basis, based on ability and time and other factors that would make things equitable in your home. Work together as a family to make dinner a pleasant time (including clean-up).

- Let children take turns experimenting in a leadership role in safe tasks at home. How will the yardwork be done this weekend? Some children are natural organizers—hand him or her a pencil and paper and see what evolves.

- After completing a boring or unpleasant task together, reward the family by going out for ice cream (wearing the clean clothes that everyone helped wash, dry, sort, and put away?).

- Don't try to be the judge in constant sibling arguments. Let them work it out—but keep your ears open!

Sincerely,

_____

Teacher

PARENT LETTER #6

RE: Relating to Peers—Making Friends

Dear Parents,

Making friends seems to come easy to most kids; however, there are times and situations in which it is difficult. Going to a new school, being in a different class, being the oldest, being the youngest, not being "good" at something—these are all complications that can get in the way of making friends.

Our lessons at school will work on techniques for making friends, including: being interested in others, being an interesting person yourself, helping others, saying nice things to others, being a good listener, and inviting others to join you.

Within your own family, you probably are part of several groups—church, community, hobbies, sports, etc. Use these activities to help your child work on the skills of making friends. For example:

- Have your child invite someone new to join you at the movies or on a family outing.

- Take advantage of community sports teams, art lessons, camping, library activities, and so on. Your child will soon be part of "a group."

- Encourage your child to have friends over to play, watch TV, or make a lemonade stand in the summer. Observe your child. Is he or she a follower? leader? cooperative?

- Ask your child questions about others in the class. Who is the best runner? Does anyone ride horses? Who won the spelling bee? Encourage your child to talk about and think about the others in his or her class. Give him or her a reason to do some talking to other children.

Sincerely,

_____

Teacher

PARENT LETTER #7

RE: Relating to Peers—Keeping Friends

Dear Parents,

It would seem that making friends would be the hard part, but often *keeping* friends is a tough task as well! Friendships change often and arguments and make-ups are hard to keep up with. Our next set of lessons involves techniques for being a good friend.

The ideas include letting others pick what to do at times, sharing friends with others, not hanging or begging too much, keeping promises, and sticking up for a friend who has a problem.

YOU will be cited often as a resource for your child to go to with a problem. You can help your child by being supportive of the ups and downs that occur with learning to be a good friend. Help by:

- quietly observing how your child interacts with others. Is he or she too pushy? Always the one to decide what will be done? Gently suggest letting someone else pick an activity.

- realizing that friendships change. Your child will have more than one friend at a given time, and those friends will have other friends. By sharing friends, everyone gets to know more people. Hang on to that special "best" friend, but encourage other friends to come over and spend time with your child.

- talking about the importance of keeping promises. Broken promises can lead to broken friendships.

- discussing loyalty and comradeship with others. When one group of kids start to badmouth someone else, help your child realize that if this is a friend, he or she should not be part of that hurtful activity.

- making your child aware that you are available to help out your child's friends, as well as your child. Listening goes a long way.

Sincerely,

_____
Teacher

CLASSROOM IDEAS FOR SECTION II
Relating to Peers

Part I. Learning and Working with Others

- Allow students to experience being a follower in a student-led group. Again, do not step in too quickly to try to solve problems; rather, let the student leader act as a leader. Compliment students who are cooperative followers for their contributions to the group. At the end, display the group's project and ask the leader to list by name everyone who contributed. **(I-1)**

- Allow students to take turns in a leadership role. It could be leading a small cooperative group, being the line leader down the hall, or even passing out papers. When members of the group try to bypass the leader to come to you with questions, give the authority back to the student. **(I-2)**

- After working on a group task, have students separately list their own contributions to the task. Have students share these lists with others in their group. Do they agree on the assessment? Students may find (by evaluating each other) that their contribution was perceived as very worthwhile, even though they themselves may feel that they didn't do very much. Always credit every member of the group, no matter how small a contribution! **(I-3)**

- Have a "You First" day or afternoon in which students actively give up their "right" to do something first. You may want to try secretly selecting two students in your class who will do this; at the end of the afternoon, see if other students can identify the ones who were chosen. Wouldn't it be great if everyone was so polite to each other that you couldn't easily guess the "plants"? **(I-4)**

- Have a "Hear and Tell" session in which students get their moment in the spotlight—2-3 minutes in which he or she can talk about something. After speaking, other students are to summarize what the student talked about. Compliment the good listeners! **(I-5)**

- When you sense that students are about to shift the blame for something to someone else, stop them and request that they begin their next sentence with the word "I." In this way, the focus is shifted to *them*; not someone else. **(I-6)**

- If you have a student who has a particularly difficult time ignoring someone or something, set up a special signal (a wink, scratching your nose, etc.) between yourself and the student to let him or her know that you noticed that he or she did a fine job of ignoring something. Just the knowledge that you are with him or her may give added power to overcome the tendency to say something about the disturbance. **(I-7)**

- If possible, find a competing behavior for a student to work on when you sense that he or she is in a mood to disturb others—particularly if you know what's coming. IF the student is about to blow up, send him on an errand. If an argument is brewing between two students, divide and conquer—time for new groups! For the student who has to have the class's attention by clowning around at the wastebasket, give him two minutes before lunch to tell his jokes and get a few laughs. Try humor. Tell the graffiti artist that you think she'd do a great job making a mural for the hallway—with her name signed on the bottom. Disturbers want attention. Try to find a positive outlet. **(I-8)**

- Have a minute of silence each day at a certain time. (Right after recess? Right before lunch?) Allow students to put their heads on the desk, close their eyes, settle themselves, and clear their heads. Teach them to enjoy the silence; to listen to the silence. If your class can't hold out for one minute, try 20 seconds. If this period is built into their day, it will only be a trial for the first few times. After the silence, classroom noises will seem very loud and disturbing. The silence will seem pleasant. **(I-9)**

- Make posters of positive touching. Find pictures in magazines of parents and children engaging in a friendly hug, friends with arms around each other, and so on. Have students make labels or captions for the posters, emphasizing that touching in a friendly way is nice. **(I-10)**

- To make the point about personal space, have all of your students cram together in a very small space (a closet? a tiny portion of the hallway?) for a short time. Then talk about how they felt with their personal space broken into. Was it fearful? Annoying? (*Caution:* Some students may not handle this activity well. Use good judgment.) **(I-10)**

- Students may like to write their own endings to a story about someone making a mistake. Start the story orally in class, perhaps choosing a problem common to your students (forgetting something, playing badly on a team) and let students make their own endings. Share stories and praise the "good forgivers"! **(I-11)**

- Explain that laughing at someone else for getting in trouble is like being an accomplice to a crime. The laughing will probably set off a bad reaction in the person who got in trouble, thereby making his or her situation even worse. By contributing to that problem, the laugher is also involving himself or herself. Whatever the consequence is for the offender, give a similar (but lesser) consequence for the laugher. Laughter may turn to sympathy. **(I-12)**

Part II. Making Friends

- Select one student at a time and have other students come up with a list of 5-10 questions that they could ask to find out more about the student. If the selected student is not too shy, have him or her sit in the center of a friendly circle and answer questions. **(II-1)**

- Have students get into partner groupings and find out as many interesting things about each other as they can in two minutes. Share findings with the group. **(II-1)**

- Have each student make a poster or coat of arms displaying things about themselves that not everyone else might know. Using the list that was made in Activity II-2 for starters, students could set up a shoebox display of pictures, mementos from the past, artwork, etc., that shows what they are like. **(II-2)**

- Have students make a class list of favorite places to go and hang out to be with friends. Students can write or make advertisements telling why or how this is a good place to go with friends or to meet friends. **(II-3)**

- Organized social groups (church youth groups, scouting, swim teams, etc.) are good places to make friends, based on common interests. Are newcomers welcome to the groups? Have students who are already members of such groups tell about their experiences—why is it fun? Does it take more than an invitation to participate? **(II-4)**

- Create a "Yellow Pages" type ad for use in the classroom with students drawing their own advertisements featuring help or assistance that they could give to others—and are willing to share with others. ("See Mark for Computer Help!") Students should realize that their services must be available to everyone and anyone in the class, not just a select few. **(II-5)**

- Students can role play examples of listening and not listening by writing and performing short skits. After each performance, have the participants explain what they were trying to show as examples of how you could tell if someone was really listening. **(II-6)**

- When students work together in small, cooperative groups, they tend to be more supportive and encouraging with each other. Assign tasks that can be worked on, turned in, and evaluated together. Watch for kids encouraging each other and make class comments such as, "I would like to be in THIS group. Boy, do they support each other and help each other out!" **(II-7)**

- Pass out stickers in the classroom to students whom you hear saying something nice about someone else. Don't comment about why you are giving so-and-so a sticker; let the kids watch and catch on. **(II-8)**

Part III. Keeping Friends

- During free time or recess, let students take turns choosing the activity with the understanding that NO ONE complains about it; everyone participates. After 12 weeks of kickball at every recess, students may be ready for a change. Let students learn to try something new. **(III-1)**

- Write anonymous stories or essays about "My Best Friend." Have students try to guess who the essay is about (if it is a classmate) and discuss the qualities that the author valued in a friend. **(III-2)**

- Role play the hanging and begging situations on worksheet III-4. Students will find that it is fun to be the culprit during the plays, but it is really annoying in real life. Have groups work on endings to the problem and give their performances in front of the others. **(III-4)**

- Make a paper chain with a sincere promise written on each link of the chain. Have students share their promises before linking them together and displaying the chain by draping it around the chalkboard or windows. Point out the symbolism of breaking the chain by breaking a promise. **(III-5)**

- If appropriate, tape a soap opera TV show and play it for the class. Count how many episodes of badmouthing or derogatory remarks are made about someone within a half hour. Use this activity as practice in identifying these types of remarks. **(III-6)**

- Use books (such as paperback series) with young characters and find examples of friends sticking up for other friends. Students may want to work in partners on this task, each taking the side of one of the friends in the story. **(III-7)**

- Assign each person in the class a "friend for the day or week." They are to look out for each other, help each other on school activities or other tasks, and perhaps even turn in assignments as a team. Rotate partners often. **(III-7)**

- Make a class list of common school problems on one side (suggested by students) and workable solutions that students may have tried on the other side. Brainstorm together to come up with ideas to try. **(III-8)**

- As a writing assignment, have students pretend to be "Dear Abby" advice-givers for other students. Have an anonymous box where students can slip in letters or notes about their concerns. Pick appropriate letters and assign students to answer them sincerely. Share results. **(III-8)**

- Invite your school counselor or principal or perhaps school nurse to talk to your class about child abuse, depression, dealing with handicaps, and other relevant topics that may pertain to your setting. Review sources of help and people who are trained to deal with these problems. Unfortunately, these situations happen. **(III-9)**

- Write a class play about friendship. The plot could be as simple as one friend betraying another in a school situation, with appropriate humor and characters thrown in to personalize it. One part of the class may perform for the other, and they could discuss thinking questions about the play and its outcome. **(III-10)**

Ralph and His Purple Face

Ralph was fun to tease. The kids in his class loved to tease him because he got very upset, and when he got upset, his face turned purple and puffs of red smoke came shooting out of his ears.

Then they really had something to tease him about. Poor Ralph.

"Look at Ralph walk," cried Billy, laughing loudly. "He walks like he has ants in his pants."

The kids started to laugh at Ralph. He felt his face getting warm.

"Stop it!" cried Ralph. "These are very nice pants and there are NO ants in them at all!"

But his face began to turn purple and the red smoke was already starting to come out of his ears.

"Ha, ha!" laughed the kids. "Purple face, purple face!"

"That's enough," said Mr. Snaggle, the teacher, in a very stern voice. "It's time for math. Everyone sit down."

Everyone sat down, but Ralph knew they were still looking at him and laughing. Billy poked Ralph in the back while he was sliding into his seat. Ralph was getting madder and madder.

"Take out your homework," Mr. Snaggle instructed the class. Then he looked at Ralph. "Ralph, what is the answer to the first problem?"

Ralph looked at his paper. "Thirteen. Oh, I mean thirty-one," said Ralph.

"Ha, ha!" laughed Pete. "Ralph doesn't even know his numbers."

"STOP it," said Ralph, turning purple.

"Stop it, stop it," sang Pete in a funny voice.

The red smoke started.

Later, on the playground, Ralph kicked the ball and ran to second base without stopping.

"Hey, purple face, you didn't touch first base," yelled Frank. "Cheater!"

"I am *not!*" Ralph yelled right back, beginning to turn purple.

Frank grabbed Ralph's shirt. "Weirdo, weirdo!"

Ralph's ears looked like a red chimney. "Quit it!" he yelled at Frank and the other kids who were coming up to laugh. "Stop teasing me!"

But the kids laughed even harder.

Mr. Snaggle called Ralph over to him. "Ralph," he began, "the kids tease you a lot, don't they?"

Ralph nodded. He didn't really want to talk about it.

"Well, listen Ralph. I have an idea. Next time they try to tease you or make you mad, just ignore them," he said.

"Ignore them?" asked Ralph in disbelief. "But they really upset me, Mr. Snaggle! I can't help my purple face and red smoke!"

"I know it sounds hard," continued Mr. Snaggle, "but they'll just give up if you pretend like you don't even hear them. Don't let them decide for you how you're going to act. *You* decide."

"It's hard," said Ralph quietly.

"They like to see your face turn purple," Mr. Snaggle continued. "And they think it's funny for red smoke to come out of your ears. Let's spoil their fun."

"OK," said Ralph. "What should I do?"

"Well," said Mr. Snaggle, "try this: when they tease you, look away and don't say anything. Not one word. Just pretend they aren't there. If you think you're going to give in, look up at me. I'll wink, and that will mean I know you can do it. Hold out."

"I'll try, Mr. Snaggle," said Ralph, feeling a little better. "I'll have them wondering what's going on!"

His first chance came later that afternoon. Amy went by Ralph's desk and whispered under her breath, "Purple face, purple face." But Ralph just scratched his head and opened his spelling book to look at the words.

"Hey, where's the red smoke?" asked Fred. Ralph just turned his head and wrote his spelling words on a piece of paper.

Amy and Fred looked at each other in surprise. Nothing was happening!

Inside, Ralph smiled. He wasn't going to get mad!

The kids didn't know what was happening. They tried all Monday afternoon to get Ralph to turn purple, but it didn't work.

They tried even harder on Tuesday. But Ralph didn't even turn light purple when they called him a bozo.

By Wednesday, the kids were getting tired of waiting for Ralph to turn purple. "He just doesn't get mad anymore," said Fred.

"Yeah," said Amy. "I don't know if we'll ever see that red smoke anymore."

By Thursday, the kids didn't even try anymore. They found out that it was more fun to play ball without fighting all the time anyhow.

On Friday, the kids found out something else about Ralph. They discovered that he was an excellent speller.

Now instead of saying "purple face," the kids say, "Ralph, would you help me with my spelling, please?"

And Ralph just smiles and says, "Sure. I'd be glad to."

Part I   Learning and Working with Others

I-1 Following the Leader

Objective:

The student will identify characters who are following the requests or instructions of the group leader.

Rationale:

When working in groups, some students may feel that they don't have to follow the instructions of anybody except for a certified adult. When working in cooperative groups, however, each student may have the opportunity to be a student leader. As such, they need to learn to function both as a leader and a follower within the group. This lesson focuses on the student as a follower.

Thinking Questions:

1. What are some activities that you can do in a group? *(work on a poster for art, do a play, play a game, spelling jeopardy, etc.)*

2. When you're working in a group, does it work well if there is no leader? *(only if everyone is cooperative)*

3. What if you were the leader of a group and your group was supposed to finish making a huge mural for the wall? How would you help your group get the project finished? *(make some goals, assign different people tasks that they were good at, oversee the project)*

4. What if you ran into some people in your group who didn't want to work on the task? Why would that be hard for the leader? *(it would jeopardize the whole project for everyone, the leader would have to "get after" them, the project wouldn't be as much fun, etc.)*

5. How can a person be a good follower of the leader in a group? *(listen to the orders, follow them, don't argue, try to be cooperative, etc.)*

Activity:

Directions: Students are to list the names of the characters on the worksheet who are being good followers. They are also to circle the student who is the leader of each group.

> *Answers:*   **#1—Leader:** Randy; **Followers:** Fred, Ben
> **#2—Leader:** Dottie; **Followers:** Nick, Luis

Follow-up: Discuss the comments of the characters in the groups. Which were helpful? *(ones that related to the topic and the project)* Which followers were most helpful?

Following the Leader

These students are working on projects together. There is one student leader in each group. Write the names of the students in each group who are good followers. Circle the group leader.

1.

We're supposed to make a poster of zoo animals. If we each draw one animal, we'll have a nice poster.

I don't like to draw. Let's go outside and play.

Cathy

Fred

I could draw a camel!

Randy

Look at me - I'm a zebra!

Hey, Randy, why don't we use some colored markers? Is that a good idea?

Ha, ha, ha!

Ben

Ann

Rick

Good Followers: _____

2.

It will be fun to play this game. We'll write questions about the story and give points to the teams for getting them right.

I want to draw zoo animals.

Renee

Hey, this is a better story. Let's do this instead.

Dottie

I'll get a pencil.

How many points should each question be for?

Nick

Maria

Luis

Good Followers: _____

© 1993 by The Center for Applied Research in Education

Part I   Learning and Working with Others

I-2 Being the Leader

Objective:

The student will identify several characteristics of a good leader for a group.

Rationale:

Being a good leader is not as easy as it looks. It is good for students, though, to have to assume a leadership role in classroom activities. Skills such as pinpointing the task, including the opinions of others, assigning tasks, keeping the group on task, etc., are all important for later leadership roles. This lesson asks students to evaluate the performance of characters in leadership roles.

Thinking Questions:

1. Do you think it is easier to be a leader of a group or a follower/participant? *(opinions will vary—the leader may have more responsibility, followers may not get to pick what they want to do)*

2. Do you think being the leader means you get to tell everyone else in the group what to do? *(no, it means "leading" or "guiding" the group)*

3. What if everyone has very different ideas about how to do something? What should the leader do then? *(listen to all of the ideas, have the group vote or come to a consensus)*

4. What should the leader know about the other people in his or her group? *(what their ideas are, what their skills are, how to ask questions about getting the task done)*

5. Why is it good to sometimes have to be a leader? *(learn to work with other people, be in charge, take responsibility for the product)*

6. If we had a list of characteristics of a good leader, what would we include? *(be clear, be fair, listen to everyone, don't be bossy, etc.)*

Activity:

Directions: Students are to read the leader's comments in the situations on the worksheet and circle the student if they think he or she sounds like a good leader.

> *Answers:*   1. no   3. no   5. yes
>   2. yes   4. yes   6. no

Follow-up: Discuss why certain characters sound like better leaders. What was the problem with the others? *(#1—not a group effort; #3—bossy; #6—not a leader at all! Has no idea what to do!)*

Being the Leader

Each of the students is supposed to be the leader of the group. Which ones do you think are the best? Circle the students you would pick.

1. OK guys, we're supposed to work together on finishing the math problems. Bob, you do all of them and let me know when you're done.

Allen

2. Let's do a good job on our play. First, we'll read through it so we know all of the words. Then we'll choose parts. Then we can practice. Does that sound good to everyone?

Rachel

3. Keith

I'm the leader, so you HAVE to do what I say or I'll kick you out.

4. I think we should listen to everyone's ideas and talk about them. Then we can pick what to do.

Linda

5. Steven

Pete - you're the best artist. Do you want to do the drawing? Who has any ideas about what to put in the background?

6. I'm not sure what to do. Just do whatever you want.

Jill

Part I   Learning and Working with Others

I-3 Doing Your Share

Objective:

The student will identify ways to split up a task fairly.

Rationale:

When working on a group project, some members just don't do their share. It is often difficult to divide up a project in such a way that all portions are equal. If everyone is cooperative, however, there is something that everyone could do to contribute to a nice finished product. In this lesson, students are to think about how they include everyone in some way in working on a project.

Thinking Questions:

1. When working in a group, what happens if only one person does the work? *(it's not fair to that person, he or she had to work harder; the project is not a group effort, it reflects only one set of ideas, etc.)*

2. What if your group had an art project to do, and only one person liked to draw? How could the others be included? *(some could do the planning, the layout, gather materials, hold books, trace pictures, etc.)*

3. Do you think everyone could be involved in some way in a project? *(probably—using their own talents to contribute)*

4. Would it be fair if the people who could draw and liked to draw did all of the drawing and other people did something else? *(yes, as long as the product included everyone's thoughts and ideas and they contributed in some way)*

5. What are some other ways everyone could become a part of a project that a group is working on? *(get things, do research, hold papers, talk about the project in front of the class, use their own talents in some way, etc.)*

6. What if no one in a group liked to draw, but you were supposed to make a poster. How could the group make a nice project? *(find another way to get pictures—use magazines, use words, use another type of talent)*

Activity:

Directions: Students are to split up task activities among members of a group in such a way that everyone is included.

Answers: (examples)

#1—read the directions/get the ingredients/stir in the ingredients/wash the dishes

#2—read the lines/work on costumes/make scenery/change the props

#3—get a partner and quiz each other/change roles and quiz each other/one person gives the quiz to everyone else

#4—rip up newspaper into strips/make the paste/put the strips on a balloon/paint the ball blue and green

#5—write the words on cards/divide the cards into four sets (two for each person)/each person draws pictures on their cards

Follow-up: Share responses. Perhaps you would like to have students divide into groups to discuss their answers and come up with the plans they liked the best. Why are some plans unworkable? What were the best/easiest/fastest/most fun ways to accomplish the tasks?

Doing Your Share

There are 4 people in each group. How could you divide up the tasks among the members of the group?

1. Bake a cake.

_____
_____
_____
_____

2. Put on a play from your reading book.

_____
_____
_____
_____

3. Quiz each other on your spelling words, then everyone will take a test on the words together.

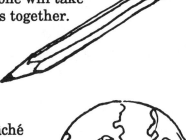

_____
_____
_____
_____

4. Make a papier-mâché model of the earth.

_____
_____
_____
_____

5. Draw pictures for each of your 8 vocabulary words.

_____
_____
_____
_____

I-4 Not Always "Me, First!"

Objective:

The student will identify characteristics of someone with a "me, first" attitude.

Rationale:

It's hard to work in a group containing someone who always has to be first, who puts his or her needs above everything else. While students may not recognize themselves in these positions, it is important to agree that this type of attitude makes things difficult for everybody and generally doesn't gain much for the pushy person.

Thinking Questions:

1. Have you ever been in a situation where somebody in the group felt like he or she had to be first? Tell about it. *(anecdotes should leave out specific names!)*

2. How does it make you feel when someone insists that he or she has to be first, line up first, or do something first, or he or she took something that should have belonged to everybody? *(angry, like you'd like to get back at them)*

3. What are some things you could do or say to someone like that without getting into a fight? *(why don't you wait your turn, could you hold on a minute—I'm almost done, etc.)*

4. Is it sometimes better to just let a pushy person have his or her way or should you always argue about it because it's not right? *(if you can let it go, let it go; some things aren't worth fighting about; on the other hand, the person needs to learn to give up that need to be first all the time)*

5. Are you ever one of the "me, first" people? How? *(listen to anecdotes—talk about how important it was to be first)*

6. What are some things that are worth arguing about if you run into a "me, first" person? *(your personal property, your safety, your school books and papers, etc.)*

7. How can students help each other get rid of the "me, first" attitude? *(remind each other to share, allow others to go first intentionally at times, take turns being first at leading the line, etc.)*

Activity:

Directions: The characters on the worksheet are all "me, first" people. Students are to write down what they think the characters might be saying.

> *Answers:* (examples)
>
> 1. Get off the swing. It's my turn.
> 2. I'm using the markers.
> 3. I'm thirsty. I'm getting a drink first.

Follow-up: Discuss how the characters who were being pushed around could handle the situations without ending up in a fight or running to the teacher. Can the "me, first" people be put in their place? How? **Ideas: #1**—the boy could negotiate ("I'll get off in five minutes. I just got on!") **#2**—the girl could ask for the markers that aren't being used; remind the pushy girl that the markers belong to everyone. **#3**—the boy could say something like, "If you and your 'me, first' attitude can't wait, go right ahead. *I* can wait." (But more likely he'll try to dunk the pushy boy's face in the water!)

Not Always "Me, First!"

These students all have "Me, First!" attitudes. What do you think each is saying? Write their words in the balloon.

1.

2.

3.

I-5 Listening to Other People's Ideas

Objective:

The student will listen to and document/state ideas from another person.

Rationale:

Sometimes in groups only the speaker is listening to himself or herself. Others are thinking about what they are going to say and are not really listening. This lesson is an exercise in listening to others' comments.

Thinking Questions:

1. When you're in a group, are you the only one with good ideas? *(no, everyone has something to contribute)*

2. What's the best way to find out the ideas of other people in your group? *(ask them, then listen)*

3. How can you tell if someone is listening to you? *(they look interested, are quiet, can repeat what you said back to the group)*

4. Tell me what I just said. *(something about how to tell if someone is listening to you)*

5. Why is repeating what someone says a good way to see if you were listening? *(you'll use the same words or ideas)*

6. Can you repeat an idea without using the same exact words? How? *(yes, paraphrasing is a higher-level skill than simply repeating; just use slightly different words that mean about the same thing)*

Activity:

Directions: Students are to divide into small groups (unless your class is already quite small) and discuss topics selected from the worksheet. After listening to the others' comments on the topic, students are to jot a few notes about the other member's comments or ideas about each topic.

Answers: (will vary) The responses don't have to be lengthy, but should make mention of each member's ideas.

Follow-up: Check with the members of the group as to the accuracy of the notes written about their comments. Was it hard to remember what each person said? Was it difficult to listen when you knew you were responsible for remembering?

Listening to Other People's Ideas

Get into a small group. Listen to each other and summarize each other's ideas about the following topics.

1. my favorite sport to play

_____

_____

_____

2. a great place to take a vacation

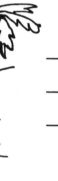

_____

_____

_____

3. a movie I would recommend to my friends

_____

_____

_____

4. what to do at your next birthday party

_____

_____

_____

5. animals that make good pets

_____

_____

_____

I-6 Accepting the Blame

Objective:

The student will identify a character in each given situation who is correctly accepting the blame for the circumstances.

Rationale:

It is important to be willing to admit to one's own involvement or contribution to a situation, especially when that situation may not be a positive one. Part of getting along with others is recognizing our own part in difficult situations so that we can correct it the next time.

Thinking Questions:

1. Did you ever mess up or make a huge mistake and feel awful about it? *(ask for anecdotes)*

2. Was it hard to take the blame for doing it? Why/why not? *(probably—fear of consequences, etc.)*

3. Why do you think people don't like to admit that they have done something wrong? *(might get in trouble, look stupid, etc.)*

4. Let's say that you broke a window. Why might it be a good idea to admit to that? *(so the people can get it repaired, so other people will be aware of it and not get hurt)*

5. What if you were only partially to blame for something being hurt or broken? Do you think you should tell who else was involved? *(perhaps! If it was a criminal situation, it would be important for the police to know who was involved.)*

6. Do you think people who admit to making a mistake could be admired for being brave and honest? *(hopefully)*

7. Do you think that accepting the blame for something means that you don't have to do anything else, such as pay for damage, apologize, make things right again, etc.? *(probably not—taking the blame is only the first step; changing behavior is the next step)*

Activity:

Directions: Students are to circle the one character in each situation on the worksheet who is accepting the blame for a problem.

Answers: 1. second student   2. third student   3. first student

Follow-up: Discuss the excuses of the other students on the worksheet. Who was being blamed? What do you think the consequences might be for the students who took the blame? Did any learning take place?

Accepting the Blame

Circle the student in each situation below who is accepting the blame for what happened.

I-7 Ignoring When You Have To

Objective:

The student will identify classroom events or disruptions that should be ignored.

Rationale:

When students are supposed to be working on a task, it is a problem when noises, arguments, or generally distracting situations occur. In this lesson, students are to identify several disturbances that are better left ignored.

Thinking Questions:

1. When you are working on something in the classroom, what are some things that might bother you or affect your concentration? *(people moving around, noises, distractions, etc.)*

2. Why would it bother you if someone was talking too loudly? *(you'd think about what they were saying rather than what you were supposed to do)*

3. Would it bother you if someone interrupted you to talk about something else? *(it would probably disrupt the task)*

4. What might happen if you got involved in someone else's argument or conversation while you were supposed to be working on something else? *(it would probably disrupt the task)*

5. Why is it hard to ignore distractions? *(they seem interesting, you have to look up when you hear something loud for safety purposes, your work might be boring, it might involve a friend, etc.)*

6. What are some ways that you could ignore or tune out the distraction? *(look at your work, turn your back on the distraction, keep your mouth shut, etc.)*

Activity:

Directions: The worksheet shows a classroom in which many disturbances are going on. The student is to put an X on the person or movement or thing that is distracting and should probably be ignored.

Answers: principal/teacher interrupting; girl tapping pencil; boy yawning; teacher discussing problem with student; boy tapping girl on the back; two boys arguing and running; girl interrupting other girl who is working on a puzzle

Follow-up: Look around your classroom. What are the problem areas as far as having difficulty ignoring things? Can you have visitors later in the day? Do students know the routine for getting help? Do you discipline too loudly in front of other students? Can you help make it easier for students to ignore problems?

Ignoring When You Have To

Put an X on each person or movement that you think should be ignored in the picture below.

I-8 Not Disturbing Others

Objective:

The student will draw a picture showing a neutral situation or task performed in a disturbing or non-disturbing manner.

Rationale:

Something as simple as walking across the room can be done in very different ways. Clumping loudly will still get the person to the other side—so will tiptoeing silently. In a classroom situation, students should be able to perform simple tasks in a non-disturbing manner.

Thinking Questions:

1. When people are supposed to be working or concentrating on something, what could be disturbing to them? *(people moving around, noises, etc.)*

2. Do you think people have some control over *how* they move, *how* loud they are, *how* quickly they do something? *(yes)*

3. If you wanted to talk to someone across the room without disturbing others, how could you do it? *(get up and go over there, talk quietly, wait until a better time, etc.)*

4. If you are supposed to leave the room and don't want to disturb others, how might you accomplish that? *(go very quietly, don't walk between every single desk on your way, etc.)*

5. How could you help yourself remember to do things without disturbing others? *(think first, look around to see where people are and what they are doing—do they require quiet surroundings?)*

Activity:

Directions: Students are given four typical classroom situations. They are to draw a picture of students carrying out that task either in a disturbing manner or in a non-disturbing manner, depending on which one is *not* already drawn. Reassure students that their artwork is not the critical factor here—stick figures plus oral explanations are fine.

Answers: (examples)

1. draw a student sharpening pencil with a small, quiet sharpener (or when everyone is out of the room)
2. draw a student passing the paper by knocking it into the head of the person in front
3. draw someone closing the window slowly and quietly
4. draw someone yelling loudly for the eraser

Follow-up: Have students share their drawings and ideas with each other. Discuss how even seemingly small tasks can be made into a major problem just by doing it too loudly, at the wrong time, or without thinking through whom might be bothered by the way it is done. Be sure to compliment students throughout the day who perform these simple tasks without disturbing others.

Not Disturbing Others

Draw a picture that shows how you could do the task on the left either by disturbing or not disturbing, depending on which square is blank.

	Disturbing	**Not Disturbing**
1. Sharpening your pencil		
2. Passing your paper forward		
3. Closing the window in the classroom		
4. Asking a friend if you can borrow an eraser		

Learning and Working with Others

I-9 Classroom Noises

Objective:

The student will identify the source of several noises in the classroom and state whether or not that noise is preventable.

Rationale:

Often, noises translate to chaos. While some classroom noises are good and healthy (students answering questions, laughing, cheering), some noises are just plain bothersome. Tapping, squeaking, burping, and scratching are all annoyances that we wish we could eliminate from the classroom when they become the center of attention. This lesson concentrates on identifying classroom noises and thinking about whether or not they can be prevented.

Thinking Questions:

1. I want you to be very quiet for 30 seconds. Then tell me what classroom noises you hear. *(rain outside, plumbing noises, footsteps in the hall, etc.)*

2. What are some noises you hear when you aren't being quiet? *(students talking, bells, papers rustling, etc.)*

3. We've already talked about ignoring classroom disturbances. What are some noisy disturbances that can be prevented? *(tapping pencils, closing books loudly, talking too loudly, etc.)*

4. Some noises can't be prevented. What are some examples? *(traffic outside, other classrooms' activities, bells, etc.)*

5. What do you think you should do about the classroom noises that can be prevented? *(stop doing them!)*

6. What could you do about classroom noises that can't be easily prevented, such as the bell ringing? *(don't let it bother you, don't think about the noises, practice ignoring, etc.)*

Activity:

Directions: Students are to list classroom noises that are typical in their classroom, as in the examples. Then they are to consider whether or not they have control (or the person responsible for the noise has control) over that noise.

Answers: Answers will vary and will produce some discussion. Can a burp be prevented? This is an argument that continues to rage and may never be settled. Allow students to explain and justify their thinking. The thinking process is more important than a yes/no answer.

Follow-up: Discuss the students' responses to the worksheet. What noises were bothersome to all students? Is some noise good for the classroom? Discuss who is in control of the noises if it is determined that someone is responsible. If no agreement is reached on whether or not a noise can be controlled, discuss what factors can be controlled—the timing? the intensity? the place?

Classroom Noises

Finish the list of classroom noises you hear. Tell if you think someone has control over that noise or not.

Noise	Can Someone Control It?
1. Door closing	_____
2. Someone sneezing	_____
3. Squeaking shoes on the floor	_____
4. Fingernails on the chalkboard	_____
5. Tapping with a pencil	_____
6. _____	_____
7. _____	_____
8. _____	_____
9. _____	_____
10. _____	_____
11. _____	_____
12. _____	_____

I-10 Touching Others

Objective:

The student will identify incidents in which touching others is appropriate or done in an appropriate manner.

Rationale:

Some people enjoy physical contact with others; others prefer to hang on to their space. While some forms of contact are generally permissible (a pat on the back, shaking hands), other forms may be too aggressive or threatening (hugs, stroking). This is one area for which many students must simply be told *not* to overdo the touching. While they may be exuberant, they must learn to express themselves without bothering others. Another problem area involving touching is that of students just not controlling their hands. Tapping others, pushing, shoving or even just knocking into someone else can be the first step towards a fight. Again, the idea of giving someone else their space is a good way to help the students limit their touching—no matter what the intention.

Thinking Questions:

1. Would you be able to work well in this room if there were 100 people in here? Why/why not? *(probably not—there wouldn't be room to move, much less get up and walk around!)*

2. Do you think having enough room or space for yourself is important? *(yes, we like to have the freedom of movement)*

3. How do you feel when others push you or knock into you, even if it is accidental? *(surprised, annoyed, invaded)*

4. Why do you think some people like to be left alone, rather than touched by others? *(gives them more space, don't have to get involved, maybe are shy or afraid of others)*

5. What are some ways that people touch each other to show affection or happiness about something? *(pat on the back, giving a friendly slap to each other)*

6. Most of the time, do you know whether or not someone would like to be touched or left alone? *(depends on how well you know the other person)*

7. If you go around trying to hug everybody, and you tried to hug someone who liked to keep their space, how would that person feel? *(closed in, unhappy)*

8. What is a good way to show you like someone without starting out by hugging them or trying to touch them? *(smile, be friendly, sit by them, etc.)*

Activity:

Directions: Several examples of touching are listed. The student is to decide whether or not that form of touching would generally be acceptable by writing OK or Not OK on the blank.

Answers:

1. not OK	6. OK
2. not OK	7. not OK
3. OK	8. not OK
4. OK	9. OK
5. not OK	10. not OK

Follow-up: Discuss the students' responses to the items. Under what circumstances could some aggressive physical contact be acceptable? *(sports, competition with friends)* Discuss why someone who liked to keep his or her space may not appreciate even subtle touching, while another person might like a pat on the back. Stress that people are different, and you must try to understand that person's feelings about touching before you get too aggressive with him or her.

I-10

Touching Others

Is this touching OK or not OK? Write <u>OK</u> or <u>Not OK</u> on each line.

1. Poking someone in the back while it's study time   _____

2. Pulling hair   _____

3. Giving a friend the "high five" slap   _____

4. Tapping someone on the other team on the back while playing
   basketball   _____

5. Shoving someone in the back   _____

6. Shaking hands   _____

7. Slapping someone on the arm   _____

8. Pushing the person you're sitting next to with your shoulder   _____

9. Giving someone a friendly pat on the back   _____

10. Sticking your foot out to trip someone   _____

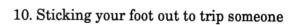

I-11 Someone Made a Mistake

Objective:

The student will identify a character in given situations who made a mistake and identify how that person would probably feel.

Rationale:

Everyone makes mistakes. When working with others, it is only a matter of time until a mistake is made. How that mistake is handled, both by the person and the others in the group, is a measure of social maturity. In this lesson students are to think about how it would make one feel to make a mistake and to come up with a socially appropriate response for others in the group.

Thinking Questions:

1. Has anyone here ever made a mistake or done something embarrassing? *(yes—listen for anecdotes)*

2. When you made a mistake, how did you feel? *(embarrassed, sad, frightened)*

3. Did anyone stick up for you or try to make you feel better? *(teacher, friends, perhaps a stranger)*

4. How would you like someone to help you the next time you get caught in a mistake or embarrassing situation? *(depends on the situation—say something nice, help pick up things, don't say anything to call attention to the mistake, etc.)*

5. Is there any difference between *mistakes* and *accidents*? *(can't help an accident; a mistake might be able to be corrected through learning)*

6. Could an accident be a mistake in judgment, like running your bike into a tree or spilling something? *(probably—learning how to ride better or to control your arms when you're at the table would prevent accidents)*

7. No matter if it's a mistake or an accident, how should you treat someone who made a mistake? *(don't laugh at them, try to help them, etc.)*

Activity:

Directions: Students are to examine four situations and to circle the person in each who has made a mistake.

Answers: 1. the girl on the left   3. the girl playing tennis
              2. the girl reading   4. the girl with the paper

Follow-up: Discuss how the circled person probably feels in each situation. How did the others in each situation respond to the person? **#1**—mean comment; **#2**—laughing; **#3**—belittling the girl; **#4**—calling attention to the problem. What would be a better response from the others in each situation? **#1**—help her clean the table; **#2**—say nothing; **#3**—encourage her to keep trying; **#4**—tell Sarah or just move the paper.

Someone Made a Mistake

Circle the person in each picture below who made a mistake.

Part I

Learning and Working with Others

I-12 Laughing When Someone Gets in Trouble

Objective:

The student will state possible feelings that he or she may experience when someone laughs at them for getting in trouble.

Rationale:

It is very tempting to laugh at others who find themselves caught, especially if the person caught is not someone you especially like. It makes us feel as though justice has been achieved. However, it is very annoying to be the one laughed at, especially when the principal is waiting. Rather than laughing (which involves the student), a student witnessing such an event should stay out of the situation and make no comment at all.

Thinking Questions:

1. How did you feel when someone you didn't like got in trouble and really got punished? *(probably pretty good)*

2. Is it tempting to laugh at someone like that? *(yes—makes us feel good to see a troublemaker caught)*

3. If you're not a part of the problem, and you're not a part of the solution, do you have a part in the situation at all? *(not unless you were a witness to something—in which case you would be a part of the solution **if asked for your input**)*

4. What usually happens when you laugh at someone who got in trouble? *(you get in trouble, too)*

5. What is a better response? *(say nothing, do nothing)*

Activity:

Directions: Students are to read the cartoon story about a boy who loves to laugh at everyone else getting in trouble—unless he is in the principal's office himself, at which point the laughing stops. At the end, the student is to write or state how the boy feels at that point.

Answers: (examples) embarrassed, sorry, angry

Follow-up: Go through the story together. You may wish to use the following questions: **Box #1**—How does Phil feel? *(sad)* How does Phil feel about Jeff's laughing? *(not pleased)*; **Box #2**—How does Rachel feel about Jeff? *(angry)*; **Box #3**—Why is Jeff so happy about the boys getting into trouble? *(wants to see them "get it")*; **Box # 4**—How is Jeff showing he is interested in what's going on? *(leaning against the door)* Why do you think Jeff is so nosey about everything going on in the office? *(likes to see others in trouble)*; **Box #5**—Now who is in the office? *(Jeff)* Why? *(skipped school)*; **Box #6**—Is Jeff laughing now? *(no)* Why? *(in trouble, sad)* How do you think Jeff feels about the other kids laughing at him? *(angry)* Do you think it's fair that the other kids are laughing at Jeff? *(students will probably answer yes, it does seem fair)* Do you think the other kids should laugh at Jeff? *(it would be better if they didn't; it solves nothing)* What should their responses to Jeff be? *(nothing)* Why is it hard for them to do nothing? *(we want to retaliate when we've been wronged)* How would Jeff feel if he walked out of the office and Rachel said, "Too bad, Jeff. Sorry you got in trouble," and Phil said, "I'll be there too, buddy." Would that change anything? *(probably less animosity between Jeff and the others; maybe Jeff would NOT laugh the next time!)*

Laughing When Someone Gets in Trouble

Read the cartoon story about Jeff. In the box, write how you think Jeff feels.

Part II   Making Friends

II-1 Being Interested in Others

Objective:

The student will identify several techniques for showing interest in others.

Rationale:

The best way to make friends is to show sincere interest in other people. People love to have other people notice them and want to know more about them. Someone could find out things about another person by asking questions, noticing what they are doing or wearing, paying attention to skills or talents of others, and making eye contact. This lesson examines these and other techniques.

Thinking Questions:

1. Why do you think it is important to have friends? *(more fun to do things together, can help each other, etc.)*

2. How could you show someone else that you would like to become friends? *(act friendly, show interest in them, share things, etc.)*

3. One good way to start is by being interested in someone else. What are some ideas for showing that you are interested? *(ask questions, hang around them, look interested, etc.)*

4. Why would this be better than just going up to someone and start talking about yourself? *(the other person might not be interested in hearing about you or what you are doing; the point is to find out about them)*

5. What's the difference between being interested in someone and being nosey? *(the other person will let you know when you've gone too far, being nosey implies you don't really care about the other person)*

Activity:

Directions: Students are to read the brief description of three characters and write or tell at least two ways to show that person that you are interested in getting to know him or her.

Answers: (examples)

1. offer to play football/ask about his family
2. ask if you could watch her ride sometime/compliment her on her clothes
3. ask if you could join in a game/hang around Alex when there is a group

Follow-up: Share ideas for showing interest in these characters. Which are good ideas? Which have potential problems?

Being Interested in Others

Here are some people who might be fun to get to know. What are at least two things you could do or say to let the person know you are interested in getting to know him or her?

1. Ramon plays football on the school team. He is from Mexico. His family just moved here this year.

_____

_____

_____

_____

2. Kris has a horse and loves to ride. She likes to wear different-looking clothes.

_____

_____

_____

_____

3. Alex always has good ideas for making up games. He makes everyone laugh and is nice to everyone.

_____

_____

_____

_____

© 1993 by The Center for Applied Research in Education

II-2 Being Interesting

Objective:

The student will list 15 things about him- or herself that would be considered unique or interesting.

Rationale:

People are attracted to interesting people. Spending a little time being introspective, digging to bring out some unusual characteristics is a worthwhile activity. No two people are alike, and things that make us different make us interesting. Help your students center on their characteristics that are unique and appealing.

Thinking Questions:

1. How are you different from everyone else in this room or group? *(name, family, physical appearance, talents, etc.)*

2. What are some differences that you are proud of? *(sports achievements, scholastic accomplishments, etc.)*

3. If you only had one minute to tell someone else about yourself, what would you be sure to include? *(most important thing—will vary!)*

4. Do you think that other people would find the "different" things about you interesting? Why? *(probably—because we tend to like things that are unusual, we notice those things)*

5. What about being "the same"? Do you think that would make you interesting to others as well? *(yes—because some groups of friends revolve around common interests)*

6. So if you were thinking about interesting things about yourself, would you include things that are the same, different, or both? *(hopefully, a good blend of them all)*

Activity:

Directions: Students are to list 15 things about themselves that others would probably find interesting. Clues on the worksheet include sports interests, skills, trips, pets, family items, and so on.

Answers: will vary

Follow-up: Have students share their lists with each other. What items appeared on most papers? What do students think is interesting about each other? Who thought of something unique to list?

Being Interesting

List 15 things about yourself that others might find interesting!

1. _____

2. _____

3. _____

4. _____

5. _____

6. _____

7. _____

8. _____

9. _____

10. _____

11. _____

12. _____

13. _____

14. _____

15. _____

Part II   Making Friends

II-3 Spending Time with Others

Objective:

The student will identify several ways that friends could spend time together.

Rationale:

People who spend time engaging in the same activity automatically have a common interest. Whether it's playing on the same team, being at the same playground, or taking art lessons, at least it is one place to start developing relationships with others. In this lesson, students are asked to start thinking about places or situations that involve spending time with others

Thinking Questions:

1. If you saw four people playing tennis together, what do you think they might be talking about? *(the game, whose turn it is, the score, etc.)*

2. What do you think two people in front of a video game would be discussing? *(what was happening in the game)*

3. Where are some places that you and other people your age might go for fun? *(museum, park, circus, county fair, bowling alley, etc.)*

4. Do you think it's true that the more time you spend with someone, the more you know about him or her? Why? *(probably—you get to observe them in many situations, see how they react, find out their likes/dislikes, etc.)*

5. Who are your favorite people to spend time with? What do you do together? *(students may list specific friends and activities)*

6. If you wanted to make some new friends, how could you spend time with people to get to know them better? *(try some new activities, go somewhere new or different)*

Activity:

Directions: Students are to read the conversations and try to decide where it is taking place and how the characters are spending time together.

   Answers: 1. at the zoo   2. riding a bike   3. playing a game

   Follow-up: Discuss what specific word clues or comments give the answers to the worksheet. Even though more than two are in each group, are they all getting along? Do they think the activities are interesting? What will happen next in each situation?

Spending Time with Others

Read these conversations. Then write on the lines how each group of friends is spending time together.

1.

_____
_____
_____
_____

2.

_____
_____

3.

_____
_____
_____
_____

II-4 Inviting Others into Your Group

Objective:

The student will cite examples of polite ways to invite someone else to join a group.

Rationale:

Sometimes groups are formed by choice; other times, by random. If a student has an opportunity to actively invite someone else to become part of a group, this is a socially mature thing to do. New students may feel hesitant or shy to break into a new group. It may be threatening to allow an outsider to merge with an already-set circle of friends. However, by enlarging the group to include others, the students are given an opportunity to share and explore new relationships—a growing experience!

Thinking Questions:

1. How would you feel if you were suddenly at a new school where you didn't know anyone? *(lost, afraid, shy, etc.)*

2. What would be a good way to help a new person learn his or her way around if this happened at our school? *(assign someone to help them learn where things are, tell everyone to be especially nice to them, etc.)*

3. What if you wanted to invite someone to sit with your group at lunch, but the others in your group didn't want that? What could you do? *(talk to the person later, sit with the new person yourself, try to convince the group to make room for one more, etc.)*

4. What good things might happen if you invited someone new to join your group? *(might make a new friend, the person might be fun and interesting, you'd feel good about it, etc.)*

5. What if the new person in your group turned out to be bossy or nasty to everyone? *(he or she probably wouldn't be asked back!)*

6. Why might it be embarrassing to invite someone who wasn't popular or who was "different" into your group? *(the others might laugh at you or the person, might kick you out of the group)*

7. What do you think you would do in that situation? *(decide if you wanted to stick with the group or if you liked the new person and wanted to be friends on your own)*

Activity:

Directions: Students are to decide which of the comments on the worksheet are good ways to invite someone else to join a group. They are to put a check mark next to the good responses.

   Answers: check mark by—1, 2, 4, 6, 7

   Follow-up: Discuss what was rude or insensitive about numbers 3, 5, and 8. (These comments make the person sound as though he or she is last choice, very undesirable as company, and difficult to be nice to.) Even if the comments express how the group truly feels, how could the person be included in a polite manner? (examples: **#3**—You're on our team, Jeff; **#5**—Let's wait for Amy; **#8**—There's room over here.)

Inviting Others into Your Group

Which of these are good ways to invite another person to join your group? Put a ✔ next to your answers.

1. Would you like to go swimming with us?   _____

2. There's room on this seat of the bus. You could sit here with us.   _____

3. Well, there's no one else left. You'll have to be on our team.   _____

4. Why don't you come with us to the playground?   _____

5. If we walk very slowly, we'll lose her.   _____

6. There's a craft time session at the library. Let's all go.   _____

7. We're all going out for ice cream. Why don't you come?   _____

8. I guess you'll have to ride with us. I'm supposed to try to be nice to you. _____

II-5 Helping Out

Objective:

The student will identify specific ways to help someone who is in a problem situation.

Rationale:

Helping others out of an embarrassing or tough situation is one way to make a friend. Not only will the student have to identify a way to help the person out, he or she will have to actually carry out the plan—the toughest part! This lesson gives students an opportunity to work on the first part of this idea.

Thinking Questions:

1. What would you do if you saw someone in a situation where he or she could use a little help? *(most will probably say they would help them)*

2. What are some problems that you might be able to help out with? *(students may name something that they are good at—working on the computer, sports, etc.)*

3. How would the person feel if you helped him or her out? *(probably grateful as long as you weren't intimidating or rude about it)*

4. If you wanted to make friends with someone, how could you do something to help him or her? *(find out what they were having trouble with, offer to help with something you're good at, etc.)*

5. Do you think that it would make someone else feel good if you let him or her help *you* out with a problem? *(probably)*

6. How can helping each other out help make a good friendship? *(people feel grateful to each other, indebted, may think more kindly about the other person)*

7. What are some ways that people could help each other out here at school or in the classroom? *(list specific classroom examples)*

Activity:

Directions: Students are to draw a picture illustrating how they could help out the person on the left who was having a problem or needed help. Encourage students to go beyond the obvious—including dialogue is fine.

Answers: (examples)

1. "I've done that before, Megan. I'll help you pick them up."
2. "Want some help?"
3. "Let's work together, OK?"
4. "I've done that program before. I thought it was hard, too, then I learned a few tricks. I can show them to you."

Follow-up: Have students share their drawings and ideas. After students have demonstrated that they can identify a way to help the character, discuss why it would be difficult for them to actually carry out the plan. (example: **#3**—Sally would slow them down too. Perhaps Sally is mean or lazy and doesn't care about the assignment.) Even if their plan is a *hard* thing to do, is it the *right* thing to do? Why should people be nice to other people who have problems? *(someday it may be their turn! Maybe their good deed will be what turns that other person's attitude around!)*

Helping Out

Draw a picture of how you could help someone out in each situation.

1. Megan dropped her bag full of crayons on the floor.

2. Andy is not very good at catching the ball.

3. Everyone is supposed to work with a partner. No one wants to work with Sally because she is so slow.

4. Carl can't figure out how to play the game on the computer.

II-6 Listening

Objective:

The student will identify comments made by a character who appears to be listening to another character.

Rationale:

Many people like to talk; few like to listen. Listening, however, is an excellent way to make friends, as most people like to be listened to. A way to show that you are listening is by making a comment that relates to what the person is talking about. In this lesson, the student is to listen (or read) and pick the character who is responding appropriately because he or she was listening to the talker.

Thinking Questions:

1. Do you think more people like to do the *talking* or the *listening*? *(opinions may vary—possibly more will think there are more talkers than listeners because they themselves like to talk)*

2. Why would listening to someone talk be a good way to make friends with them? *(you'd find out something about them, their concerns, show that you are interested in them, etc.)*

3. Why is it hard to listen? *(we want to do the talking, we feel that we have something more important to say)*

4. How could you show that you are listening to someone who is talking? *(look at them, be quiet)*

5. What could you say to someone after they are done talking that would show you were listening? *(ask a question about what they were talking about, ask for more details about their situation, etc.)*

6. Do you think you should *pretend* to be interested in someone and what they're saying even if you really aren't? *(perhaps by pretending at first you might really get interested later, this may still be a polite way to make a friend, realize that not everything you say or do is interesting to everyone else)*

Activity:

Directions: Students are to match the two participants in a conversation—the listener on the left with the one who is listening (and then commenting appropriately) on the right.

   Answers: 1. b   2. d   3. e   4. a   5. c

   Follow-up: How did the listeners show that they were listening? How were their comments polite and appropriate? Which ones asked for more information? How did each make the talker feel?

Listening

Match each student on the left who is talking to the student on the right who is listening.

1.

My dog is so pretty - she's black and tan. Her name is Callie. I like to take her for a walk in the park.

_____

a.

I think you look fine. Just ignore the other kids.

2.

I really hate it when we have to get up and talk in front of the class. I get so nervous!

_____

b.

Where did you get your dog?

3.

My stepfather is so mean. I don't like it when he tries to tell me what to do all the time.

_____

c.

Could I read it next? What is the name of it?

d.

What do you have to talk about?

4.

These glasses are so big and ugly. Sometimes the other kids make fun of me.

_____

e.

What does he ask you to do?

5.

This is a great book! I could read it again and again!

_____

II-7 What Is Encouragement?

Objective:

The student will identify a character giving an encouraging statement to another.

Rationale:

Many students do not know what encouraging others is. The idea of "me, first" or being out for yourself takes precedence over giving another person a little boost of confidence or stepping aside to let someone else have the spotlight. This lesson discusses what encouragement is and how to recognize an encouraging statement.

Thinking Questions:

1. What does it mean to be "discouraged"? *(feel lost, hopeless, like you try but just can't get anywhere)*

2. When have you felt discouraged? *(ask for anecdotes—poor test performance, lost at a game, etc.)*

3. Did someone say anything nice to you when you felt discouraged that really cheered you up? What? *(perhaps a parent gave some support, a friend may have said "nice try" or something like that)*

4. What does "encouragement" mean? *(the opposite of discouragement—when you say something that makes the other person feel like there is hope)*

5. When you say something to give another person hope, how would the other person probably feel? *(perhaps a little better)*

6. How would that person feel about you, the encourager? *(would look at you as a friend)*

7. Even if what you said didn't make a difference or change anything, how would it still help the discouraged person? *(let him or her know you care)*

Activity:

Directions: The student is to circle the student in the pair on the right who is giving encouragement to the discouraged student on the left.

Answers:	1. second student	4. first student
	2. first student	5. second student
	3. first student	

Follow-up: Discuss the specific comments of the encourager in each example. How did the comment give the discouraged person hope? How realistic (or valued) was the "hope" given? Does it really help to be encouraging or is it just a nice thing to say?

Name _____   Date _____

II-7

What Is Encouragement?

Circle the student in each pair who is saying something encouraging to the student on the left.

1.  I'm so stupid - I got a bad grade on this paper.   You <u>are</u> stupid.   You'll do better next time.

2.  I wish I could run as fast as you.   Keep trying.   I'm the best.

3.  No one likes me.   I like you.   You're bossy and unfriendly. That's why.

4.  I try and try, but I just can't get this math down! It's so hard!   Would you like me to try to help you?   So?

5.  I'm scared - I don't know anyone here. . .   This is a huge school. It will take all year to get to know anyone.   You'll make friends quickly. The kids are nice.

II-8 Saying Nice Things

Objective:

The student will state an example of a polite comment that could be made in given situations.

Rationale:

Another good technique for letting someone know that you would like to be friends is simply that of making a nice comment to them. If students could accept the fact that a compliment, given in sincerity, is a perfectly fine way to approach someone else, perhaps they would try it more often. People like to hear nice things about themselves. Given the opportunity, we should do this consciously more often!

Thinking Questions:

1. What is a compliment? *(something someone says that is nice, a comment that praises something you've done, etc.)*

2. When someone gives you a compliment, how does that make you feel? *(pretty good)*

3. Are there situations you can think of in which you could say something nice to someone else to make them feel better? *(ask for anecdotes)*

4. Would saying nice things about someone or to someone be a good way to make friends? Why? *(yes—it lets the other person know that you are friendly, positive, and interested in him or her)*

5. Why is it hard to say something nice about someone, especially after someone else has said something rude or negative? *(then that person might think you're trying to be less of a friend to him or her, shows that you disagree)*

6. What would other people start to think about you if you said nice things about other people all the time? *(they'd respect you; maybe they would stop saying mean things about others because they know you would disagree with them)*

Activity:

Directions: Given four cartoon situations, the student is to fill in the speech balloon to show what an appropriate "nice" comment might be.

Answers: (examples)

1. It's a very pretty color.
2. No, that might really hurt him. Leave Robert alone.
3. That kid is really good at softball.
4. Yes, I sure would—let me see your book.

Follow-up: Go through each situation and try to view it through the eyes of the potential "friend" in each situation. How would the girl with the strange dress respond? What about Robert? He seems to be unpopular. Even if you didn't want to be friends with him, how would saying something nice make you a better friend to the speaker? In #3, the girl is talking right in front of the new boy. How would both kids respond to a friendly comment? Discuss how your kind comments might be received by others who would overhear you.

Name _____ Date _____

II-8

Saying Nice Things

What is a nice thing that you could say in each situation below? Write your answer in the balloon.

Part III   Keeping Friends

III-1 Let Others Choose Sometimes

Objective:

The student will identify reasons for letting someone else choose what to do.

Rationale:

Some students like to be in charge, always in control of what everyone in the group will do. While this may be satisfactory in a group full of complacent followers, it is nice to let others have a say in what will be done and how it will be accomplished. This lesson asks students to think about how someone might feel being paired with a bossy partner.

Thinking Questions:

1. When you are working or playing with a friend, who usually decides what you both will do? *(might name someone or state that they take turns)*

2. What if you disagree on what to do; how do you work it out? *(one will give in, there might be an argument, do something else)*

3. What if you were always with someone who wanted to make the decisions and decide what to do—how would you feel? *(might get tired of never having a voice in the situation)*

4. Why might it be important to let someone else decide what to do sometimes? *(they will feel important, the other person might have some good ideas)*

5. What are some good ways to make sure that you're not too busy and are always the one to decide what to do? *(plan to be quiet and step back, systematically take turns, ask everyone for their opinion before starting, etc.)*

Activity:

Directions: The student is to think about the four situations presented on the worksheet involving one student who is the decider of what to do. The student is to write down what he or she thinks the other student is feeling or thinking about.

Answers: (examples)

1. I don't even want to play baseball!
2. I ate there last night. I don't like the food.
3. He's so bossy; I don't want to work with him.
4. I'm tired. I played tennis this morning.

Follow-up: Go through each situation again, this time rephrasing the bossy person's desires into statements and questions that take into consideration the other person's feelings.

Let Others Choose Sometimes

Some of these students always want to choose what to do. What do you think the others in each situation below are thinking? Write your answer in the balloon.

III-2 Be a Fair Friend

Objective:

The student will state that being a "fair" friend means sharing the friend with others and not putting restrictions upon the other person.

Rationale:

Some students view a friend as their own personal property. Therefore, that person cannot talk to anyone else, play with anyone else, and must always be available for whatever reason the student wishes—to help with work, to be there to play, etc. Being "fair" with others means allowing the other person freedom to live his or her own life, understanding that friendship does not come with unrealistic ties.

Thinking Questions:

1. How would you feel if you were only allowed to have one friend? *(restricted, hard to pick only one, etc.)*

2. What if you were not allowed to play with anyone else, talk to anyone else, and you always had to help this person out whenever he or she wanted you to? Would this be fun? *(not really—it would be very limiting)*

3. What are some ways people might finish this sentence: You can be my friend if...? *(you give me that toy, you let me come over, you help me with something, etc.)*

4. Why do you think it is important to have lots of friends? *(one might move away, get to know more people, some things are more fun in groups, etc.)*

5. What do you think being a "fair" friend means? *(letting your friend do things on his or her own, having other friends, not saying "if" to them, etc.)*

6. Can you give some examples of not being fair with others? *(telling them who they can or cannot hang around with, changing friendships quickly—not really being sincerely interested in the other person)*

Activity:

Directions: The student is to match the student who is being "unfair" with the reason why on the right.

Answers: 1. d   2. c   3. e   4. b   5. a

Follow-up: Discuss how each student who was taken advantage of by the unfair friend could have responded—politely, but with fairness in mind. How could each situation be remedied with both sides working together or still having fun?

Be a Fair Friend

None of these students are being fair friends. Match the students with the reason why they aren't being fair.

1.

You can't play with Sarah. You can play with Beth, though. _____

a. It's not fair to always expect someone to do things your way or at your house.

2.

You can be my friend if you let me have that ball. _____

b. It's not fair to make your friend do your work or it's his fault.

3.

I have to clean out the garage. You better help me. _____

c. It's not fair to make your friend give you things (or you won't be friends anymore).

d. It's not fair to tell a friend who he can or can't play with.

4.

Don't leave me! You are the only one who can help me with this paper! You have to help me or I'll get a bad grade! _____

e. It's not fair to make your friend do chores that you don't like, just because he's your friend.

5.

Why do I always have to go over to your house? Why don't you ever come over to my house to play? _____

Part III   Keeping Friends

III-3 Sharing Friends

Objective:

The student will identify ways that a friend can be shared with another person or situation.

Rationale:

When someone has a "best" friend, it is often hard to see that friend with someone else, having a good time. However, friends are not property and it is reasonable to expect a friend to have other friends or to participate in an activity with someone else. A good friend won't make a big deal of this, but will accept the fact that at some point he or she will do something with someone else.

Thinking Questions:

1. How many of you have a "best" friend? *(show of hands)*

2. Why is it fun to have a best friend? *(someone you can count on, someone you especially enjoy being with, someone who lives close to you, etc.)*

3. Have you ever had a really good friend get invited to something that you were not invited to? How did you feel? *(probably left out, jealous)*

4. Is it really fair to expect a best friend to be your only friend? *(no, situations change and there are lots of other people around who might be fun to get to know)*

5. Why do you think it is hard to "share" your friend with other people? *(might fear that they will like someone better than you, that you'll be forgotten)*

6. How could making a big deal about your friend going off with other people hurt your relationship? *(your friend might be mad at you for being upset about it, you might miss out on something if other people want to invite you to something too)*

7. If your friend does get to do something that you can't do or aren't invited to do, how could you handle it? *(be a good sport, tell your friend you hope he or she has a good time, find something else to do)*

Activity:

Directions: Students are to view each situation on the worksheet from the perspective of the character with a star beside him or her. They are to write or draw a response that shows how the student could share the friend with others.

Answers: (examples)

1. Show all three girls riding bikes.
2. "You could help me another time. Have fun at the party."
3. Tony (who wasn't picked) could say, "I'll wait for you after class, Mike."
4. The girl on the left could say, "Can I watch you, Sandy? I'd like to learn to dive, too."

Follow-up: It's hard to be the person who is left out, but learning to be gracious and accepting is a real step towards social maturity. Discuss how each person who was starred might feel left out or rejected at first, but then discuss the positive ways that he or she could handle the situation.

Sharing Friends

How could this student (⭐) share his or her friend with others? Write your answer or draw a picture to show a way.

1.

> We're going to the park to ride our bikes.

> Let's ask Nancy to go too.

2.

> I can't come over tomorrow. It's my friend's birthday party.

> But you said you'd help me with my model.

3.

> I need two people to wash the blackboards. David, pick someone.

> Andy.

4.

> Swimming is so much fun.

> Sandy, would you help me dive?

III-4 Don't Hang or Beg

Objective:

The student will identify situations in which the character considered is hanging or begging on another person.

Rationale:

Some students want to have a friend so badly that they actually "smother" the other person with attention. A good friend not only can share another person, but is also not so demanding of the other's attention that he or she actually hangs on the other or becomes annoying by begging for the person's attention.

Thinking Questions:

1. What happens if you want your friend to do something with you really badly but he or she can't? What do you do? *(some will probably say they give up, plan for another time, etc.)*

2. What would happen if you kept insisting that your friend do something with you, even if the friend already said he or she couldn't? *(the friend might become annoyed with you)*

3. How do you think your friend would feel if you kept pulling on his or her arm, trying to get him or her to do what you wanted to do? *(really irritated, might start a fight, etc.)*

4. Why would begging over and over also be annoying? *(same kind of thing— verbal hanging)*

5. If your friend already tells you "no" or that he or she can't spend time with you right then, what are some good ways to show that you can handle the situation without hanging or begging? *(agree to do something together another time, let your friend go without a hassle, ask once and then stop asking, etc.)*

Activity:

Directions: The student is to look over the five situations on the worksheet and decide whether or not the character is hanging on another person or begging for something. They are to draw a smile on the face for the characters who are being good friends (in that they are not hanging or begging) or draw a frown for not showing good friendship skills.

Answers: 1. frown   2. smile   3. frown   4. frown   5. smile

Follow-up: Discuss what alternatives the hangers and beggers could use to convey their wishes to the other person involved. At what point should they just give up? Which situations do the other people have control over? *(possibly #1—if the girl had the option of letting someone go with her; #2—they could have worked out a way to rotate players; #3—the person might choose to look at records. The other situations seem to be pretty well decided already.)* If they can't control the situation, what point is there in hanging or begging?

Don't Hang or Beg

Draw a smile on the face if you think the person talking in each cartoon below is being a good friend. Draw a frown if you think he or she is not.

1. **Please let me go to the store with you! Come on, let me go!**

2. **I'd like to play basketball with you, but I see that you have enough players. I'll find something else to do.**

3. **Let's look at the records in this store. Oh, let's go over here! Look at this!**

4. **Don't go to Kathy's party on Saturday. Come to my house instead. OK? Please? Please?**

5. **I wish you could spend the night, but your mom said no. See you later.**

Part III   Keeping Friends

III-5 Keep Your Promises

Objective:

The student will identify realistic promises that a friend could make and keep to another friend.

Rationale:

Some students make elaborate, unrealistic promises to others as an attempt to keep someone a friend. While this may seem appealing to the person who is wanted as a friend, it is likely to result in disappointment and arguments once the promise is broken. Friends do promise each other things, and it is important to keep those promises. It is also important not to try to win a friend with enormous promises that can't be kept.

Thinking Questions:

1. What kinds of promises do friends make to each other? *(not to tell secrets, to help each other out, to share things, etc.)*

2. What if you really wanted someone to like you and you promised to give them an expensive present if they would be your friend—is that a good way to make friends? *(probably not—what if you didn't come through?)*

3. How could you tell if the friend really liked you or just liked what you could do for them or give them? *(a real friend would like you without all those things)*

4. How would it make you feel if your friend promised you something and then forgot about it or changed his or her mind? *(angry at the friend, sad, betrayed, etc.)*

5. Why is it important to keep your promises? *(someone is counting on you, you should keep your word)*

6. If it is important to keep promises, why should you be careful what kinds of promises you make? *(make sure you can keep them, make sure you're not just trying to impress someone, etc.)*

Activity:

Directions: Students are to look over the list of promises and put a check mark by the ones that someone could probably keep.

Answers: check marks by—2, 5, 7, 9

Follow-up: Discuss why the promises that were not checked are unrealistic or not "safe" promises. Can you make a promise for someone else? *(3, 8, 10)* Why are "absolutes" risky promises? *(**always** and **never** promises)*

Keep Your Promises

Which of these are promises that you think someone could keep? Put a check mark by the promises that are good. Add your own promises to keep.

1. I'll never eat lunch with anyone but you. Ever. _____

2. I'll ask my dad if you can go with us to the beach. _____

3. I'll have my big brother beat up Ricky for you. _____

4. I will always wait for you after school so we can walk home together. _____

5. I'll save a seat for you on the bus if I get there first. _____

6. Let's steal some candy from the store. I won't tell anyone if you get caught. _____

7. You're sick, so I'll return your library book for you. _____

8. If you'll be my friend, I'll have my father buy that remote control car for you. It's only $150! _____

9. I won't tell Debbie that you got a bad grade on your test. _____

10. I'll make our teacher give you an A on that poster. _____

11. _____

12. _____

13. _____

14. _____

Part III Keeping Friends

III-6 Don't Badmouth

Objective:

The student will identify statements that are badmouthing or derogatory to someone else.

Rationale:

Sooner or later, if you say something bad about someone else, it will get back to you. It is important to realize that when you share your opinions about someone to another person, that person might tell someone else. The person being talked about might overhear what is being said as well. To keep friends, students should learn to be careful about what they say about others.

Thinking Questions:

1. What does it mean to "badmouth" someone? *(say bad things about them, usually talk behind their back, etc.)*

2. When you badmouth someone, does it usually change anything about the person? *(not if it is a characteristic about the person or they don't know it)*

3. Can people change the way they look or act? *(to some extent, if they want to and have some means of making a change)*

4. What do most people badmouth other people about? *(the way they look, act, irritating habits)*

5. How would you feel if everyone in a room was saying bad things about a friend of yours? *(angry, annoyed)*

6. Why do you think some people say bad things about a person behind their back instead of to their face? *(don't really want a confrontation; just want to gossip or bring out the mistakes of other people)*

7. Have you ever badmouthed someone and later regretted it? Tell about it. *(listen to anecdotes about how someone was embarrassed, got in trouble, etc.)*

Activity:

Directions: Students are to put an X on the characters on the worksheet who are badmouthing someone else.

Answers: X on—1, 6, 7, 9

Follow-up: Discuss characteristics of Sam, Mary, and John. Can these students control the problems that the badmouthers are talking about? Instead of badmouthing them, how could the characters change the outcome of the situations?

Don't Badmouth

Which students below are saying something bad about someone? Put an X on them.

III-7 Stick Up for Your Friend

Objective:

The student will identify ways to show support for a friend in various situations.

Rationale:

Friends stick up for each other—especially when the friend cannot defend him- or herself in a situation. Friends should not be friends only when it is easy. Sticking up for a friend does NOT mean fighting. This lesson examines ways to show support for a friend.

Thinking Questions:

1. What would you do if you heard people badmouthing your best friend? *(ignore, tell them to stop, threaten them, etc.)*

2. Why would it bother you if someone was saying bad things about a friend of yours? *(you like your friend and don't want other people challenging your taste in friends!)*

3. How could you stick up for your friend without getting into a big argument or fight? *(state what your opinion is, then walk away, etc.)*

4. What if your friend is in a situation where people are picking on him or her and your friend is too shy or scared to do anything about it? What could you do without fighting? *(tell someone, talk to the offenders, help your friend think of things to do, etc.)*

5. What if it didn't bother your friend one bit that other people were talking about him or her? Should you do something then? *(if the friend doesn't care, you might talk to the friend to make sure he or she really isn't bothered; otherwise it might be better to just leave the situation alone—let the offenders get tired and just quit)*

Activity:

Directions: Students are to consider several situations involving a friend in trouble and write down their answers as to what they would do in each situation.

Answers: (examples)

1. say that you are watching them and tell the teacher if they take your friend's things

2. stay with your friend

3. tell Nancy to be careful when she walks past the desk, she might hurt her arm by knocking your friend too much

4. tell Antonio that you will wait for him after school and help him get caught up

Follow-up: Discuss students' responses. How many went straight to fighting and violence as their way of sticking up for the friend? Discuss the idea of sticking up for a friend by *being* a friend, rather than having a confrontation with the other people.

Stick Up for Your Friend

What would you do in each situation below? Write your answer on the lines.

1. Your friend is sick at home one day. Two kids want to go
through your friend's desk and look for pencils and money.
They ask you not to say anything to anybody.

_____

_____

2. You and your friend Bob are walking home from school
together. Another friend rides past you on his bike and asks if you want
to ride to the lake with him. You want to, but the two other kids don't like
each other. You ask if Bob can go too, but the other friend says no.

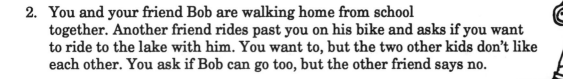

_____

_____

3. Nancy keeps knocking into your friend whenever she
passes by her desk. You know that she is doing it just to
be mean. Your friend is too shy to tell the teacher or say
anything to Nancy.

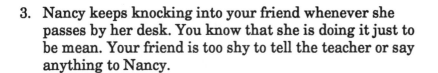

_____

_____

4. Antonio had to go to detention for not doing his homework. Two
girls go by the detention room and make fun of him. They are
calling him names and saying that he is stupid. You know that
Antonio was sick last night and that's why he didn't do his
homework.

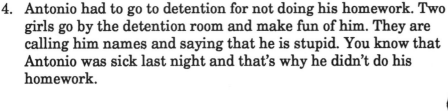

_____

_____

III-8 Helping Someone with a Problem

Objective:

The student will identify possible strategies for helping a friend with a specified problem.

Rationale:

Friends share their problems with other friends, and at times students may find themselves in a position to help out a friend with opinions or advice. This lesson involves the student in evaluating ideas for helping a friend with a problem.

Thinking Questions:

1. Have you ever had a friend come to you with a problem? If so, what did you do? *(probably—listen to them, give advice, etc.)*

2. Does your friend expect you to solve the problem or just give your ideas? *(probably just give ideas and helpful comments)*

3. When you want to help a friend solve his or her problems, do you think there is more than one possible way to work things out? Why? *(probably; there are usually several alternatives available)*

4. How did it make you feel to be able to help out a friend? *(good, powerful, happy)*

5. If you can't actually DO something to help a friend with a problem, what are some other ways you could help? *(listen, talk to another friend, be there for your friend instead of leaving him or her alone, etc.)*

Activity:

Directions: The student is to evaluate several different ideas for solving a friend's problem. There may be more than one possible good answer. The student is to write YES or NO indicating his or her thoughts about the answers.

Answers: 1. second, fourth answers
　　　　　　　2. first, fourth answers
　　　　　　　3. third, fourth answers

Follow-up: Discuss why certain answers were discarded and why others were more reasonable alternatives. Come up with a generalized list of "helping" responses, such as: listening, being sympathetic, offering to help practice a skill, etc.

Helping Someone with a Problem

Your friend comes to you with a problem. What could you say? Write YES or NO on the line to show good answers.

1.

> **I just hate my sister. She is always taking my stuff and trying to get me in trouble.**

You could move into my house. I have a nice sister. _____

Can you talk to your parents about her? _____

Let's go through her stuff and hide everything. _____

I'll help you talk to your sister and explain how you feel. _____

2.

> **I know I won't make the football team. I'll be the only one who doesn't make it.**

Why don't you practice with me after school? _____

Football is stupid. Just give up. _____

Move to another school district. Maybe you could make the team there. _____

I'll help you work on passing the ball. _____

3.

> **I need some money. I have to pay for the window I broke.**

I'll take some out of my mother's purse. _____

Don't say anything about the window. They won't catch you. _____

I could lend you some, but I have to put some in the bank. _____

You better tell your parents. I'll go with you. _____

Section II

III-9   Telling Someone If a Friend Needs Help

Objective:

The student will identify an appropriate source if a friend indicates he or she is in need of serious help.

Rationale:

If the situation is such that friends listening and being sympathetic is enough, that's great. Some situations may arise, however, that call for involvement of someone else who can do more to help the problem. In this lesson, the student is asked to suggest others who can help.

Thinking Questions:

1. If your friend broke his pencil, would you be able to help him? How? *(yes—lend him one, buy one for him, etc.)*

2. If your friend broke his ankle, could you take care of the problem? Why or why not? *(probably not—that's a serious medical problem, but the student could call for help, stay with his friend while waiting, etc.)*

3. Why is it harder to handle the second broken incident than the first? *(much more serious to have a broken ankle than pencil)*

4. When you know your friend has a problem that is more than you can handle, who are some people who could help? *(parent, teacher, doctor, counselor, etc.)*

5. If your friend is not willing or able to get help by himself or herself, what could you do to convince your friend to let you get help or how could you actually go for help? *(explain to your friend that the problem requires more expert help, promise to keep it confidential if that is a problem, talk to your own parents if that is appropriate, etc.)*

Activity:

Directions: The student is to identify an appropriate source of help for each of the situations that his or her friend is experiencing on the worksheet.

Answers: (examples)

1. school counselor, teacher
2. older friend or sibling
3. teacher, principal
4. school counselor, principal, teacher
5. nurse, doctor, parent
6. bus driver

Follow-up: Go through each of the situations and evaluate them in terms of the seriousness of each. Which involve emotional problems? Which are physical problems? Why are these problems more serious than those on the previous worksheet?

Telling Someone If a Friend Needs Help

Who is someone that you could go to if your friend needed help?

1. I feel so sad. I hate school. I don't like my family. I just don't want to live anymore.

   _____

2. Allen wants me to try some drugs. I don't really want to, but I'm afraid he'll make fun of me if I don't.

   _____

3. The other kids are making fun of me because I'm in a wheelchair. I don't even want to go to school anymore.

   _____

4. Someone at home is hitting me. I'm afraid. I don't know what to do.

   _____

5. Oh no - I think I broke my arm! It really hurts!

   _____

6. Those big kids said they were going to punch me out after school in the back of the bus. I'm afraid.

   _____

© 1993 by The Center for Applied Research in Education

III-10 Friends Don't Get You in Trouble!

Objective:

The student will recognize characteristics of friends who do not try to involve him or her in situations that could cause problems for the student or get him or her in trouble.

Rationale:

Students need to watch out for friends who are users; whose intent for the friendship is to manipulate and end up getting their own way. If a so-called friend's ideas always involve getting a person in trouble, it is definitely time to reevaluate that relationship!

Thinking Questions:

1. Have you ever been in a situation when a friend asked you to do something wrong for him or her? Tell about it if you can. *(students may relate anecdotes—no names!)*

2. How did you feel when that person was asking you to do something that would possibly get you in trouble? *(may state that they would do it for their friendship, some may feel uneasy, threatened, etc.)*

3. Have you ever had friends who were nice to you when they wanted something, but didn't care when you got in trouble later for helping them out? *(listen to anecdotes)*

4. What do you think of a friend who is constantly letting you get in trouble or asking you to do hard things that put you in a bad situation? *(not a very caring friend, selfish, etc.)*

5. Is there a difference between getting in trouble with a friend and getting in trouble because a friend asks you to do something while he or she sits back and waits for you to finish? *(yes—in the first situation, both people made a mistake; in the second, the friend used the other person to "test the waters" or see what would happen)*

Activity:

Directions: Students are to read the brief descriptions of the students and decide whether or not that person is a good friend, based on whether or not they asked someone to get into trouble or created a situation that would involve getting a person into trouble.

Answers: Allen, Sandra, Anita

Follow-up: Discuss what was wrong with what the other students asked the friend to do. How could you tell your friend that you didn't want to get involved in that situation? What could you say to your friend to help resolve the friend's problem?

Friends Don't Get You in Trouble!

Which of these students below is a good friend? Write their names in the box below.

1. MARIE wants you to go to the mall with her and try to put some jewelry in your purse without paying for the stuff.

2. ALLEN has an extra ticket to a basketball game and asked you to go.

3. RANDY got in trouble for breaking a window and he told the police that you were with him, even though you were at home.

4. SANDRA picked up your books from school and brought them to you when you were sick for a few days.

5. TODD broke the fender on his bicycle so he took the part he needed off of your bike without asking. Your parents just bought you the bike and you promised to take good care of it.

6. KAREN knows that you aren't supposed to talk on the phone for more than 5 minutes, but she won't hang up. She wants you to listen to a record over the phone while your dad is waiting to use it.

7. ANITA brought extra cookies to school to share with you.

8. BRIAN hid his guinea pigs in your room so his parents wouldn't find out about them. He made you promise not to tell your parents.

III

Developing

Positive

Social Skills

Much time is spent in typical classrooms on devising ways to deter negative student social skills, yet it is just as important to replace them with positive ones. We all have our role-models whom we hope will inspire students to become successful in their endeavors. There are certain qualities that we admire and desire in others and for ourselves.

In some cases, a child may never become a terrific athlete, the best academic achiever in any subject, or become totally independent. Yet having a pleasant attitude and being a considerate, thoughtful individual may be a more worthwhile contribution to society in the long run.

Not everyone is outgoing and popular, but there is no excuse for anyone to be rude, nasty, or hateful to others. Special children may carry the extra weight of dealing with embarrassment, an inferiority complex, and failure at school. The development of a strong self-esteem is extremely important for these children. Not only do they need to know how to act socially, they need to be confident—to *know* that they know. Success breeds success, and teaching children to handle social situations confidently is a wonderful first step to build upon.

Section III focuses on the positive attributes of fitting in socially. The story for this section is *The Accident,* about a girl with an abrasive, rude personality and her friend who is passive and gives in easily. When they collide at school (the accident), they exchange attributes about their personality and eventually learn to temper the original with aspects of the other.

In Section III, "Developing Positive Social Skills," you will find:

- Parent Letters 8 through 11
- Classroom Ideas
- "The Accident" *(story)*
- Part I: Understanding Social Situations Correctly *(activities)*
- Part II: Positive Personality Attributes *(activities)*
- Part III: Getting Along with Others at Home *(activities)*
- Part IV: Everyday Etiquette *(activities)*

**RE: Developing Positive Social Skills—Understanding
Social Situations**

Dear Parents,

Have you ever walked into a room and felt that you had no idea what was going on? By listening to the conversation, looking around for clues, and relying on past experiences, you probably pieced together what was happening before too long.

For some children, it is a difficult task to understand what is involved in many social situations. Whether it is at school, at home, going to a friend's house, or talking to people in a store, it may be a confusing experience to the child who is not good at recognizing moods in people, knowing what to expect in a situation, or toning down his or her own voice to sound friendly.

These lessons give ideas for behaving appropriately around handicapped individuals, respecting others' opinions, and paying attention to tone of voice, facial expressions, and the current setting before making demands on others.

Help at home by:

- discussing your expectations for your child's behavior in social situations. Will Aunt Bertha try to kiss him? Should she ask to use the pool? Prepare your child for what's coming.

- call attention to your own moods, facial expressions, and behavior as clues to how you are feeling. Ask your child to tell you what he sees. How do you feel? Why? Is this a good time for added stress?

- make your values clear to your child. If he cheats at school, does this upset you? Is fighting permissible? What do you mean by right and wrong? Where will your child learn the values that will guide him or her through life? Decide!

Sincerely,

_____

Teacher

PARENT LETTER #9

RE: Developing Positive Social Skills—Positive Personality Attributes

Dear Parents,

When you think of someone with a nice, pleasing personality, what do you think of? Most likely your thoughts include someone who is friendly, understanding, interesting, and perhaps someone who takes an interest in others.

The next set of lessons deals with developing positive qualities as a way to make friends and get along with others. These include developing interests, being a good sport, being tolerant of others, accepting the blame when appropriate, and being organized.

You can help reinforce as well as teach these ideas at home. Here are some suggestions.

- Encourage your child to seek out new experiences and find new interests. Check into sports programs, craft lessons, volunteer opportunities.

- Model good sportsmanship. When something goes wrong, show your child how to handle it in a responsible manner. Show that there is no shame in being a good loser. It's easier to be a good winner; being a good loser takes work and a good attitude!

- If your child is a leader, use this ability to help organize the other children in the family. Ask this child to help you plan the family picnic, sort through the piles of clothing, help make lists.

- When your child is at fault, help make it a little easier for him or her to accept the blame by treating the matter fairly and without extreme punishment, if appropriate. Thank him or her for coming to you honestly—although you still expect amends to be made!

Sincerely,

_____
Teacher

© 1993 by The Center for Applied Research in Education

PARENT LETTER #10

RE: Developing Positive Social Skills—Getting Along with Others at Home

Dear Parents,

This part is for you! Though we don't get to see our students in their homes very often, we know that what goes on at home can affect what happens at school and vice versa. Hopefully, if we are all stressing getting along with others in our day-to-day lives—whether it is at school or at home—we are teaching the same ideas: developing good relationships.

The lessons in this section will cover areas such as getting along with parents; fitting into a family of siblings as the oldest, youngest, or middle child; dealing with chores and homework; and having fun as a family. You can help by:

- explaining your family rules clearly to your child. You might want to discuss the need for rules and the consequences if rules are not followed.

- realize that your child is a unique individual, not simply "the youngest" or "my other son." Praise your child for his or her special accomplishments and encourage interests.

- be systematic and fair when it comes to chores. Everyone lives in the house—everyone can contribute in some way to getting things done. It doesn't have to be viewed as punishment! It's just a responsibility that can make it easier for everyone if we all lend a hand.

- realize that your children will probably not be in the house forever. Use the time you have with them to create a happy childhood, lots of good experiences, and the memory of a family who supports each other and loves each other. Look for ways to have fun together as a family.

Sincerely,

_____

Teacher

PARENT LETTER #11

RE: Developing Positive Social Skills—Everyday Etiquette

Dear Parents,

Our final set of lessons deals with teaching social skills that are used in everyday settings. We all hope that our children will grow up to be polite and respectful to others, as it is a good reflection on us! Other skills, such as washing hands before eating, using good table manners, using appropriate language, and writing thank-you notes are also included.

Perhaps the most important social skill covered in this series of lessons is the final one: discussion of the "Golden Rule," which is simply to treat others as you wish to be treated. It says it all!

Help your child learn good manners at home:

- Specifically instruct them how to introduce others and meet your friends when they come into the house. It doesn't have to be a formal thing, but make sure names are exchanged and there is good eye contact.

- Make hand washing, use of silverware, and passing plates around the table a part of your structured mealtimes. It's cute when a small child dives into the peas, but not so funny when someone who should know better attacks his or her food. Even if you don't have structured meals often, use the times that you do to work on these skills.

- Look for opportunities to teach your child about common courtesy when using public facilities such as a phone, transportation, or sitting in a crowded waiting room. Look for ways to show kindness to others.

- Take pride in the times when your child demonstrates courtesy to others. Compliment him or her on the thoughtfulness shown (even though it may surprise you!).

Good luck!

Sincerely,

_____

Teacher

CLASSROOM IDEAS FOR SECTION III
Developing Positive Social Skills

Part I. Understanding Social Situations

- Before you go to the gym, attend a school play in another classroom or go to an assembly and discuss expectations. Make predictions as to what will happen. After the event, go through your list. Was the event predictable? Did planning ahead for it make things go smoother? **(I-1)**

- Plan a surprise party for your assistant or someone you know well who is connected with your classroom. Discuss how *lack* of expectations is the key to having a good surprise. Show how taking away the clues of predicting makes the event a surprise. **(I-1)**

- When someone (or if you catch yourself) is unnecessarily rude in talking to someone, ask for an immediate rephrasing of the response. "Could you try that again?" or "I'm sure you didn't mean that the way it sounded; would you like to repeat that?" might be ways to alert the speaker (or use yourself as an example) to be more polite. **(I-2)**

- Modified assertiveness training might be helpful for some of the meeker, milder students who are continually taken advantage of by others. Working in small groups, perhaps with the assistance of the counselor as coach, have students practice standing up for themselves, saying "no" appropriately, and sticking up for each other. **(I-3)**

- Have a "Handicapped Awareness" week in your class, emphasizing how handicaps can be overcome. Read stories of famous athletes who overcame handicaps, share articles about devices invented to help lessen handicaps, and invite a guest speaker who might be willing to talk about his or her handicap with the students. **(I-5)**

- Invite speakers who are from other countries or who have ties to another country to come in and talk about the customs, language, schools, games, etc., of another country. **(I-6)**

- Make a tape recording of speakers demonstrating various tones of voice. Speakers could be in the midst of an argument, cheering at a ballgame, etc. Have students use the clues to figure out what the speaker's mood is and where the speaker is at the time. Use comedy if appropriate. **(I-7)**

- Cut out magazine pictures showing facial expressions. Have students write appropriate (even comical) captions to go with the expressions. **(I-8)**

- Set up mini-debates in which students have 30-60 seconds to make a point about an issue, then listen to someone from the "other side" make their points. The topics should be as simple as: The Best Pet, The Most Important Holiday, A Great Meal, etc. It is more important that students make good points and are clear in their presentation than what their choices truly are. Have other students in the audience discuss which side was more convincing and why. **(I-9)**

- When you are in an especially good or down mood, explain to your students how you are feeling and why (if appropriate). Give them a chance to learn to respect your feelings by allowing them to see how you are feeling. Show them you appreciate their concern. Respect is reciprocal; ask them to alert you to their moods or a particularly bad day that they are having. Communicate. **(I-11)**

- During reading, stop often to reflect how the character in the story is probably feeling at that moment. Students may enjoy keeping a diary for a few days *as* a favorite character. What would Little Red Riding Hood be thinking about after her first visit with the wolf? Would Goldilocks be worried about breaking the chairs? Create an awareness of feelings in others. **(I-12)**

- Collect articles from the newspaper about local events that illustrate right and wrong. Perhaps there are some local heroes who helped someone out, as well as a few who got caught for hurting someone else or destroying property. What would a student court decide as a sentence for the destruction? What penalties were given? **(I-14)**

- If appropriate, discuss the Code of Hammurabi (king of Babylon), which was an ancient system of legal codes. How would his system work today? **(I-14)**

- Have students write creative stories with the general theme of EMERGENCY! Although the story can be fictional, have students show how an emergency situation could be handled correctly in the story. They may have to do some research (What's the treatment for rabies? How do firefighters put out a fire? What do you do if someone swallows cleaning fluid?) to be accurate. **(I-15)**

Part II. Positive Personality Attributes

- Have an "Interest Fair" in which students can set up a booth displaying their hobbies by using pictures, displaying trophies and ribbons, or books showing something about their hobby. Let students work at their booths for half of the class on one day; then switch and let them be visitors the second day. **(II-1)**

- Students can practice being good sports by making it a policy for both teams to slap hands with the other team after a game is played. During this time, there is to be no grumbling or arguing over the game; only "nice job" or other words of praise. **(II-3)**

- Gather information from newspapers and magazines about local Good Samaritans who have done something noteworthy to help out someone else. Display the articles and pictures on a bulletin board and keep adding to the collection. **(II-4)**

- Assign students to think "you, first" for a week, allowing someone else to go first or be the recipient of thoughtful behavior. By doing at least one good deed every day for a week, this may become a habit. Encourage students to talk about the "rewards" that they experienced at the end of the week. **(II-5)**

- Research famous political individuals and decide whether or not they were good leaders. Upper elementary students might be assigned someone from a particular country who has been newsworthy in the past. Based on the outcome of the individual's leadership, would they be considered "good" leaders? **(II-6)**

- Have students write fan letters to an admired individual. It could be a sports figure, popular musical star, or someone in the news. What do students find to admire in these individuals? **(II-7)**

- Set a good example for your students by admitting when you make a mistake. It's hard for adults to apologize to a child or to take the blame for something when it is deserved. This is the kind of example that really makes an impact on children. **(II-8)**

- Have a class day in which everything gets cleaned up and organized! Demonstrate that time spent in organizing things is time well spent. Assign students a "buddy" to help them check things out to make sure everything's in place. **(II-9)**

- As an experiment, give the students all of their written assignments at one time, first thing in the morning. Tell students that they are to come up with a WRITTEN plan telling how they will accomplish all of the tasks. Afterwards, discuss how it worked. Is it easier for some to have the whole picture and chip away at tasks or do some do better by being given small doses of assignments with lots of teacher support? Discuss how the day went. Some very well-organized students may want to do it this way all the time! **(II-10)**

Part III. Getting Along with Others at Home

- Assign students the research task of finding out about the childhood life of an admired adult. Using biographies, have students relate how incidents from the person's childhood helped shape him or her as an adult. **(III-1)**

- To help students understand that everyone answers to someone else, make a class chart starting with the students, going through the teacher, principal, school board, governor, etc. You may want to use the line of questioning such as: "And who would that person have to answer to?" No one, even the president, has the total power that controls others. By demonstrating that respecting others is endless, students may realize that it is part of our system and our life. **(III-2)**

- Have students compile a list of requests that their parents have given to them in a one-hour (or one-afternoon or one-day) period of time. Discuss the requests. Are they mostly for chore-related incidents? Are the requests unreasonable? Should they be obeyed? **(III-3)**

- Assign a creative writing task with the title: The Day I Didn't Obey. Look for lots of interesting consequences! **(III-4)**

- Send home an informal survey to parents requesting lists of family rules. Are the rules similar among families? Would students like to trade family rules for a week? **(III-5)**

- Over a period of a week and with parental support, have students make a checklist of the rules for each room of the house. After he or she has followed the rules for a week (with parental initials to verify), have the student bring the list to school for a small prize. **(III-6)**

- Designate a holiday for honoring siblings and make cards in class for students to give to those at home. You may wish to have students prepare small gifts such as a small plant or a cupcake. Discuss how it went over at home when students return the next day. Were they surprised? **(III-7)**

- With parents' help, have students make a photo-autobiography. Here is the chance for students to shine by concentrating on THEMSELVES. If desired, have students put their projects on a table and let students browse through each other's. **(III-8, 9, 10)**

- As a homework assignment, have students sit down with a parent and talk for at least 15 minutes every night. (You may have to adjust this to fit specific needs.) To get things started, give each student a question or topic to be discussed each night. Require parents to sign a little sheet to indicate that they had their nightly "conversation." Both students and parents might enjoy this homework activity and keep it up beyond the week or two assigned. **(III-11)**

- Compile a job description booklet of chores that students may do around the house. What is involved in cleaning out the closet? Ask students to be very specific. It is often lack of being specific that complicates a simple job. **(III-12)**

- If you don't normally assign homework, choose one or two days a week in which you will. Alert parents to the system so they can watch for the assignments. Make sure that you give homework that can be done at home without requiring extensive research or mess. Get students used to the idea that homework will be assigned, they will work on it at home, parents will sign the homework, and then it will be returned to school. It's never too early to get used to this system. If your point is to get students used to taking things home and remembering (rather than actually completing a written assignment), make your homework fun. Assign them a television show to watch, or finding out three jokes going around school, or cutting out three pictures from the newspaper. **(III-13)**

- If students in your class have a copy of a family tree or have a family Bible in their possession with this information, ask if it could be brought to school. You may locate a geneologist who could come into your class and explain how to search for relatives. **(III-14)**

- If you have a class camera (or are willing to donate yours for the project), send it home with each child in your class, one day at a time, and ask them to have a family picture taken. They may want to "stage" it, with the family doing something fun together. As an alternative, you could ask for vacation pictures or even drawings showing how a family has fun together. **(III-15)**

Part IV. Everyday Etiquette

- Have a class party in which students are in contact with other students whom they may not have met. You could engineer an activity by arranging for another class at a different school to come over to view a play, participate in a kickball tournament, or share artwork. During this time, arrange for students to systematically meet each other and practice their meeting skills. **(IV-1)**

- Allow children to bring their parents to school to read a story, share a hobby, or answer questions about some area of expertise to the class. (This could be done every Friday afternoon, for example.) Make sure students introduce their parents to the class by giving their names and telling a bit about them. **(IV-2)**

- Ask all students to have a small box of tissues to keep close by in their desks during cold season. Use these periods of sneezing and coughing to show students how to keep their germs to themselves. **(IV-3)**

- If you find a student in a position where he or she is interrupting, bothering someone, or about to step on toes, just clearing your throat can be a signal that something is expected of them: a polite "excuse me." Make a small deal about this instead of insisting that they have done something terribly wrong. **(IV-4)**

- Invite a guest speaker to your class to be interviewed. This could be a person with an interesting occupation, recent journey to another country, or someone who is willing to be interviewed. Before the speaker arrives, have students compile a list of appropriate questions that would help them get to know the guest without being overly inquisitive or asking embarrassing or impolite questions. **(IV-5)**

- Many comedians get their laughs from mimicking famous people. Allow students to videotape APPROPRIATE comics from television and demonstrate why mimicking is funny in these situations. Perhaps you have an aspiring comedian in your class who would like to do some imitations of famous people. **(IV-6)**

- Get some examples of caricatures and explain that they are cartoon representations of people with exaggerated features. If you have some good sports for volunteers, have a class artist or the art teacher draw some caricatures featuring celebrities around the school (basketball star with a ball in his hand, someone who likes to swim wearing fins, etc.). **(IV-6)**

- Invite a public official (the mayor?) to visit your class to give a brief explanation of how your city or community is run. What public facilities are available in your town? Why is it important for everyone in the community to take pride in how the area looks? How expensive is it for graffiti to be removed? Use this opportunity to ask for suggestions for projects that the class can become involved in for showing community spirit. **(IV-7)**

- Set aside a time (daily) for students to wash their hands before eating. By making this a routine, you will help students automatically wash their hands before eating—at least at school! **(IV-8)**

- Have an interested student or two get a behind-the-scenes look at how school meals are prepared. How much hand contact is involved? What cleanliness procedures are followed by the people who work in the kitchen? **(IV-8)**

- Some fast-food restaurants offer tours of behind-the-scenes procedures for food preparation. If possible, take a tour and ask about health standards for personnel. **(IV-8)**

- At Thanksgiving or another occasion, prepare a semi-formal meal for the class to assist in and practice good table manners. With parental help, plan a menu, select jobs for the students, list materials and food items needed, and dig out the tablecloths and silverware. (You may wish to invite parents and have them work with their children to bring a table setting.) Go through each of the table manners before the meal and practice using those good manners. **(IV-9)**

- Assign students to create a restaurant by working together in small groups. Each restaurant-group can make menus, set up a table for customers, and maybe even make a billboard for advertising. Have volunteer students "attend" the restaurant, order food from a "waitress," and fill out a comment card. Throughout the entire skit or experience, have students practice the eating-out skills and have non-participating students evaluate the others who are in the performance. **(IV-10)**

- Let students take turns being the official door holder at times when the class leaves to go to another room or location. In this way there will be less confusion about going through the door when there is a fire drill, emergency, rush to reach the buses, etc. **(IV-11)**

- With parental permission and assistance, have students make a phone call using a public phone. Have parents fill out a summary or rating sheet indicating how the student did on the skills listed (e.g., voice level, polite voice on the phone, etc.). **(IV-14)**

- If appropriate, bring in a newspaper tabloid that contains articles of gossip about celebrities. Discuss why this constitutes gossip and how it can be harmful to people. **(IV-14)**

- Explain the difference between rhetorical questions that expect no response and legitimate questions that do. Collect examples of rhetorical questions (e.g., Isn't this a nice day? What is the world coming to?). **(IV-15)**

- Designate a class word to express frustration, such as "oh, fudge" or "jumping jelly beans," or something equally absurd but funny. **(IV-16)**

- Have aspiring designers compile a portfolio of popular clothing including recent fads for wearing at school and occasions that might come up for students. **(IV-17)**

- Some students may want to put on a fashion show, displaying what's "in" at your school. Take photographs for advertising and for scrapbooks. **(IV-17)**

- Send a class thank-you note to guest speakers, parents who have sent treats or helped on field trips, and other individuals who have done something for your class. Involve all students by including signatures and brief comments on a single card. **(IV-18)**

- Have students bring in or fill out samples of invitations to events or parties, including the R.S.V.P. Students may enjoy designing invitations to attend their penthouse on the moon, breakfast with the NFL team of your region, or cruise to Europe. Let imaginations go! **(IV-19)**

- Design a class pin that will stand for the "Golden Rule." Spray paint the item with gold paint and attach pins so students can wear the pin on their shirts. When students have indicated that they will agree to abide by the rule, have a small ceremony in which the pins are put into place and worn for a week or two (or longer if interest is there). Remind students often what the pin stands for. **(IV-20)**

The Accident

Cynthia and Linda were both students in Mrs. Clark's class, but that was about all they had in common. Linda was very tall; Cynthia was short. Linda liked to play baseball; Cynthia liked to draw. And they both had very different ways of telling people "no."

When Linda didn't want something, she would take a deep breath and holler "NO!" at the top of her lungs. One day Michael asked if he could borrow her eraser. She yelled "NO!" so loudly that the force of her breath knocked the poor boy on the ground.

When she said, "no," she means "no." There was NO question about that.

But when Cynthia wanted to tell someone "no," she always ended up saying, "Well, OK," which is not really "no" at all.

One day Nancy came up to her and asked if she could copy Cynthia's reading answers. Cynthia really didn't want to give Nancy her paper, but she said "Well, OK," and handed it over to her.

Mrs. Clark was watching them on the playground one day. Steven walked up to Linda, who had been playing on the swings for quite a long time, and asked politely if he could have a turn. Linda violently shook her head, took a deep breath, and yelled, "No! Now get out of here!"

So, Steven went down to the next swing and asked Cynthia the same thing. Cynthia had just gotten on the swing, and she didn't really want to get off, but she said, "Well, OK" and got off.

Mrs. Clark shook her head. She turned to Mrs. Smith and said, "I sure wish a little bit of Linda would rub off on Cynthia and a little bit of Cynthia would rub off on Linda. Then they'd both be able to say 'no' without upsetting other people and themselves."

She walked over to Steven to tell him to give Cynthia her swing back. But Steven wasn't happy with that idea, so when Mrs. Clark's back was turned, he gave Cynthia's swing a really hard push! Actually, it was a lot harder than he meant to push it and the two girls were headed right for each other!

© 1993 by The Center for Applied Research in Education

The girls started screaming! They knew they were going to collide! The last thing that Linda yelled was "NOOOOO!" and the last thing Cynthia yelled was, "Well, OK!"

They hit. Hard! And both girls sat on the ground, rubbing the huge bumps that were already beginning to form on their heads.

"Are you all right?" asked Mrs. Clark, rushing up to them.

"Well, OK," said Linda.

"NO!" yelled Cynthia.

The girls looked at each other, startled!

"What did you say?" asked Mrs. Clark. "Did I hear right?"

Cynthia said, "NO!" and Linda said, "Well, OK."

The girls stared at each other with their mouths wide open. What had happened?

"Do you need to go home?" asked Mrs. Clark, looking a little worried.

"NO!" yelled Cynthia, sounding a lot like Linda. She covered her mouth with her hands. She meant to say "yes," but it came out wrong.

"OK," said Mrs. Clark, holding up her hands. "I was just asking. Don't yell at me. What about you, Linda? Shall I call your mother?"

Linda shook her head because she knew her mother was planning to go out for the day, but the words came out, "Well, OK," and Mrs. Clark headed for the phone. She had sounded an awful lot like Cynthia.

As it turned out, Mrs. Clark called both parents and both girls went home for the rest of the day with huge bumps and an ice pack.

It was not long before both girls figured out that all they could say was the last words that each had spoken before their swings had collided. Somehow in the accident their voices had gotten mixed up and stuck on "no" or "well, OK."

"Do you want to take a nap?" asked Linda's mom when they got home.

Linda, of course, didn't want to take a nap - she wanted to go out in the back yard and play baseball, but the words came out, "Well, OK," and her mom pushed her into her bedroom.

"It's so nice to hear you using a quiet voice," she said. "I like that, Linda."

Linda crawled into bed and found out that she really was pretty tired.

That night, Linda's mother fixed a big dinner. "Would you like to try some of this broccoli and spinach casserole?" she asked her daughter.

The only thing Linda hated more than broccoli was spinach, but she was unable to say anything but, "Well, OK," and was faced with two heaping portions of the green stuff on her plate.

"I really like how you're trying new things, Linda," said her mom, smiling. "I always thought you didn't like these vegetables."

And it turned out that the stuff wasn't too bad.

After dinner, Linda's little brother Jimmy came up to her and asked, "Linda, would you help me with my homework? It's math." He stuck out his tongue.

Linda couldn't think of anything more boring than helping Jimmy with his homework, but she said, "Well, OK," and sat down next to him. Her little brother was so happy, he ran and got his favorite toy truck to give to her. Linda didn't care about the truck, but she felt good about helping Jimmy.

© 1993 by The Center for Applied Research in Education

Meanwhile, at Cynthia's house, her mother was getting out rolls and rolls of bandages to wrap all over Cynthia's body, even though only her head hurt. "You poor dear," she said. "We're going to have to wrap you up and make sure you're OK, right sweetie?"

Cynthia groaned inside. She hated it when her mother covered her with bandages when only one little band-aid was needed, but she was so used to saying, "Well, OK," that she opened her mouth and startled herself when she said, "NO!"

"What?" gasped her mother. "You don't want these bandages?"

"NO!" said Cynthia, almost falling off the couch with the force of her voice.

"Well, OK," said Cynthia's mother, putting the doctor's kit away.

Cynthia couldn't believe it! The bandages were gone! This was great! Maybe this meant she wouldn't have to ride around in a wheelchair for a day either! Cynthia's mother sometimes went overboard when it came to taking care of Cynthia.

Later, Alice, the girl next door, came over to play with Cynthia. Cynthia liked Alice most of the time, but she didn't like it when Alice took her bicycle and rode it in the mud. But she always told Alice, "Well, OK," when Alice asked to borrow it.

This time, however, when Alice asked about the bike, Cynthia kind of enjoyed saying "NO."

"Really?" asked Alice. "Well, if you don't want to. . . I guess I'll just go home then, and ride my own bike."

Cynthia didn't want to say "NO!" right then, so she closed her mouth tightly and cheered inside her head!

Later that night, Nancy came over to copy Cynthia's homework (like she did every night). Cynthia smiled as she saw Nancy walking up to the house. She was going to enjoy this.

"Hi there, Cynthia," called Nancy, waving her blank paper. "May I - "

The neighbors must have been pretty surprised when they saw a young girl blowing across the front yard!

At school the next day, the girls sat together in class. Cynthia wrote Linda a note that said: "Are you having as much fun with my voice as I am with yours?"

The note came back: "No! But I'm learning a lot!"

It turned out that both Cynthia and Linda had to work with the speech teacher for a few weeks before their voices completely returned to normal.

Linda worked on saying "no" in a quiet voice, but it still meant "no."

Cynthia worked on saying "no" when she really didn't want to do something, instead of letting people take advantage of her.

"I'm so proud of both of you," Mrs. Clark told them. "I think this has been a rather good experience for both of you, don't you agree?"

The girls looked at each other, smiled, and said together: "YES!"

I-1 Having Clear Expectations

Objective:

Given a specific social situation, the student will correctly identify at least one plausible outcome or expectation.

Rationale:

Many embarrassing social problems result in not clearly understanding the social situation itself. While this skill generally improves with practice and lots of social experiences, it is helpful to stop and think about what is involved in a specific social situation even before you are in the situation. For special students especially, thinking through the situation before it comes up is a real benefit to planning what will happen and how to prepare for what is expected of the student.

Thinking Questions:

1. If you were invited to the circus, would you show up in skis and a tennis racquet? *(probably not)*

2. If you were supposed to give a speech, how would you feel if you walked into an empty room? *(confused, relieved!)*

3. How does it help you prepare for something by knowing what you are supposed to do ahead of time? *(you can rehearse, get things ready, buy something if you need to, etc.)*

4. How would you prepare if you knew you were going to the White House to have dinner with the President? *(might get new clothes, wash your hair, etc.)*

5. Why might it be embarrassing to show up at a party wearing the wrong clothes or coming at the wrong time or not bringing something you needed? *(makes you look silly or different from everyone else)*

6. Why might it be helpful to know as much as you can about something, such as a party or game or other event, before you go? *(so you can figure out what you'll need)*

7. Have you ever been disappointed because you expected something to happen at a social event and it didn't? Tell about it. *(perhaps a surprise party that wasn't or expecting someone to be there who didn't show up)*

Activity:

Directions: The student is to read each of the four social situations and to pick out the best answer that tells a logical expectation. Inform students that there is only one answer for each

> *Answers:* 1. c
> 2. a
> 3. b
> 4. c

Follow-up: Discuss why the unselected answers were not logical expectations. Why wouldn't the neighbors have a swimming suit ready for you? At what point are you expecting too much of someone else? Sometimes illogical things happen and we are quite surprised; however, in most situations there are certain things that we expect of others. Emphasize what is typical or normal in most situations, allowing for the fact that strange things do happen!

Having Clear Expectations

Read the following situations. What would you expect would happen in each? Check the best answer.

1. You got an invitation to a swimming party at a neighbor's house. You are supposed to arrive at 4 o'clock and stay for a cookout. Would you expect. . .

   _____ a. the neighbors to have your suit and towel for you?

   _____ b. to bring dinner for everyone there?

   _____ c. to bring your suit, dry clothes, and maybe some chips?
   _____

2. The principal walks into your classroom while the teacher is talking about growing plants. She stops to go over to talk to the principal. Would you expect. . .

   _____ a. to be quiet and wait for the teacher to return?

   _____ b. the teacher to throw the plants on the floor?

   _____ c. the principal to go through the teacher's desk?

3. There is a new person in your class. At recess time, he comes up to you and asks if he could join your group for kickball. Would you expect. . .

   _____ a. him to go around hitting everyone?

   _____ b. to let him be on a team and play?

   _____ c. everyone to ignore him?

4. Your older sister lets you borrow her very expensive red sweater to wear to the football game. Would you expect. . .

   _____ a. to let your friend use it to clean up spilled soda?

   _____ b. your sister to let you keep it?

   _____ c. to be very careful not to get it dirty?

© 1993 by The Center for Applied Research in Education

I-2 Saying "NO" Without Sounding Rude

Objective:

The student will identify polite or acceptable ways to tell someone "no."

Rationale:

Many times we are in situations where a refusal is perfectly acceptable. However, turning someone down or telling someone they can't have their way or wants can sometimes be done in a hostile manner. Students should be aware that they can say "no" without conveying rudeness, anger, or hostility.

Thinking Questions:

1. If someone came up to you and asked for all of your money, your best jeans, and your favorite toys at home, what would you tell him or her? *(forget it, no way, are you crazy? etc.)*

2. How could you let that person know the answer is "no" in a very polite way? *(rephrase the above comments to things like "sorry," "I can't do that," etc.)*

3. What are some situations that you probably would say "no" to someone for? *(sharing something you're not supposed to, not being able to go somewhere with someone, etc.)*

4. If you said "no" to someone politely, would you have the same result? *(probably, although some people might require more persistence)*

5. How could telling someone "no" in a rude or mean manner make the situation worse? *(the other person might become angry, might be less likely to share something with you, etc.)*

Activity:

Directions: The student is to circle the characters on the worksheet who are saying "no" politely and to X the ones who are sounding rude. Stress that even though the characters may not intend to be rude, the way the words come out make it sound impolite.

 Answers: **Circle**—#2, #3, #6; **X**—#1, #4, #5

Follow-up: Have students rephrase the impolite-sounding refusals to make them more polite. The tone of voice used to refuse someone also conveys your intention. Have students practice using a pleasant or neutral voice quality when reading the characters' words.

Saying "NO" Without Sounding Rude

These students are all saying "NO" about something. Circle the ones who are being polite. Put an X on the ones who sound rude.

1.

What? You want to use my markers? Forget it, creep! No!

2.
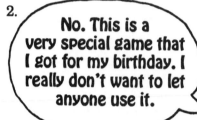
No. This is a very special game that I got for my birthday. I really don't want to let anyone use it.

3.

No - I'm not supposed to let anyone else use my hairbrush. Sorry.

4.

No. You can't be on our team - you're a horrible player!

5.

No, I won't pass you the ketchup. Get it yourself.

6.
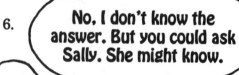

No, I don't know the answer. But you could ask Sally. She might know.

I-3 Don't Say "Yes" If You Mean "No"

Objective:

The student will demonstrate telling someone "no" appropriately by drawing or explaining a solution to a specified problem.

Rationale:

Some students have a somewhat different problem with the word "no." They tend to be agreeable or to commit to a situation even when they are unable to do what they just agreed to do. The skill of saying "no" instead of "yes" when it is called for is the focus of this lesson.

Thinking Questions:

1. Have you ever agreed to do something for someone else even though you really didn't want to do it? Tell about it. *(have students relate anecdotes)*

2. Did it turn out to be a problem for you? If so, how? *(if so it might have taken more time, been a hard task, involved something the student didn't like, etc.)*

3. Are there times when you really should say "no" to someone when they ask? What? *(if they ask you to do something wrong, if you know you could be in danger, etc.)*

4. Why do you think people agree to do things when they know it isn't the right time or could be dangerous? *(don't want others to laugh at them, be picked on, look foolish, etc.)*

5. What's the worst thing that might happen if you told someone "no"? *(they'd laugh at you, wouldn't be your friend, etc.)*

6. Is it better to put up with an embarrassing consequence than to find yourself in trouble or danger? *(yes!)*

Activity:

Directions: Students are to draw a picture of a character saying "no" in each of the situations on the worksheet. The pictures can be explained in class or students can use speech balloons or other forms of writing to get their points across.

Answers: (examples)

1. "No, I just don't want to do that."
2. "No, that's not fair."
3. "I really can't tonight; it's my birthday and I already have plans."
4. "I'm not feeling well; I think I should go home."

Follow-up: Have students share their ideas. Why were the situations on the worksheet potential problems? *(danger, cheating, etc.)* Is the greatest fear that the other person in the situation will not understand or accept the answer of "no"?

I-3

Don't Say "Yes" If You Mean "No"

How could you say "no" in each of these situations? Draw a picture and write how you would handle the problem.

1. An older kid wants you to smoke a cigarette or he'll call you a baby.

2. Your best friend wants to copy your homework.

3. It's your birthday, but your neighbor asks you to babysit all evening instead of going bowling with your friends.

4. You don't feel very well, but your teacher asks you to stay after school to work on the school newspaper.

I-4 Not Hurting Feelings of Others

Objective:

The student will identify comments that potentially could hurt the feelings of someone else in that they are thoughtless or rude.

Rationale:

It is very easy to make offhand comments about other people or their situations without realizing that they may hurt the other's feelings, whether we intended to or not. Before speaking impulsively, students who are prone to do this should be conscious of how their words may affect the feelings of others.

Thinking Questions:

1. Think for a moment about the things you are sensitive about regarding yourself. Without being specific, what are some areas that people might be touchy about? *(weight, looks, school inability, athletic inability, etc.)*

2. Can you think of any situations in which someone said something about another person's mistakes or weaknesses? *(ask for examples)*

3. How did the other person react? *(hurt feelings, anger, etc.)*

4. Do you think most people try to hurt other people's feelings? *(depends on the situation and person)*

5. How could you tell if what you said hurt another person's feelings? *(the person might look sad, cry, leave the group, etc.)*

6. How do people try to disguise their hurt feelings? *(act like nothing happened, change the subject, etc.)*

7. Whether you hurt someone's feelings or not, there are comments that are just plain hurtful and mean. Can you think of examples? *(comments about someone's weak areas, habits, home situation, etc.)*

8. Does anything good ever come of being hurtful to others? *(not directly)*

Activity:

Directions: The student is to read the list of comments and to draw a sad face next to the ones that are hurtful. They do not need to draw anything on the positive or neutral comments.

   Answers: **Sad faces**—#1, #2, #5, #6, #9, #10

   Follow-up: Discuss students' reasoning for drawing the sad faces. Why were the comments hurtful? What weak area did the comment target? *(looks, inability, hygiene, finances, etc.)*

Not Hurting Feelings of Others

Which of these comments might hurt someone's feelings? Draw a sad face next to the ones that are hurtful.

1. You're really fat.

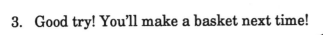

2. Don't you know how to read that word? You must be really slow.

3. Good try! You'll make a basket next time!

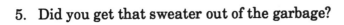

4. Would you please pass me my pencil?

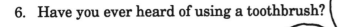

5. Did you get that sweater out of the garbage?

6. Have you ever heard of using a toothbrush?

7. I like your tennis shoes.

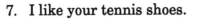

8. Ronald is the fastest runner in our class.

9. We don't want Sarah to be in our group.

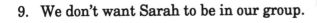

10. Is that a big rip in the back of your shirt? Or is it just a stain?

I-5   What Is a Handicap?

Objective:

The student will identify physical or mental handicapping conditions that he or she may be likely to encounter in his or her environment.

Rationale:

Most of us feel uncomfortable at first in interactions with individuals who have an obvious handicap. It is awkward to know what to do or say. The more students know about handicaps and are comfortable discussing situations involving people who are so challenged, the more likely they will handle these situations appropriately.

Thinking Questions:

1. What do you think of when you hear the word *handicapped*? *(someone who is blind, in a wheelchair, crippled, retarded, etc.)*

2. There are lots of types of handicaps. Can you think of some that are physical? *(blindness, deafness, loss of limbs, etc.)*

3. Do people with those handicaps ever get better or does the handicap last their whole lives? *(may be improved somewhat, but the physical handicap will always have to be dealt with)*

4. Can you think of any people who were physically handicapped but were still able to do most everything they wanted to do? *(students may know of a local person, famous athlete, Helen Keller, etc.)*

5. Just because someone has a handicap, does that mean they are sick or can't do anything fun? *(not necessarily—they find ways to adapt to their environment)*

6. Other kinds of handicaps might not be so obvious. Can you think of mental handicaps? *(Down's syndrome, autism, learning disabilities, etc.)*

7. There are lots of students who may have to work even harder in school because of reading disabilities or learning disabilities. You can't tell by

looking at someone, but these students, too, have to overcome special problems. Can you think of how this would make things in school tough for a student? *(harder to get through all of the assignments, might take longer to read, other kids might make fun of them, etc.)*

8. How do you feel when you see someone who is obviously handicapped on the street or at a restaurant? *(awkward, staring, etc.)*

9. How do you think that person might feel? *(embarrassed, angry, etc.)*

10. If you didn't know whether a handicapped person was bothered by his or her situation or not, how might you talk to that person at first? *(don't discuss the handicap, listen before talking, don't stare, etc.)*

11. Do you think everyone who has a handicap wants you to rush right in and help them, such as opening a door? *(no—some can probably handle the situation quite well)*

12. A handicap might make things harder, but do you think it would have to slow someone down completely? *(no—there are many examples of people who have achieved much despite—or because of—a handicap)*

13. How could you try to understand what a handicapped person's life is like? *(read about it, talk to someone, observe, think through a day as a handicapped person, etc.)*

Activity:

Directions: The student is to read the list of handicaps and nuisances, and place a check mark next to those that are true handicaps.

Answers: check mark—#2, #3, #6, #7, #8, #11

Follow-up: Go through each item on the list and discuss why or why not it would be considered a handicap. *(having a hangnail is a temporary condition, being tall might make it harder to sit in a little car—but it would be possible to perform most everyday tasks, etc.)* Then, consider the handicapped items one by one with the thoughts of how a person with that disability could function well in everyday life, thereby not letting the handicap make them seem handicapped. *(being in a wheelchair limits mobility to some extent, but there are ramps, specialized cars, other motorized devices to make things accessible; deaf people can function well by signing, relying on vision, using special telephones that have written cues, etc.)*

What Is a Handicap?

All of the things on this list might make life a little harder for someone. Which of these could be considered handicaps, not just a nuisance that you have to deal with for a short time? Put a check mark next to your answers.

1. having a hangnail   _____

2. being in a wheelchair   _____

3. not being able to hear very well   _____

4. having red hair   _____

5. being tall   _____

6. being blind   _____

7. having only one arm   _____

8. not being able to read because the
   letters and words seem all jumbled up   _____

9. having a cold   _____

10. having a bloody nose   _____

11. having an artificial leg   _____

12. sneezing from hay fever   _____

I-6 People Who Are Different

Objective:

The student will identify at least one characteristic of a person who is different from him- or herself and state at least one commonality.

Rationale:

When we encounter a person who is different from ourselves, whether by race, interest, oddity, or any other feature, we may at first stress the difference. With special children, this may manifest itself as staring, embarrassing questions, or intense curiosity. Differences can be interesting and understood. This lesson focuses on finding common areas that a student could explore with a person who is perceived as "different" from him- or herself.

Thinking Questions:

1. Is everyone in this room exactly alike? *(no)*

2. In what ways are people different? *(race, physical characteristics, sex, emotions, etc.)*

3. Sometimes you may run into a person who is really different from yourself, like someone from another country. What kind of differences might there be between you and that person? *(language, culture, interests, clothing, etc.)*

4. Do you think there would be anything in common between you? What? *(might like to eat the same things, play games together, laugh at same things, etc.)*

5. Some people are different not only in the way they look, but in how they act or what they believe. What are some different church groups? Political groups? Clubs that people can join? *(Baptist, Catholic; Republican, Democrat; Elks, Lions, etc.)*

6. Just because someone is different from you in some way, does that mean you have nothing that you could do or enjoy together? Explain. *(no—we all have differences, but we have common points as well)*

7. Do you think if you tried hard and thought hard you could find something in common with almost everyone? *(probably)*

Activity:

Directions: Six characters are pictured on the worksheet. Students are instructed to choose one who is different from themselves in some way and to list at least three activities or topics of conversation that they could possibly have in common.

Answers: (example) #1—Maria is from another country, but we could probably play house together, jump rope, toss a ball, walk in the woods, or play with dolls.

Follow-up: Have students discuss why they selected the particular character that was chosen. What aspect was very different from a characteristic you possess? What topics or interests seem to appeal to almost every child, no matter what country or social status?

People Who Are Different

Pick someone on this page who is different from you. List at least three things that you could do together or talk about.

1. Maria is from Bolivia. She does not speak any English. She has eight brothers and sisters.

_____

_____

_____

2. Frank is in a wheelchair. He was born with a spine injury and will never be able to walk.

_____

_____

_____

3. Carolyn goes to a different church than everyone else in your class. Her church service is different from yours.

_____

_____

_____

4. Tommy is an American Indian. His skin is dark and his grandparents know how to do old dances.

_____

_____

_____

5. Carlos lives in a mansion. His parents have eight cars and an enormous swimming pool. He travels to other countries in the summer.

_____

_____

_____

6. Rachel has a huge scar on her face from a car accident. She is good at roller skating.

_____

_____

_____

I-7 Tone of Voice

Objective:

The student will correctly identify the intended meaning of a statement by applying tone-of-voice cues.

Rationale:

Words are just words unless the meaning behind them is conveyed and received by the listener. Students sometimes focus only on the words without listening to the tone that carries the word. The speaker may say something angrily, teasingly, laughingly or with some other emotion that may change the entire meaning of the words. To correctly understand social situations, students must be able to use the speaker's voice to help interpret the situation.

Thinking Questions

1. Listen to this: Shut...the...door. What do I want you to do? *(shut the door)*

2. How could you say those three words and make it sound like I was really angry? *(SHUT THE DOOR!)*

3. How could you say that and make it sound as though I thought it was the funniest thing I had ever heard? *(with laughter)*

4. How could you make it sound as though I thought you were going over to close the window? *(Shut the **door**.)*

5. Can you think of a situation in which I would say "Shut the door," but I really didn't want you to shut it at all? *(to stop the principal from coming into the room, if it were really hot in the room and you wanted to get a reaction from the students, etc.)*

6. How does the way you say something change what you actually say? *(you emphasize different parts of the sentence)*

7. How would paying attention to someone's voice as he or she were talking help you understand the situation? *(you'd get clues from their face, clues from what words were emphasized, clues from the loudness or sharpness of their voice, etc.)*

Activity:

Directions: Students are to read what the characters are saying, using picture clues and context clues to determine the tone of voice the speaker probably is using. Then they are to check the answer below that matches with the speaker's true message.

Answers: 1. a   2. b   3. b

Follow-up: Have students take turns reading the character's comments in an appropriate tone of voice. Discuss how the words that are emphasized change the meaning of the message, as well as how the other clues (dogs' tails wagging, teacher's expression, etc.) help figure out what the speaker means.

Tone of Voice

Read what each person below is saying. Check the answer below that explains what the person means.

1.

> Good morning, Mark. I said GOOD MORNING, Mark. Aren't you talking to anyone today?

_____ a. The girl wants Mark to pay attention to her.

_____ b. The girl wants Mark to have a good morning.

_____ c. The girl wants Mark to talk loudly.

2.

> I just can't stand dogs. I hate them all. They are real pains to have around.

_____ a. The boy hates dogs and is not enjoying himself.

_____ b. The boy is teasing. He loves the dogs.

_____ c. The boy was hurt by one of the dogs.

3.

> The bell rang already... Find your seat.

_____ a. The teacher thinks the boy does not know what the bell means.

_____ b. The teacher wants the boy to sit down right away.

_____ c. The teacher wants the boy to look for a chair.

Part I   Understanding Social Situations

I-8 Facial Expressions

Objective:

The student will identify feelings or emotions from a facial expression on a character.

Rationale:

The way a person looks can give clues as to what he or she is thinking or feeling. An open mouth, gritted teeth, furrowed brow, red cheeks, and so on are all bodily expressions of inner feelings. Giving the student practice in identifying possible emotions based solely on a facial expression is a good exercise for reading social situations

Thinking Questions:

1. How can you tell if someone is really, really mad at you, even if he or she doesn't say a word? *(red face, tight mouth, clenched fist, etc.)*

2. Without words, how could you tell if someone was really sad? *(might have tears in eyes, mouth in a frown, etc.)*

3. Can you tell a lot about how someone is feeling even if he or she isn't talking? *(yes—bodily clues)*

4. What are some other ways a person's face expresses feelings? *(eyes might be tight if they are angry, nose flaring, mouth pouting, etc.)*

5. What are some other types of feelings that might be easy to detect by looking at someone's face? *(sadness, happiness, surprise, etc.)*

Activity:

Directions: The student is to match the facial expression on the left of the worksheet with the probable emotion on the right. Remind students to look for facial cues, such as eyes and mouth.

Answers: 1. c   2. d   3. a   4. e   5. b

Follow-up: Have students take turns imitating some of the expressions on the worksheet. How does it feel? Does making the facial expression help you feel angry, surprised, puzzled? Would making your face smile and look happy help you to feel happier?

Facial Expressions

Match the facial expression on the left with what you think the person is feeling on the right.

1.

      _____

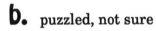 **a.** very angry

2.

      _____

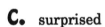 **b.** puzzled, not sure

c. surprised

3.

      _____

d. pouting, feeling sorry for self

e. bored, not thinking about anything

4.

      _____

5.

      _____

I-9 Other People's Opinions

Objective:

The student will identify characters who are treating another person's opinion with respect.

Rationale:

All through our lives we will run into people who have different opinions from ours. Whether we agree with these opinions or not, it is nice to acknowledge them and allow the other person to express what he or she thinks. In this lesson, students are to identify people who are listening respectfully to another's opinion.

Thinking Questions:

1. Who do you think is the best basketball player/rock singer/teacher, etc.? *(students will express opinions)*

2. Why were there different answers to that question? *(different opinions)*

3. Is there only one correct answer, or could different people have different ideas or opinions about that question? *(different opinions)*

4. If someone disagrees with your opinion about something, does that mean he or she is wrong? *(no—just another opinion)*

5. Does it mean you are wrong? *(no, again it's just another opinion)*

6. If someone says something that is not at all how you feel about the matter, what good would it do to tell him or her that you don't agree? *(probably very little good, may lead to an argument)*

7. Is it okay for you to express to someone else how you feel, even if you know he or she will disagree? *(sure, depending on the situation and your motive—not trying to start a fight)*

8. If two people totally disagree on something, having very different opinions, can they still be friends? *(yes, but they'll have to accept differences in each other)*

Activity:

Directions: The worksheet shows five situations in which students are involved in listening to another person's opinion. The student is to note whether or not the starred (*) student on the worksheet is respectfully listening to the opinions or not by writing YES or NO on the lines.

Answers: 1. no   2. yes   3. no   4. yes   5. no

Follow-up: Discuss how you could change the "no" responses to make them respectful or kinder. Were the characters who gave opinions being obnoxious or were they simply stating how they felt? What experiences could the characters have had with Mrs. Jones or with dogs to make them feel the way they said they felt? How would our experiences shape our opinions?

Other People's Opinions

Which of these students (☆) are listening to another person's opinion with respect? Write YES or NO next to each situation.

1. *I like this game. It's really fun.* *This is a stupid game. You don't know how to have fun!* ☆ _____

2. *I don't think it's fair for one person to always be the captain of the team.* *What do you think we should do that is fair?* ☆ _____

3. *I like Mrs. Jones.* *I do, too.* *You're both nuts.* ☆ _____

4. *Collies are the smartest dogs of all the dogs.* *Collies are nice. Other dogs are nice, too.* ☆ _____

5. *That movie was really scarey!* *Are you kidding? You must be a real baby if you were scared by that!* ☆ _____

I-10 Is This the Right Time?

Objective:

The student will identify whether or not the situation given is an appropriate interruption or action.

Rationale:

Often an action or question in itself is perfectly fine, but depending on the setting, it may or may not be the best time to ask or do something. Students should first consider whether or not their "need" is appropriate to be dealt with at any given time before going ahead with making a demand on someone.

Thinking Questions:

1. If you were in the middle of a busy street, would that be a good time to stop and play checkers? Why or why not? *(no—lots of commotion going around, dangerous, etc.)*

2. Is playing checkers dangerous? *(not by itself)*

3. What would make that situation dangerous? *(the setting—**where** it was being played)*

4. Is there anything wrong with asking questions, asking someone to get something for you, or telling someone about what you did last night? *(probably not)*

5. In what situations would those things be difficult or bothersome for someone else? *(if the other person was busy, talking to someone else, etc.)*

6. Before you interrupt someone, why would it be helpful to check out the situation to see if it was the right time to interrupt? *(the other person won't pay as close attention if he or she is busy, might make a situation dangerous if they have to stop to listen to you, etc.)*

Activity:

Directions: The student is to read each situation on the worksheet and decide whether or not it is the right time to complete the task. They are to check YES or NO.

   Answers: 1. no   2. no   3. yes   4. no   5. yes

   Follow-up: Discuss the appropriateness of the actions in each of the examples. For each situation, decide when or where the action is best completed. Is it the action itself that is the problem or the timing?

Name _____   Date _____

Is This the Right Time?

Read each situation below and decide whether or not it is the right time for the character in the cartoon to do something. Check YES or NO.

1. The fire bell just went off! The class is supposed to line up quietly at the door and get ready to go outside. Is this the right time for Marsha to ask her teacher if she can call her mother to bring her doll to school?

   YES _____   NO _____

2. It is quiet time and everyone is reading a book. Is this a good time for Bobby to take out his squirt gun to show his friend?

   YES _____   NO _____

3. There is a guest speaker in the room, talking about how to take good pictures with a camera. Is this a good time to ask how to use a flash with your camera?

   YES _____   NO _____

4. A new student is sitting at your lunch table. Everyone at the lunch table is good friends and you do a lot of things together. Is this a good time to talk about how you are all going to go bike riding together?

   YES _____   NO _____

5. You are eating spaghetti at a friend's house. The sauce is watery and spilling all over. Is this a good time to put your napkin on your lap and be careful while you're eating?

   YES _____   NO _____

I-11 Understanding the Teacher's Moods

Objective:

The student will identify the most probable mood of the teacher depicted on a worksheet, given facial and verbal cues.

Rationale:

Part of a good teacher-student relationship is mutual understanding of the current mood that each is operating under. Teachers are human beings and are subject to responding to situations differently. By recognizing the mood of a teacher, a student can better assess the appropriateness of his or her requests and needs at that time.

Thinking Questions:

1. What kinds of moods does your teacher get in sometimes? *(happy, angry, impatient, funny, etc.)*

2. What kinds of things might bring on those different moods? *(a bad day— losing something, a good day—pay check, well-behaved students, etc.)*

3. When is the best time to talk to your teacher about problems with your work? *(when he or she isn't busy or stressed, during a designated time, etc.)*

4. If you had a problem that maybe wasn't urgent and your teacher was very tired, why wouldn't that be the best time to talk to him or her? *(may not be as concerned or pay as much attention or listen as well, etc.)*

5. How can you pick the best time to approach your teacher with school problems? home problems? just general conversation? complaints? arguing about something? *(figure out what kind of reception you are likely to get—does the teacher listen more sympathetically when it's quiet and controlled in the class?)*

Activity:

Directions: The students are to use picture and verbal clues to determine which word best describes the teacher's present mood or feeling. They are to circle the word on the worksheet.

Answers: 1. tired   2. upset   3. excited

Follow-up: Some of the word choices may be perceived as quite similar in meaning (tired/angry, upset/sad, surprised/excited). Discuss the subtle differences in these words and why the selected answer is a little bit more specific.

Understanding the Teacher's Moods

Which word describes how the teacher in each cartoon below feels? Circle your answer.

1.

It's very hot in here and it's been a long day. Let's work quietly until it's time to go home. No talking.

happy   angry

tired

2.

I do not like how you behaved yesterday when the substitute was here! You made things very difficult for her!

upset   tired

sad

3.

This is a wonderful story, Mary! Let's hang this out in the hall where everyone can see it!

surprised   excited

quiet

I-12 Understanding How Other People Feel

Objective:

The student will depict an example of each of the following emotions: jealousy, sadness, fear, excitement, happiness, and fatigue.

Rationale:

Not everyone is either happy or sad. There are lots of emotions or "ways of feeling" that affect how we operate on any given day in different circumstances. In this lesson, students can show how someone might experience a certain feeling by depicting a situation or event.

Thinking Questions:

1. Have you ever been really, really happy? Tell about it. *(anecdotes about parties, gifts, events, etc.)*

2. Have you ever been extremely frightened or afraid? When? *(anecdotes)*

3. What are some situations in which someone might feel impatient or short-tempered? *(waiting for someone who is always late, being in a hurry to get to a game, etc.)*

4. Does everyone feel the same way about the same events? Why would some people react differently? *(some people may love parties, others be shy in a crowd; a roller coaster may terrify one person, but cause great excitement in another)*

5. Do you think people can control their moods or do you think what happens to people has a lot to do with how they feel? *(a debate topic)*

Activity:

Directions: Students are to draw pictures of people involved in situations that might affect their moods. They are to draw pictures that depict given moods in others.

Answers: (examples)

1. two friends playing together with a toy; one left out
2. a sick puppy
3. seeing a robber
4. a great big present under the Christmas tree
5. swimming
6. shoveling snow

Follow-up: Share students' pictures and ideas with the class. Search for common threads as well as situations that depicted very different emotions from different students.

Understanding How Other People Feel

Draw a picture of a situation that might make someone feel one of the following moods:

1. **Jealous**	2. **Sad**
3. **Frightened**	4. **Excited**
5. **Happy**	6. **Tired**

I-13 What Are My Choices?

Objective:

The student will state at least three possible alternatives for a character in a given situation.

Rationale:

There is rarely one correct answer or behavior in most situations. Since students may tend to look for only one right answer, this is an activity in extended thinking—going beyond the obvious to think of other possible choices for the character in the situation.

Thinking Questions:

1. Let's say you're sitting at the kitchen table with a pizza in front of you. What are you going to do? *(eat it, wait, smell it, etc.)*

2. How many different responses did we come up with for number 1? *(several)*

3. In most situations in which you have to make a choice, do you think there are only one or two possible choices? *(no, if you think about it there are usually lots of alternatives)*

4. When you're faced with a problem, is there only one thing you can do? *(no, you can think through several possible solutions before deciding on one)*

5. What if two friends both wanted you to go to the movies with them and they selected different movies? What are four or five different choices that you have? *(go with one, go with the other, don't go at all, invite another friend to go with you, invite the two to go with you, etc.)*

Activity:

Directions: Each of the characters is in a situation in which he or she must consider several choices. Students are to list three additional options for the characters.

Answers: (examples)

1. Mark can swim another time; Mark can ask if his other friend can swim too; Mark can swim first, then see his friend.

2. Jessie can borrow a book; Jessie can call home; Jessie can talk to the teacher later.

3. Sam can talk to his teacher; Sam can confront the boy; Sam can ask a friend to walk with him.

Follow-up: Discuss choices that the class wrote for each situation. Which choices are most logical or likely to cause the least conflict? Have students circle their best answer for each situation or the answer that they would choose in that situation.

What Are My Choices?

These students are in situations in which they must make a choice. List at least three other choices that each has in this situation. One choice for each is already given.

1.

Mark is invited to a swimming party, but his friend is not.

_____

_____

Mark can go to the party by himself.

2.

Jessie forgot to bring her book to school. Her teacher seems to be in a bad mood right now.

_____

_____

Jessie can talk to her teacher politely and explain.

3.

Sam is being teased by an older boy on the playground.

_____

_____

Sam could ignore the boy.

I-14 What Is the Right Thing to Do?

Objective:

Given several situations involving a right/wrong choice, the student will identify the right answer.

Rationale:

It seems that it's getting harder and harder to find clear-cut right and wrong answers to problems. Everything is complicated by situational ethics, different standards of moral behavior at home, school, church and other settings, as well as unclear values. In this lesson, the premise is that it is *not* right to hurt others, cheat, steal, or lie.

Thinking Questions:

1. What is wrong with stealing? *(taking something that doesn't belong to you, it leaves the person who was stolen from with problems, not fair to have something for free when someone else had to pay for it)*

2. What about cheating? *(it's not fair to use someone else's thoughts or ideas and pass them off as your own, cheats you out of a fair evaluation of your work, etc.)*

3. What are some other behaviors that most people tell you are wrong? *(killing, lying, hitting, etc.)*

4. Why do you think those are always wrong? *(involve infringing on other's rights, not character-building activities, can get you in bigger trouble, etc.)*

5. When someone says, "Don't you know the difference between right and wrong?" what does he or she mean? *(some things are clearly right or wrong; some things are always considered the right thing to do, etc.)*

6. What kind of trouble could someone get into for lying, cheating, or hurting someone else? *(trouble at home, trouble with authorities, could lose a friend, could be responsible for damages, etc.)*

7. Why do you think some people choose to do the wrong thing, even if they know better? *(thrills, fun, really angry at something, don't think about it, etc.)*

Activity:

Directions: The student is to put a check mark next to the response that shows the right thing to do in each situation. The situations involve ethical choices—choosing not to lie, cheat, hurt someone, etc.

Answers:		
	1. second answer	4. second answer
	2. first answer	5. first answer
	3. first answer	

Follow-up: Discuss why someone might choose the incorrect answer as his or her choice of behavior in each situation. What motive might be involved? *(revenge, fear, embarrassment, etc.)* What are the rewards of choosing to do the right thing? Why should anyone choose the right thing if he or she wouldn't get caught or noticed anyhow?

What Is the Right Thing to Do?

Put a check mark next to the right thing to do in each situation below.

1. A boy has been hit on the head on the playground and he is knocked out.

    _____ Go after the kid who hit him and beat him up.

    _____ Run for a teacher or adult who can help.

2. Your test is very hard and you are afraid you won't pass.

    _____ Do your best anyway and keep trying.

    _____ Copy the answers from your friend who sits by you.

3. Your best friend wanted you to come over for a birthday party this weekend and you said you would.

    _____ Go to the party.

    _____ Go, unless another friend has a better idea for doing something fun that day.

4. A girl went into the teacher's desk while the teacher was out of the room. The teacher said some money was missing.

    _____ Give the teacher some of your money.

    _____ Tell the teacher what you saw.

5. You said you would bring Kool-Aid® to school but you forgot. Now the kids are mad at you.

    _____ Tell them you are sorry and will bring it tomorrow.

    _____ Tell them that your house was robbed last night and the robbers stole the Kool-Aid®.

© 1993 by The Center for Applied Research in Education

I-15   Going for Help

Objective:

The student will identify a person or method to alert someone when help is needed in a given situation.

Rationale:

Some social situations involve recognizing danger and potentially dangerous conditions. In these situations, students should have some idea of who could help or what they should do to assist.

Thinking Questions:

1. What would you do if there was a runaway car going through your neighborhood? *(get out of the way, call the police, etc.)*

2. Would you try to jump in the car and stop it yourself? *(hopefully not)*

3. What if you encountered someone who had stopped breathing? What would you do? *(call emergency number, police, some might say they know how to do CPR, etc.)*

4. If you encounter a dangerous or emergency situation, who are some people who might be available to help? *(fire department, police, adults nearby, etc.)*

5. What are some emergencies that could happen in your neighborhood? *(car accident, fire, broken glass, etc.)*

6. What is the emergency procedure in our city for accidents, fires, or need for police? *(review your situation—call 911 or whatever system is in effect)*

Activity:

Directions: There are five situations on the worksheet that are potentially dangerous or at least bothersome. Students are to draw a picture depicting how they could go for help or alert someone to the problem.

Answers: (examples)

1. call fire department
2. take the little girl to her parents
3. tell an adult at the party
4. tell a security guard at the mall
5. call home from a public phone/walk bikes together to a public place

Follow-up: Discuss what could happen if someone tried to solve the problem alone. For example, what if Danny tried to put out the fire? Or Rita tried to capture the dog? Discuss why the best first step is to alert someone else to help.

Going for Help

Each character below needs to go for help for some reason. Draw a picture of the way the person could go for help or get help.

1. Danny saw some smoke coming from an empty building on the way to school.

2. Rita saw a little girl get bitten by a big black dog in her neighborhood.

3. Alison is at a party. Her friend is crying because she swallowed something that doesn't taste right. It might be poisonous.

4. Ricky is walking through the mall parking lot. He comes up to a little girl who is crying because she can't find her mother.

5. Sandy is riding her bike through the park. Her friend rides through some glass and gets a flat tire. They are a long way from home.

© 1993 by The Center for Applied Research in Education

Part II   Positive Personality Attributes

II-1   Developing Interests and Hobbies

Objective:

The student will identify at least five interests or hobbies of importance to him- or herself.

Rationale:

Part of what we share with each other is things about ourselves that make us interesting or unique. Having a hobby or spending time pursuing our own interests are ways that we can develop our own personalities. This lesson encourages students to explore new interests as well as to identify current areas that are important to them.

Thinking Questions:

1. What is a *hobby?* (*something that you spend time doing for enjoyment, a favorite activity, etc.*)

2. What are some examples of hobbies that people might have? (*golfing, collecting things, painting, etc.*)

3. What are some examples of things that people might collect? (*shells, rocks, stuffed animals, etc.*)

4. Why do you think it is important to have hobbies and interests? (*makes you an interesting person, might lead to new friends, can learn a lot about something you are particularly good at, etc.*)

5. How could you go about learning a new hobby or getting involved in something new that interests you? (*look for classes, do some reading, talk to people, visit a library or museum, etc.*)

6. Have you ever been in a situation where you thought you wouldn't be interested in doing something or trying something but after you did—you were hooked? Tell about it. (*ask for anecdotes*)

7. What good things could come about from trying new things? (*find out you're really good at something, meet new people, etc.*)

Activity:

Directions: Students are to check at least five items from the list (including ideas of their own) that they are interested in.

Answers: will vary

Follow-up: Have students share their ideas and hobbies with the class. What discoveries did they make about each other and themselves? Who had an unusual interest or hobby? What experiences did they have with a certain hobby or activity?

Developing Interests and Hobbies

Here is a list of some things that you might be interested in doing or learning more about. Add your own ideas to the list. Then check five that you are most interested in.

playing softball   _____

playing basketball   _____

collecting coins   _____

training dogs   _____

painting   _____

reading books   _____

riding a bike   _____

putting on a play   _____

writing stories   _____

swimming   _____

cooking   _____

making things out of clay   _____

sewing   _____

doing cross-stitch   _____

riding horses   _____

archery   _____

bowling   _____

playing piano   _____

_____   _____

_____   _____

_____   _____

_____   _____

Part II   Positive Personality Attributes

II-2 Being Patient with Others

Objective:

The student will identify characters on the worksheet who are exhibiting patience with someone else.

Rationale:

A nice personality attribute in others is patience, whether it is with circumstances or with others. If students want to be well on the road to getting along with others, the virtue of patience is well worth developing.

Thinking Questions:

1. How do you feel when you're in a big hurry and you have to wait for someone to find his or her shoes or make a phone call? *(impatient, angry, etc.)*

2. What are some times that you can remember where you were very impatient with someone? *(ask for anecdotes)*

3. Can you control how fast other people move or what other people are doing all the time? *(no)*

4. When you find yourself being impatient and you can't do anything about it, what are things you could do? *(do something else, talk to someone, tell the person that you are in a hurry and to be ready next time, try to calm yourself down, etc.)*

5. If someone is making you impatient and feels badly about it, what could you say or do to let the person know that it's okay? *(tell them it's okay, help them do whatever is keeping them busy, act like it doesn't bother you, etc.)*

6. How do you feel when you are the one who is making someone late or frustrated? *(frustrated also, afraid they will be angry, etc.)*

Activity:

Directions: There are eight situations on the worksheet that depict students in situations involving another person. The student is to circle the characters on the worksheet who are showing patience to someone else.

   Answers: **Patient People**—Carlo, Liz, Joanne, Brian

   Follow-up: Discuss the circumstances in each of the situations on the worksheet. How did the impatient people come across to the students? How did the patient people handle the situations and turn the inconvenience into something positive?

Being Patient with Others

Which of these students is being patient or trying to be patient with someone else? Write the names in the space at the bottom.

1. It takes so long for the dentist to get to me. I'm enjoying reading this magazine, though.

Carla

2. Where is Martha? We're going to be late! I'm going to give it to her when I see her!

Ann

3. HURRY UP! We're going to leave without you!

Sam

4. Mark really bugs me. I'll try to find somewhere else to sit.

Mike

5. I'm angry, but I won't say anything. Maybe my anger will go away.

Liz

6. Why does it take her so long to read?

That word is bicycle!

Fred

7. While I'm waiting I'll talk to Sandy. I don't know her very well.

Joanne

8. You seem to be having some trouble reaching that. May I give you a hand?

Brian

Patient People: _____

Part II   Positive Personality Attributes

II-3 Being a Good Sport

Objective:

The student will write an appropriate comment to show that the character is being a good sport in frustrating situations.

Rationale:

It is hard to be a good sport in situations that are disappointing, difficult, and annoying. People who show good sportsmanship, however, are much nicer to compete with and probably end up having a better experience. In this lesson, students are given the opportunity to demonstrate good sportsmanship by writing comments that indicate acceptance of the disappointing outcome.

Thinking Questions:

1. Have you ever played a game of basketball or soccer and lost the game by only one point? How did that make you feel? *(angry, sad, frustrated, etc.)*

2. What are ways to show that you are a good sport, even if you or your team loses a game? *(congratulate the other players, don't say bad things about the other team, don't blame the referees, etc.)*

3. What are some ways that people show poor sportsmanship? *(just the opposite of the above answers)*

4. What are some situations, besides playing sports or games, that might make someone feel like being a bad sport about something? *(not getting a grade you thought you deserved, losing a contest, being caught doing something you are embarrassed about, etc.)*

5. When you show good sportsmanship, how does that affect you and other people? *(you—makes you a better person, shows good judgment; others—sets a good example, contributes to good mood, shows you are a good competitor, etc.)*

Activity:

Directions: Students are to write comments that reflect good sportsmanship in the situations on the worksheet.

Answers: (examples)

1. We'll win next time!

2. I'll send Alison a card anyway.

3. I'll thank my uncle for the gift.

4. I'll just pay the fine without complaining.

5. I guess you're the fastest runner, Tim.

Follow-up: Not all of the situations involve sports or playing a game. Discuss how good sportsmanship applies to all sorts of situations, not just sports. How does being a good sport in the situations help the person out, even if he or she must accept the disappointment?

Name _____   Date _____

II-3

Being a Good Sport

What could each of these people say in these situations to show that they are good sports?

1. Joe's basketball team lost by one point.

_____

_____

_____

2. Mary is the only girl in her class who wasn't invited to Alison's birthday party.

_____

_____

3. Jack wanted a game for Christmas from his uncle, but instead he got a shirt and a tie.

_____

_____

4. Catherine forgot her library book and had to pay a fine. Her little brother was the one who hid the book from her.

_____

_____

5. Both Tim and Lisa want to sit in the front of the sports car, but Tim got there first and won't move.

_____

_____

_____

II-4 Helping Others

Objective:

The student will show examples of ways that he or she could help out another person who is in need of assistance.

Rationale:

People who help other people are often shown appreciation—although sometimes they are not. We should help others, not because we want the rewards, but because we are all members of the human race and it's the decent thing to do. Encourage students to look for opportunities to give someone else a hand.

Thinking Questions:

1. When was the last time you needed help with something? *(carrying something, understanding something, going somewhere, etc.)*

2. How did you feel when someone helped you? *(appreciative?)*

3. What are some ways that you could help someone out, either at school, at home, or in the community? *(ask for examples)*

4. If you are able to help someone, and do help them out, how do you think the other person would feel towards you? *(grateful, willing to help you out some other time, etc.)*

5. If you knew that someone wouldn't even say "thanks" if you helped them, would you help them anyway? *(hopefully yes, but some might feel they need the reward of gratitude)*

6. Have you ever forgotten to thank someone who helped you? Tell about it. *(anecdotes)*

7. How do you think you would feel about someone who was helpful even if they didn't want thanks or a reward? Would you admire them? *(hopefully yes—they are doing things for the right reason, not for money or rewards, but because it's good to help each other)*

Activity:

Directions: The student is to write or draw a response that shows how he or she could help someone out in a problem situation involving assistance.

Answers: (examples)

1. Here, take mine.
2. I'll show you where the gym is.
3. I'll get it for you.
4. I can explain that.
5. I'll look it over for you.
6. I see the problem—it's not plugged in.

Follow-up: Discuss students' responses. Did anyone come up with an unusual or insightful way of helping?

Helping Others

What could you do in each of these situations to help someone out? Draw or write what you could do.

1.

I need a blue marker to finish my map. That's the only color I don't have.

2.

I'm new in this school. Am I close to the gym? That's my next class.

3.

These bags are heavy. I don't think I can get that door open.

4.

I just don't understand what we're supposed to do on this sheet.

5.

Do you think all these words are spelled right?

6.

Why did the computer shut off?

© 1993 by The Center for Applied Research in Education

II-5 Thinking of Others

Objective:

The student will identify situations that show consideration for someone else.

Rationale:

It is almost unusual for people to put others' needs in front of their own in this "me, first" world. A very positive personality attribute is the ability to show consideration for others; to put the needs of others in first place, even if yours must wait. This lesson gives students examples of consideration and the lack of this quality.

Thinking Questions:

1. If you and a friend were out running in the heat and were both thirsty, how would you decide who got to drink from the water fountain first? *(first one there, might let the friend go first, might decide who was thirstier, etc.)*

2. What if another person was heading for the water fountain who was holding his throat and choking and coughing? Who would go first? *(probably the person in distress)*

3. Why is it nice to let someone else go first if he or she is in pain or in a hurry? *(their needs are very important to them, might be a more critical situation, etc.)*

4. What does it mean if someone says you are very *considerate*? *(you consider—or think about—other people)*

5. What are some ways that you could think about other people's needs before your own at home? school? the community? *(pick up your room / be quiet when someone is working / don't litter, etc.)*

Activity:

Directions: The students are to check each example that shows consideration of someone else's needs or situation.

Answers: Check marks by 1, 2, 4, 6, 8, 10

Follow-up: Discuss specifically how consideration was shown in each of the above examples. How was the other person put first in each case? In the examples of inconsiderate behavior, what could have been done to show thinking of someone else first?

Thinking of Others

Which of these behaviors shows that you are thinking about someone else and their needs? Put a check mark by each answer.

1. You let someone go ahead of you in line for a drink because you know he is in a bigger hurry than you. _____

2. It's your mother's birthday and you made her a special card. _____

3. You want to go out for pizza for dinner so you make sure everyone knows what you want to do. _____

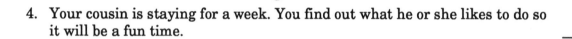

4. Your cousin is staying for a week. You find out what he or she likes to do so it will be a fun time. _____

5. The bathroom is a mess! You make sure your mother knows so she can clean it up for you. _____

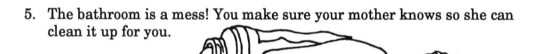

6. Your sister has a flat tire on her bike. You pump it up with air for her. _____

7. You have to get up earlier than anyone else in your family to catch the bus. You make a lot of noise so someone else will wake up and keep you company. _____

8. It's time to change the bedding in the guinea pig's cage. It's Tom's turn, but you know he has not been feeling well, so you take care of it. _____

9. You are really tired after playing tennis so you put your tennis racquet on the kitchen table instead of in the hall closet. _____

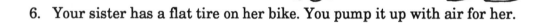

10. You are really good at jumping rope all by yourself. Your friend wants to jump double with you. You don't really want to, but you know she likes to jump with you. _____

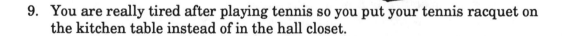

© 1993 by The Center for Applied Research in Education

Part II   Positive Personality Attributes

II-6 Being a Good Leader

Objective:

The student will identify leadership qualities in a person as someone who steers a group in a positive or helpful direction.

Rationale:

If we start with the premise that a leader is someone who directs the activities or thinking of the group, then we would expect a good leader to be someone who leads others in a positive direction. Someone might be particularly good at getting the group to follow some bad advice and get them in trouble, and although the leadership might be effective, the end result is not good. Emphasize that a good leader steers the group towards some end result that is positive and helpful to them.

Thinking Questions:

1. Who are some people you can think of who are good leaders? *(president, captain of sports teams, class leaders, etc.)*

2. Why is that person a good leader? *(helps others out, makes good decisions, listens to everyone in the group, etc.)*

3. How would you feel about someone who was a good leader, and got everyone to follow him or her, but everyone ended up in trouble? *(angry, wouldn't want to follow them again, etc.)*

4. Is someone a good leader if they can get everyone to do what they want, but duck out or disappear when the group gets in trouble? Why/why not? *(no—the leader should stick with the group, not abandon them; otherwise, the leader is just using them)*

5. What could we use as a definition of a good leader? *(someone who is good at leading and leads toward good or positive results)*

Activity:

Directions: The student is to select the character from each pair who is demonstrating good leadership in each situation. Remind students of the definition of a good leader.

Answers: 1. second student   3. first student
            2. first student   4. second student

Follow-up: Discuss the possible outcome of each situation if the first person's advice was followed, and then under the leadership of the second. How does this help decide who is the good leader?

Being a Good Leader

Which student in each pair is being a good leader? Circle your answer.

1.

2.

3.

4.

Part II   Positive Personality Attributes

II-7 Admiring and Complimenting Others

Objective:

The student will provide examples of statements that show admiration for another person.

Rationale:

There's nothing like getting a sincere compliment to help a friendship grow! This lesson gives students opportunities to think of appropriate compliments to give others in typical situations.

Thinking Questions:

1. Has anyone ever admired you for anything? Tell about it. *(ask for examples)*

2. Why does it feel good to have someone give you a compliment? *(it emphasizes the good things about you, shows that someone noticed you, etc.)*

3. Do you think it is hard or easy to give compliments to others? *(sometimes hard if you don't know the other person well; others might be easy if they are good at doing many things)*

4. Is there anyone who wouldn't like to be admired or complimented sometimes? *(maybe someone who was very shy and didn't want the attention)*

5. If someone does something that you admire, how could you let them know without embarrassing them or calling a lot of attention to them if they were shy? *(say it quietly, find the right time and place, be sincere, etc.)*

Activity:

Directions: Students are to write an example of what they could say in the given situations to express admiration or a sincere compliment.

Answers: (examples)

1. You did a nice job.

2. You played really well last night.

3. I like your drawings. Could I see some more?

4. You've got a great bike.

5. You're a good speller, Dottie!

6. Good luck tonight, Miguel!

Follow-up: Discuss how a good compliment avoids calling attention to anything bad. For example, instead of mentioning that Amanda only messed up once, don't mention the mistake at all. Share ideas for making sincere, appropriate compliments in these examples.

Admiring and Complimenting Others

What is a compliment you could give or something nice you could say to each of the following people? Write what you could say.

1. Amanda just played a piano piece in front of the class. She only messed up once.

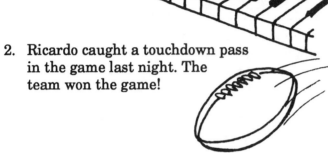

2. Ricardo caught a touchdown pass in the game last night. The team won the game!

3. Shelley is really shy. You know that she is a really good artist from the sketches all over her notebook.

4. Mike got a new 12-speed bike.

5. Dottie won the spelling bee for her class.

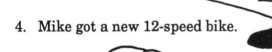

6. Miguel is the fastest runner in the whole school. He will be in the track meet after school tonight.

II-8 Apologizing and Accepting the Blame

Objective:

The student will identify characters who are sincerely accepting the blame or apologizing for a given situation.

Rationale:

Another quality that we admire about others is the ability to admit when they are wrong and accept the blame. Consider this in contrast to someone who believes that he or she is never wrong, never guilty of anything, always looking for someone to pin the problem on. There is no disgrace in admitting to have done something wrong, especially when you are willing to go a step farther and make amends.

Thinking Questions:

1. Have you ever been in a situation in which your parents or some other adult made you apologize to someone even though you felt you did nothing wrong? Tell about it. *(ask for anecdotes)*

2. How did that make you feel? Were you really sorry? *(probably not)*

3. Why do you think people expect other people to apologize for making a mistake? *(it's polite, lets the other person know that you realize you made a mistake, shows that you were concerned about what happened, etc.)*

4. Even if someone says the words, "I'm sorry," how can you really tell if that person is sincerely sorry about what happened? *(look for facial expression, what they do about the problem, etc.)*

5. Why is it important to accept the blame if you are in a situation in which you did something wrong? *(shows that you are grown-up, responsible enough to admit to doing something wrong, takes the blame off of someone else who might be blamed, etc.)*

Activity:

Directions: Students are to decide whether or not they think the character who is apologizing is truly sorry and accepting the blame or not. They are to write YES or NO on the lines.

Answers: 1. no 2. yes 3. yes 4. no 5. no 6. no 7. yes 8. no

Follow-up: Discuss how each of the "no" students handled the situation. What excuses were given? Who was blamed for the problem? How did the "yes" students try to take care of the problem?

Apologizing and Accepting the Blame

Some of these students are apologizing or accepting the blame for something that they did. Write YES or NO if you think they are sincerely sorry.

II-9 Being Organized

Objective:

The student will recognize and list ideas for organizing an activity.

Rationale:

Often the hardest part about accomplishing something is identifying the first step—and then taking it. This lesson gives the student several situations to consider by asking him or her to list helpful ideas for accomplishing the task.

Thinking Questions:

1. What would an organized desk look like? *(pencils in place, books neatly stacked, everything in order, etc.)*

2. What would an organized bedroom look like? *(no clothes on the floor, everything in the dresser in place, etc.)*

3. Why do you think it is important to be organized in most things? *(so you can find things quickly, so things don't get lost or destroyed, so it looks nicer, etc.)*

4. What are some problems that could occur at home or school if you were constantly disorganized? *(lose homework assignments, make yourself late looking for something, get in trouble for losing something that belongs to someone else, etc.)*

5. What are some ways to help yourself become better organized? *(decide where everything will go, replace something when you are finished with it, throw out unwanted or unneeded items periodically, think ahead!, etc.)*

Activity:

Directions: Students are given several situations in which a character is experiencing anxiety because of his or her disorganization. The student is to list ideas for helping the character become organized.

Answers: (examples)

1. clean out the desk, get a few extra pencils, keep books on one side

2. find clothes the night before school, think about what you'll do that day

3. bring books home, spend time studying before the test, keep an assignment notebook

4. keep the list on a bulletin board in the kitchen, check off the items on the list

5. make a list, decide what to do first, do it

Follow-up: Have students come up with a class list describing the most common areas of their lives that need organization. Discuss how this could be tackled and begin!

Being Organized

How could these students be better organized? List some ideas that you think would help them.

1. *I can't find my pencil. I can't find my paper. Have you seen my workbook? I think I saw my lunch from last week around here somewhere. . .*

2. *Do my socks have to match today? I only have one shoe. I think we have gym today and I'm supposed to bring a t-shirt.*

3. *We have a test today? Did I know that? Where's my pencil? What's it on? What chapter?*

4. *Here is the list of things I'm supposed to bring to the slumber party. Where did that list go?*

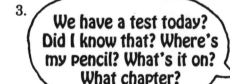

5. *I'm supposed to write a letter, clean my room, walk the dog, and start on my homework. But I think I'll just find the cookies and then take a nap.*

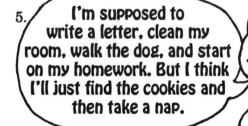

© 1993 by The Center for Applied Research in Education

II-10 Managing Your Jobs

Objective:

Given a list of possible tasks, the student will outline a plan or list of ideas for accomplishing the tasks.

Rationale:

It's nice to be able to entrust a job with a responsible student, knowing that it will be accomplished and will be done right. The student is given a list of fictitious tasks to accomplish in this lesson and is to plan how it will be done.

Thinking Questions:

1. Have you ever been in a situation where you had so many different things to do you didn't know where to begin? Tell about it. *(ask for anecdotes)*

2. How did it make you feel? *(confused, frustrated, not knowing what to do first)*

3. When you are given a lot of responsibility, why is that somewhat harder than just having someone tell you exactly what to do, step by step? *(you have to do the planning and the thinking, not someone else)*

4. If you are given a job to do, who will be the ones to check up on you? *(the one who assigned the job, probably a teacher or parent)*

5. If you have lots of little things to do and not much time, how could you figure out what to do first to get everything done? *(decide how much time each task will take, which tasks are most important, can you delegate to other helpers, etc.)*

Activity:

Directions: Students are to plan out how they will accomplish the set of activities that they have been given and list their ideas in terms of priorities, delegating, and other factors to consider.

Answers: (examples)

1. consider—coats for the little kids, locking the house, taking a watch so you'll know the time

2. look over the list, get your bike, plan to come straight home

3. tell your friend you'll call back later, perhaps do the dishes with TV on in the background, then do homework

4. pick someone to take photos, list what he'll need, pick people to do the writing and typing, look over the finished product

5. after the teacher leaves, walk over to the student and explain you're there to help and follow the instructions your teacher gave you; if the other student is uncooperative, try once more, explaining that you're trying to help; try your best so the teacher won't blame you if it doesn't work out

Follow-up: Have students tell about their responses to the situations. What possible problems did they anticipate running into on each? How would they handle them?

Managing Your Jobs

Here are some jobs you are supposed to do. How will you handle each situation to complete the job?

1. After school, you are supposed to take your little brother and sister to the park. It's really cold out today. Be sure to lock the house - there are no extra keys. Be home before dark.

2. Your mother wants you to go to the store and pick up some things for dinner. You'll have to take your bike to carry everything. Make sure nothing melts.

3. It's your turn to wash the dishes while your parents go to a meeting. You know they won't be home until late. Your favorite TV show will be on in a few minutes. You also have a lot of homework today. Your best friend is on the phone. Looks like a busy evening!

4. You are the leader in your group that is writing a report about the animal shelter. Someone needs to type it up. It would be nice to have photos or pictures, too. Everyone is waiting for you to decide what to do.

5. Your teacher, Mrs. Ryler, has asked you to help the class nerd with his spelling. You don't like him at all, and sure don't want to work with him. He doesn't like you either. Then Mrs. Ryler left the room.

III-1 Being an Adult

Objective:

The student will complete a survey by interviewing an adult and relate interesting responses.

Rationale:

Talking can pave the way to communication between adults and children. Before real understanding takes place, both parties should be willing to ask and answer questions about the other. This lesson gives students a survey to complete by asking questions of an adult, preferably a parent or someone at home.

Thinking Questions:

1. Do you think it is more fun to be an adult or a child? Why? *(adults may be perceived as powerful, rich, or dominant, but children may seem to have more fun in life, etc.)*

2. What are some responsibilities or rights that are reserved for adults? *(driving, getting married, smoking, voting, etc.)*

3. What do you think adults worry about? *(making payments, raising children, etc.)*

4. Who are some adults who you admire? Why? *(athletes, perhaps a teacher, author, leader in the community, etc.)*

5. Do you want to grow older or do you wish you could stay the age you are now? *(ask for comments)*

6. What do you think is the prefect age to be? Why? *(answers will vary)*

Activity:

Directions: Students should select a responsible adult—preferably someone at home—to interview. They will ask general questions of the respondent concerning what it is like to be an adult.

Answers: will vary

Follow-up: Make a chart reflecting the responses to the survey and try to draw conclusions. Did most adults want to be the age they were right then? What was perceived as most fun? most regretful? what other insights did students observe about the adults in general and their own specific interviewee?

Being an Adult

Complete this survey by asking these questions of an adult whom you know.

Person _____

1. What do you think is the best thing about being an adult?

2. What are some things that are hard for an adult to deal with or are not fun?

3. What do you think is the best age to be? Why?

4. What are some things that you wish you could have changed about being a child?

5. What advice would you give to someone about enjoying being a kid?

6. What advice would you give about preparing to be an adult?

7. What are some things you wish you could change about your life now?

8. How do you think most adults feel about children and teenagers?

9. How do you feel about children and teenagers?

10. What do you think are good ways for adults to communicate with or get to know younger people?

III-2 Respecting Adults at Home and in the Community

Objective:

The student will identify behaviors that show respect of adults in the home or community settings.

Rationale:

Though some students may show respect to teachers in the classroom, it is a different scene outside of the building. Students hopefully will generalize the idea of respect to all adults, whether or not they have a direct link to the student in terms of authority or personal relationship.

Thinking Questions:

1. Who are some adults besides your parents whom you see around town or in public places? *(police officers, checkout cashiers, waitresses, etc.)*

2. What are some reasons that these people might have contact with you or tell you what to do? *(you might be buying something from them, need their services, etc.)*

3. How can you show respect towards an adult who asks you or tells you to do something? *(do it)*

4. Why should you obey someone who isn't your parent or teacher? *(they might know more about the situation than you, might be an authority figure, etc.)*

5. Are there times when you shouldn't listen to an adult? *(if it is a stranger, if the request seems wrong or odd, if it contradicts what your parents have instructed you, etc.)*

6. How does it show good manners to show respect to an older person, especially someone who may not hear well or see well or even understand what's going on? *(older people have earned the right to be respected even though they may not be functioning well, as in the case with nursing home residents or older relatives)*

Activity:

Directions: Students are to check the items on the list that are examples of showing respect to an adult in a home or community situation.

Answers: Check mark by 2, 3, 5, 8, 10

Follow-up: Discuss responses, especially how the items that were *not* checked show disrespect to someone, even if the person is not actually there (the owner of the car, the waitress).

Respecting Adults at Home and in the Community

Which of these behaviors is showing respect to an adult? Put a check in front of the respectful behaviors.

1. laughing at a lady whose hair is slightly blue   _____

2. noticing a man planting flowers in the front of his yard and being careful
    to walk around them   _____

3. being quiet after a man and woman turn around in the movie theatre and
    ask you and your friends to be quiet   _____

4. sticking your tongue out at your mother after she tells you to clean your
    room and then shuts the door   _____

5. crossing the street where the crossing guard tells you to   _____

6. leaving a penny on the table at a restaurant for a tip      _____

7. taking a glass bottle and putting it under a tire in a parking lot   _____

8. staying home to see your aunt and uncle and cousins even though you
    would rather go out with your friends   _____

9. saying "I don't have to listen to you" to your father when he tells you to take
    an umbrella to school   _____

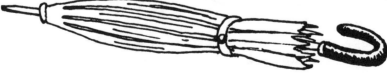

10. holding the door open for your mother who is carrying an armful of dry
    cleaning   _____

III-3 Obeying Parents

Objective:

The student will identify characters who are complying with a request from a parent.

Rationale:

Obedience—or lack thereof—is at the heart of so many social problems! A first step towards learning obedience is acknowledging the command or order, then hopefully deciding to comply. Parents make many requests of children every day, and the child's response may depend on his or her mood, appetite, choice of activities, time of day, or even learned negativism. One lesson will not teach a child to become obedient. This lesson is simply concerned with the student's ability to identify obedience on the worksheet in common examples.

Thinking Questions:

1. What are some orders or requests that your parents give you at home? *(pick up clothes, don't yell, wipe your feet, etc.)*

2. What do your parents expect you to do when they ask you to do something? *(do it, obey)*

3. Why do you think your parents like it when you obey them? *(shows that you can follow directions, shows respect to them, makes their job easier, etc.)*

4. Have your parents ever asked you to do things you didn't want to do? *(probably)*

5. What happened when you didn't obey? *(got in trouble, some sort of punishment, were ignored, etc.)*

6. Why do your parents ask you to do things? *(want you to learn how to do something, learn how to work, do your share, etc.)*

7. Have your parents ever asked you to do something that would put you in danger or hurt you? *(hopefully not)*

8. Why is it a good idea to obey your parents? *(they know more than you, shows respect, it is expected!)*

Activity:

Directions: The worksheet shows six examples of children who have been given requests by their parents. Based on the drawings and comments, the children are or are not obeying their parents. Students are to circle the ones who are and put an X on the ones who are not.

Answers: **Circle**—1, 3, 5; **X**—2, 4, 6

Follow-up: Discuss the potentially harmful or dangerous consequences that could occur by the child's disobedience in these circumstances *(sister could get in trouble if left alone at home; an unused seat belt could result in a severe injury if there was an accident, etc.).* In the less serious instances, why is it important to good family functioning for the children to comply with the request? *(helps everyone get along with each other, family members share jobs, etc.)*

Obeying Parents

Which of these children are obeying their parents? Circle the children who are; put an X on those who are not.

1. Go to bed at 9 o'clock.

   Ok, Dad. I will.

2. Be sure to take your sister with you to the library.

   I will.

   Stay here. You'll only get in my way.

3. Put your seat belt on.

4. Stop teasing your brother right now!

   I'm not teasing him.

   THE TIMES

5. I want you to clean your room when you get home from school.

6. It's your turn to take out the garbage.

   Maybe she'll forget. . .

III-4 Consequences of Disobedience

Objective:

The student will identify a likely consequence for a given disobedience.

Rationale:

It may be annoying when a child ask "why?" or constantly questions an order given by a parent; however, if the child is able to understand how the obedience is beneficial to him or her, it may help the child comply. On the other hand, "because I said so" is sometimes the only answer that is necessary. In either case, it is important for the child to be able to think through the consequences of not being obedient.

Thinking Questions:

1. Have your parents ever asked you to do something that you really didn't want to do? What? *(probably—a distasteful task, something that took a long time, etc.)*

2. What happens if you ask "why?" after a parent tells you to do something? *(might take time to explain, might tell child to do it without questioning, etc.)*

3. Do you always have to know why you are supposed to do something? *(no—in a fire you wouldn't stop to ask questions, you'd just follow instructions to get out)*

4. Why do you think some people don't like to have their orders questioned? *(might be questioned in a haughty way, defiant, might think you are looking for a way out, etc.)*

5. How do you think your parents feel when they find out you have been disobedient, especially to another adult? *(probably ashamed, angry, mad!)*

6. Most of the time when you have been disobedient, did it turn out that you regretted it? *(hopefully)*

Activity:

Directions: The children on the worksheet have been disobedient. Students are to draw a picture or write something to show a possible consequence of this disobedience.

Answers: (examples)

1. Rachel's parents will worry and call the police.
2. Mike will spend the night cleaning out the garage instead of camping.
3. Amy will be late for the bus, looking for her shoes.
4. Randy will have cold hands and head.
5. The dog will eat the donuts.

Follow-up: Discuss the consequences suggested by the students. Were some of the consequences the result of the parent imposing punishment? Or were the consequences a result of naturally-occurring circumstances? Do students think that the only negative consequence to disobedience is getting in trouble with the parents?

Consequences of Disobedience

These children have been disobedient to someone or to an order. Draw a picture or write what could happen because of this disobedience.

1. Rachel went to her friend's house after school instead of going straight home.

2. Mike wanted to go on a camping trip overnight but he didn't clean out the garage like he was supposed to.

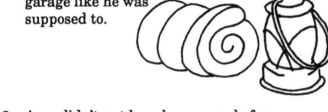

3. Amy didn't put her shoes away before going to bed. Her mother told her that the bus would be coming earlier the next day.

4. Randy's dad told him to wear a hat and mittens to school, but Randy didn't. Then the snowstorm hit!

5. Tara's grandmother asked her to put the donuts on the table where the dog wouldn't get them.
   Tara didn't.

© 1993 by The Center for Applied Research in Education

III-5 Family Rules

Objective:

The student will identify at least three rules that are in effect in his or her home or are good typical family rules.

Rationale:

Every family has some sort of structure to keep it together and organized—even if it is minimal! There are rules within a family as well, whether or not they are stated or written in stone. This lesson asks students to think about the underlying structure of "do's" and "don't's" within his or her family.

Thinking Questions:

1. Are there any rules at your house? What? *(hopefully yes—ask for examples)*
2. Do you think that having rules is a good idea? *(probably—helps everyone know what to expect)*
3. Who makes the rules? *(parents, family council, father, etc.)*
4. What would it be like in your family if there were no rules at all—everyone did whatever he or she wanted to? *(chaos, a mess, one person might get stuck doing everything, etc.)*
5. Are the rules ever changed? How? *(probably—as needs of the family change; family vote, parental discretion, etc.)*

Activity:

Directions: Students are to make a list of rules that are in effect in his or her family. At this point, the rules can be very general and can apply to any type of situation—bedtime, wiping feet, doing chores, keeping family secrets, etc. Make the distinction between *rules* and *chores*; the former being an attitude as well as an action.

Answers: (examples) Obey your parents. Don't talk back. Don't bring friends into the dining room. First one up takes the dog out.

Follow-up: Share family rules with the class and discuss why these rules are important to keep a family functioning well. Note similarities between families. Did students confuse rules with chores?

Family Rules

Make a list of rules that apply to your family or rules that you think are good family rules.

Rules:

1.

2.

3.

4.

5.

III-6   Rules for the House

Objective:

The student will list or state at least five rules that apply in his or her house.

Rationale:

There are rules at every house, though some are stated more clearly and powerfully than others. Is it acceptable to wear shoes in the living room? Are dirty clothes supposed to be brought to the laundry room? Who takes out the garbage? This lesson focuses on general household rules as well as specific rules for different sections of the house.

Thinking Questions:

1. What are some of the different rooms in a house? *(kitchen, closet, bedroom, bathroom, etc.)*

2. What are some rules for each of the different rooms in your house? *(bathroom—flush the toilet, wash your hands, etc.)*

3. Why are there different rules for the different rooms? *(each room serves a different purpose, different needs, etc.)*

4. Which rooms do you think are the easiest/hardest to take care of? Why? *(ask for opinions—some students may think cleaning is difficult, others may think organizing or sorting is harder, etc.)*

5. Do you think the rules for the kitchen are the same in every household? *(somewhat similar perhaps—clean up your own dishes, mop the floor, don't leave the drawers open, etc.)*

6. What are some rules for outside the house? *(wipe your feet, don't leave toys outside, etc.)*

7. How does having rules at home help everything to get done in a better way? *(people can share the chores, people know what's expected of them, might get an allowance for helping, if no one breaks the rules everyone benefits by having a cleaner house, etc.)*

Activity:

Directions: Students are to look at the floor plan of the house on the worksheet and write at least one good family rule for that room. This can be expanded to include yard rules, basements, a garage, etc., depending on the student and the house. The idea is to look for *family* rules, not specific chores for one person.

Answers: (examples) **Front porch**—wipe your feet; **kitchen**—wash hands before eating; **bathroom**—put a new roll of toilet paper on the holder when necessary; etc.

Follow-up: Expand the rule-making by including activities that usually take place in the room as well as taking care of the room and its furnishings. For example, eating and talking might occur in the kitchen, so rules about having polite conversations during meals and no yelling at the table might be appropriate for the kitchen area.

Rules for the House

Write at least one good rule that you or your family might have for the rooms in the house. Add other buildings (garage, pool house) or places if your family has rules for other things.

III-7 Sharing with Siblings

Objective:

The student will identify the item or place that is being shared with a sibling in given examples.

Rationale:

Most siblings have to share things—clothes, parents' time, a bedroom, or even other siblings. Part of getting along at home, especially if the student has brothers and sisters, is finding his or her place among the family by getting along with the other people who reside there. Sharing with others is not often easy, but it is part of being a family.

Thinking Questions:

1. What are some things that you might have to share with brothers and sisters at home? *(a bedroom, clothing, toys, etc.)*

2. How do you share your parents with brothers and sisters? *(you might talk to them at different times, have them spend time with you at different activities, etc.)*

3. Who decides how things get split up among your brothers and sisters? *(parents, perhaps the kids themselves, etc.)*

4. Why is it necessary to share things with others at home? *(don't need two or three of everything, too expensive to duplicate, convenient to use same items, etc.)*

5. What are some things you could learn by having to share with others at home? *(need to pace yourself, accept rations, learn patience, learn to leave things in good condition, etc.)*

Activity:

Directions: Students are to read the conversations between siblings and try to figure out what item is being discussed and shared. There are several possible answers to the situations—have students think of alternative answers for later discussion.

Answers: (examples)

1. sweater, jacket
2. baseball, mitt
3. bedroom, back of the car
4. a game, toys
5. comic book, bubble gum wrapper

Follow-up: Have students share their responses. What clues were given on the worksheet? Why could different answers fit the description?

Sharing with Siblings

Read each conversation between brothers and sisters. What is being shared in each situation? Write your answer on the line. There may be several possible answers for each item!

1.

"Oh, please could I borrow that? I love the red color and it's almost my size!"

"Sure, just don't get it dirty."

_____

2.

"Hey, we're playing outside in the park. But guess what we forgot?"

"You can use mine. I'll get it from the closet."

_____

3.

"You stay on your side and I'll stay on mine."

"OK, but don't mess up my half!"

_____

4.

"It's your turn."

"Hmmm. I'll move this guy over here."

_____

5.

"Ha ha ha! This is so funny!"

"May I read it when you're done?"

_____

III-8 Being the Oldest

Objective:

The student will identify common characteristics of children who are the oldest of siblings.

Rationale:

There are differing responsibilities for children in a family with several siblings. Birth order affects how that child is treated within the family as well as how the child relates to others. This lesson discusses characteristics or situations common to the oldest child in a family.

Thinking Questions:

1. Is anyone here the oldest child in a family? What is it like? *(ask for general comments)*

2. Do you enjoy being the oldest? Why/why not? *(some may like the responsibility and leadership, others may feel that the younger kids get more attention, etc.)*

3. What responsibilities might the oldest child have that others in the family wouldn't have? Why? *(watching the younger children, doing more around the house; older children may be more responsible, know how to do things that the younger ones don't, etc.)*

4. What might be some drawbacks to being the oldest? *(might not want the responsibility, resent being a leader, no role-model to follow among other children in the family, etc.)*

5. How is being an only child like being an oldest child? *(there is only one to do chores and take responsibility, this child is the first one in both cases, etc.)*

6. Why might it be harder to be the parent to an oldest child? *(the parent is going through parenting for the first time, may make "mistakes" or be unsure how to handle things, etc.)*

Activity:

Directions: Ten statements are listed on the worksheet. Students are to put a check mark by those that could describe a person who is the oldest in the family. Caution children that these are general statements; their own situations may be quite different, and there will be time to discuss their own experiences.

Answers: (general—allow for discussion of individual experiences) Probably 1, 2, 3, 5, 6, 7, 9, 10

Follow-up: Discuss students' responses and personal experiences with being the oldest. Each situation may be different in terms of what it is truly like to be the oldest, but look for common threads. Is it different if the oldest is a boy or girl? Are younger siblings treated differently? How and why? Would the older children trade places with someone else in the family who is younger?

Being the Oldest

Which of these statements could describe someone who is the oldest in the family? Put a check mark next to each one.

1. You might have younger children in the family.   _____

2. You are expected to act grown-up and set a good example.   _____

3. You might have to babysit for others in the family.   _____

4. You are the youngest of the children.   _____

5. Your parents count on you to be responsible.   _____

6. You are the first one to get new clothes.   _____

7. You get to do things that younger children in your family don't get to do.   _____

8. You have to go to bed before everybody else.   _____

9. You might be bigger and stronger than the other kids in your family.   _____

10. You know more about school than the others in your family.   _____

© 1993 by The Center for Applied Research in Education

Part III   Getting Along with Others at Home

III-9 Being the Youngest

Objective:

The student will identify at least two characteristics common to the youngest child in a family of several siblings.

Rationale:

The youngest child in a group of siblings may be the "baby"; he or she may be ignored because there are many others; possibly this child is extremely special because he or she represents the last child that will be born in the family. Being the youngest has perceived advantages and disadvantages, which will be discussed in this lesson.

Thinking Questions:

1. What is it like having older brothers and/or sisters? *(ask for opinions, examples)*

2. What might be nice about being the youngest in the family? *(may be treated better, spoiled, don't have to do as much work, etc.)*

3. Are there things that the youngest might not be allowed to do? What and why? *(handle knives, stay out alone longer, ride a two-wheeled bike in the street, etc.—element of danger, lack of skill)*

4. What if you had older brothers or sisters who constantly got into trouble at school? How could that be a problem for the youngest? *(teacher may expect that child to have problems at school, too, that child will have bad examples to follow, indicates family problems, etc.)*

5. What if your older siblings were smart and good at everything? Do you think people would expect that of the younger child, too? Why? *(probably—we tend to group family traits a lot because they come from the same parents and environment)*

Activity:

Directions: The student is to fill in a simple chart by listing ideas about what would be advantageous to being the youngest in the family and then what would be a disadvantage. Clues are given for ideas to start with. Again, inform children that you are seeking general responses, though you want them to draw from their own experiences if applicable.

   Answers: (examples) **Good**—last to have to go to school, have older brothers and sisters to help you with problems, parents might spend more time with you, etc. **Not as Good**—have to go to bed early, last one to get the clothes (if handed down), perceived as "too little" to do things, etc.

   Follow-up: Encourage discussion of what it is like to be the youngest in the family. How does it compare to being the oldest? What is it like having older siblings with good/bad reputations? Do they feel that parents treat them differently than the other children in the family? Is it harder or easier to get along with others if you are the youngest? The same?

Being the Youngest

What are some good things about being the youngest? What might be some drawbacks to being the youngest? Fill in your ideas on the chart.

think about. . . bedtime, having pets, going to school, doing chores. . .

Good: Not as good:

III-10 Being in the Middle

Objective:

The student will identify at least one characteristic of given children on the worksheet that is unique to that child.

Rationale:

Middle children are not the oldest or the youngest, but may have characteristics of both. Especially if there are many children in the family, these children have to be good at handling relationships from both chronological sides. Sometimes they are the "big brother"; other times they must defer to a sibling who is older than they. Each child is an individual with special characteristics. Middle children, in particular, may need to recognize their own uniqueness from the others in the group.

Thinking Questions:

1. What is it like to be a middle child? Can anyone give some experiences? *(some may enjoy it, others may feel lost or not noticed, etc.)*

2. How would being a middle child be similar to being the oldest? youngest? **(oldest:** *would have others younger than you in the family;* **youngest:** *still have older siblings around)*

3. How would being a middle child be different from being the oldest? youngest? **(oldest:** *maybe wouldn't have quite as much responsibility as the oldest in the family;* **youngest:** *both are treated as younger members of the family, not allowed to do as much)*

4. If there were lots of kids in a family, do you think each one would be special in some way to the parents? How or why? *(hopefully yes—because each has different abilities, interests, personality traits, etc.)*

5. How would having to get along with lots of children in the family help that person get along in life—at school, when they're grown-up, around other people, etc.? *(getting along means just that—being able to "get along" with others. That's something that people need to learn to do throughout life. Having siblings means sharing, negotiating, getting attention, and experiencing things together.)*

Activity:

Directions: Students are to select one unique quality about the characters who are pictured on the worksheet and write it on the line.

   Answers:

   1. plays piano
   2. has brown hair
   3. sings rock and roll
   4. drew cartoons that were printed
   5. loves animals a lot

   Follow-up: Discuss the responses to the worksheet. Besides the distinction for each student on the page, what similarities were given between the character and the other siblings? Do most siblings share some kind of ability? Are physical traits noticeable in families, such as the same hair color, skin color, height, etc.?

Being in the Middle

Being in the middle means you might be compared to other kids in the family, but you are still an individual! What is different or unique about these children? Write your answer on the line.

1. **Everyone in my family plays basketball but me. I'm good at playing the piano.**

_____

2. **My brother has red hair and my sister has red hair. But I have brown hair.**

_____

3. **Everyone in my family likes to sing. My two sisters sing in the school choir, but I sing rock and roll with my friends.**

_____

4. **My brother can draw anything. My sister is a real artist. I like to draw, too. I drew some cartoons that got printed in the paper. No one else did that!**

_____

5. **My sister likes animals. My other sister likes animals sort of, but not as much as I. I love horses and other animals! I collect them and draw them and think about them all the time. I want to work in a zoo!**

_____

III-11 Talking with Parents

Objective:

The student will identify characters who are attempting to talk to their parents in a rational, pleasant manner.

Rationale:

Talking to parents at home may be more of a challenge than we realize for some students. Some students simply do not know how to get their parents' attention in an appropriate way. Instead, they beg, whine, demand, or yell. Parents are not likely to listen happily to such forms of communication. Other students may not feel that they can approach their parents when they need help or just want to talk. Encouraging students to try to talk to parents and to do it in a pleasant manner is one step towards opening up lines of communication at home.

Thinking Questions:

1. If you had a problem or were really worried about something, would it be easy to talk to your parents? *(ask for comments)*

2. Some people find it difficult to talk to their parents. Why do you think that might be the case? *(feel parents aren't interested, don't know how to approach the topic, don't want to reveal their thoughts to an adult, etc.)*

3. Do you think most parents are interested in what's happening with their children? *(hopefully!)*

4. Have you ever heard anyone say, "My parents just don't understand"? What does that mean? *(might mean that the parents aren't trying to understand the child, or that the child hasn't done a good job of communicating with the parents)*

5. Do you think the age difference between parents and children has anything to do with a different viewpoint? *(in some cases, yes—the music, fads, clothing, etc., might be different)*

6. How would having different experiences affect the way someone feels about something? *(if someone wasn't interested in something or had no knowledge about it, that person couldn't really understand how someone else might feel)*

7. Do you think it's important for parents and kids to talk to each other? Why/why not? *(hopefully yes—to express different viewpoints, to understand each other, to keep up with what's going on in each other's lives, etc.)*

8. What are some ways that kids and parents can communicate or talk to each other about important things? *(sit down and talk, spend time listening, think about the other's point of view, etc.)*

9. What are some ways that you could get your parents' attention if you wanted to talk to them? *(ask for time alone, write a little note, go to their office, etc.)*

10. What are some ways that you could understand how your parents feel about something? *(ask them, observe them, try to think from their point of view, etc.)*

11. If you feel that your parents aren't listening to you, what else could you do? *(try again, talk to someone else if the problem is serious, try at a different time, etc.)*

12. If you and your parents don't understand each other or agree on things, what are some things your family might do together to work out the problems? *(set aside time to talk with just the family, cool off and talk later, see a family counselor, etc.)*

Activity:

Directions: Students are to circle the children on the worksheet who are truly talking to their parents, as opposed to arguing, whining, begging, etc.

Answers: 2, 4, 5

Follow-up: Have students determine why the children in 1 and 3 were not concerned about talking to their parents, but rather getting their own way, actively and passively. How did the children in the other examples convey their concerns to the parent without being sidetracked by immature behaviors? Is the character in number 4 arguing with his mother or trying to convince her to see his point of view? Even though the mother in number 5 was busy, she wanted to listen to the poem. If the daughter had asked at a different time, would the mother's response have been different? Encourage students to talk to their parents, keeping in mind the setting as well as the approach.

Talking with Parents

The situations below show children who are really trying to talk to their parents and some who are not. Circle the children who are trying to talk to their parents, not just trying to shut them out.

1. "Give me that toy! I have to have it! I want it right now!" "We told you it was very expensive..."

"I want it! I want it!"

2. "Mom, I can't see the board at school. Everything looks blurry. Can you help me?" "Well, we better get your eyes checked right away."

3. "Steve, I asked you to clean up your room. What's the problem?"

4. "No, you can't go to the park with your friends. We have plans for the family tonight." "But I had plans, too. Remember you told me I could go out tonight? For just a short time?"

"Oh yes. Now I do remember."

5. "Would you like to hear the poem I wrote in school today? Are you busy?" "No - I'd love to hear it."

III-12 Doing Chores at Home

Objective:

The student will identify several household chores and state the person responsible for completing the task at home.

Rationale:

Most families (by necessity!) have some sort of division of labor. It used to be that mom washed the dishes and clothes and dad mowed the lawn and filled up the car. Now, however, it's pretty much anyone's guess who will do what—provided that people are willing to help out to keep the household running. This lesson attempts to remind students that there are many tasks involved, and for the student to be willing to assume a place among those who are needed to fill in to help out.

Thinking Questions:

1. What are *chores*? *(tasks or things that you do around the house, maintaining or taking care of jobs that are necessary to keep the household functioning on a physical level)*

2. Why do families usually divide up the chores? *(so no one person gets stuck with everything, it's a fairer system, some people might be better at doing one chore than another, etc.)*

3. What are some examples of household chores? *(washing the clothes, setting the table, cleaning out the garage, etc.)*

4. What are some fair ways for a family to divide up the chores? *(take into account amount of time available, other responsibilities, alternate doing the dishes, everyone cleans their own room, etc.)*

5. How does having a good attitude about doing chores make things easier? *(perhaps everyone will be more willing to pitch in, you feel like your family is working together, makes things go faster, etc.)*

Activity:

Directions: Students are to look at the list of typical household chores and write down who is primarily responsible for doing it at their house. You may wish to add your own chores to the list.

Answers: will vary—a lot!

Follow-up: Discuss the different individuals who are responsible for the chores at students' houses. Is it always the mother who washes the dishes? How do students feel about the chore schedule at their own house? What would they change to still be fair?

Doing Chores at Home

Here is a list of common chores. You may wish to add your own ideas to the list. Who is responsible for completing them at your house?

Who?

1. mopping the kitchen floor   _____

2. cutting the grass   _____

3. washing the clothes   _____

4. feeding the pets   _____

5. cleaning the bedrooms   _____

6. washing the car   _____

7. washing the dishes after dinner   _____

8. picking up the newspaper/mail   _____

9. sweeping the front porch   _____

10. taking the aluminum cans to
    the recycle center   _____

III-13 Homework at Home

Objective:

The student will identify the problem in each situation given that makes doing homework difficult.

Rationale:

Doing homework in a home setting is very different from doing schoolwork in a school setting. Parents do not always have time to supervise, students must rely on their own initiative to a greater degree, and there are many types of distractions at home. This lesson illustrates a few of the distractions and gives students a chance to think of ways to get around them.

Thinking Questions:

1. Why do you have homework? *(didn't get it done at school, have a test coming up, teacher wants you to do extra work to learn, etc.)*

2. How can doing homework help you do better in school? *(it's a second time around to think about the material; extra time might help it sink in; more time you spend studying, the better you'll do; etc.)*

3. How can people at home help you with homework? *(quiz you over the material, sit next to you and do the homework, be quiet so you can study, answer questions you may have, etc.)*

4. How is studying at home different than studying at school? *(quieter, less structured, you can eat, etc.)*

5. What are some distractions that you might run into at home? *(TV, people, pets, etc.)*

6. What are some ways that you can reduce the distractions to make studying at home easier? *(go in another room, shut your door, tell your parents to hold your calls, work first then eat, etc.)*

7. What are some things that could help make doing homework easier? *(do it at the same time, same place everyday, study with a friend, etc.)*

Activity:

Directions: Each situation shows a character who is not getting his or her homework done because of a problem or distraction. The student is to write down the problem in each situation on the line.

> *Answers:*
> 1. too tired
> 2. wrong book
> 3. wants to play with friends
> 4. giving up because of lost crayon
> 5. talking on the phone
> 6. not understanding the homework

Follow-up: Have students discuss their responses, then talk about ways to avoid the problem. In each situation, what could the student do to get the homework done? What could prevent it from happening again?

Homework at Home

What is the problem in each situation below that is making getting homework done very difficult?

1. *Yawn. . .it's almost midnight. I can't think about this anymore. . . Zzzzzzzzz*

_____

2. *I'm supposed to copy spelling words from my spelling book. Spelling book? This is my math book!*

_____

3. *Hey - can I play too? Toss that football over here!*

_____

4. *I can't do my homework. I'm supposed to color the water blue and I don't have a blue crayon.*

_____

5. *And then Mary said to Liz. . .*

_____

6. *I don't have any idea what I'm supposed to do.*

_____

© 1993 by The Center for Applied Research in Education

III-14 Being Part of a Family

Objective:

The student will make a simple family tree, showing siblings, parents, and grandparents.

Rationale:

We all came from somewhere, and it is often quite interesting to trace family roots back a few generations, especially if there are people around to make the names come alive. In this lesson, students are to think about their immediate family and to find information from the preceding two generations. Even if the child is adopted or from a blended family, he or she fits into a family in some way.

Thinking Questions:

1. Who are the members of your family? Tell the relationships, i.e., aunt-uncle, brother-sister, etc. *(students may cite grandparents living with them, cousins, step-family members, etc.)*

2. How are aunts and uncles related to you? *(they are the sisters and brothers of the parents)*

3. What are cousins? *(children of your aunts and uncles)*

4. What is a family tree and what is it for? *(it shows the relationship of people in a family, helps to show who is related to whom for several past generations, etc.)*

5. How can someone find out about his or her ancestors or family tree? *(talk to parents and grandparents, check birth records, old Bibles, etc.)*

Activity:

Directions: Go over the example of using a circle and triangle to represent the student. The circle is for a female; the triangle is for a male. In the example, Ann and Sue are sisters, with Ricky being their brother. The parents are Alice and Mark. Make sure students understand that each line represents a different generation. You will only be looking at three generations (the student, parents, grandparents) in this lesson.

Answers: will vary according to the student

Follow-up: Have students share their family trees with others. What interesting information did they find out about their families by talking to their parents? Did anyone find out that they had someone famous in their family tree? Was it difficult to find the information? How did they go about it?

Name_____ Date _____

III-14

Being Part of a Family

Can you fill out your family tree? The circle stands for a woman or girl; the triangle stands for a man or boy. Ask your parents to help you fill in the names.

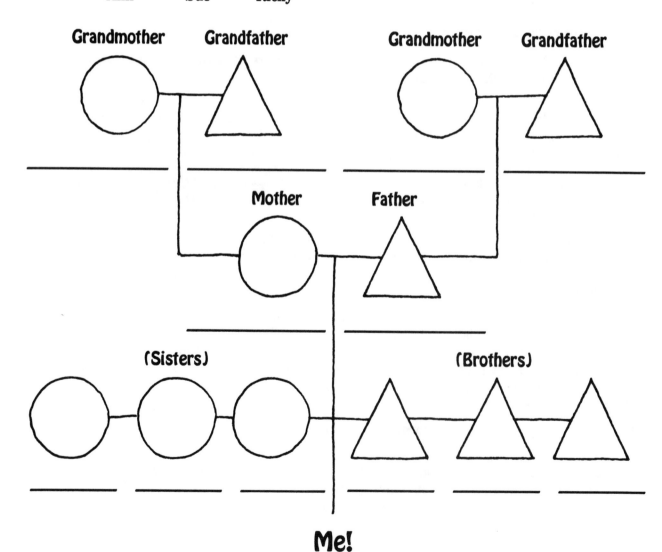

Example:

Alice   Mark

Ann   Sue   Ricky

Grandmother   Grandfather   Grandmother   Grandfather

Mother   Father

(Sisters)   (Brothers)

Me!

Part III   Getting Along with Others at Home

III-15   Family Fun

Objective:

The student will identify several activities that a family could do together for fun or leisure.

Rationale:

The times that a family can do things together may seem rare, considering all of the different activities and schedules. Nevertheless, it is important for a family to spend time together. There are many family activities that can be done on any budget, any time. Hopefully, students will realize that their family is a social grouping that can be a lot of fun!

Thinking Questions:

1. What are some ways that a family could have fun together? *(going on a picnic, taking a vacation, riding bikes, etc.)*

2. Has anyone ever taken a family vacation? Where was the destination? *(ask for examples)*

3. What are some things that a family could do together in the house or same city? *(play cards, basketball, go swimming, go to the zoo)*

4. Even though you might fight with siblings occasionally, what are things that you can do with brothers and sisters that are fun? *(board games, basketball in the back yard, riding bikes, building models, jumping rope, etc.)*

5. How is being part of a family different from being part of a group of friends? *(you will always be related by blood, always have the same background; with friends you're about the same age, but may change friendships with time and as you move, etc.)*

Activity:

Directions: The left side of the worksheet lists parts of a conversation from a family engaging in a fun activity. The student is to decide what the activity is and write the letter of the answer on the line.

   Answers: 1. d   2. c   3. b   4. e   5. a

Follow-up: After discussing the answers on the worksheet, have students think of and list other activities that a family could do together for fun. What conversational clues would give it away?

Family Fun

Match the way the family is having fun together with the clues in the conversations on the left.

1. Yea!! You got them all down! It's a strike! _____

a. watching TV

2. Please pass the potato chips. Watch out for the ants! _____

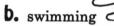
b. swimming

3. Don't splash me! _____

c. having a picnic

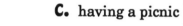
d. bowling

4. Do you have any fives? Quit looking over here! _____

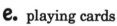
e. playing cards

5. Ha ha ha! I love this. Oh, here's a commercial. Let's get something to drink. _____

Part IV   Everyday Etiquette

IV-1 Meeting Other People

Objective:

The student will identify characters who are meeting other people by looking at the person, smiling, and saying hello or other greeting.

Rationale:

Though most introductions are contrived and probably somewhat awkward for most students, it is a polite ritual to say "hello," put on a smile, and look the other person in the eye. In this lesson, students will concentrate on identifying those behaviors from characters on the worksheet.

Thinking Questions:

1. When do you think you might meet new people? *(new kids at school, at a friend's party, church youth group, etc.)*

2. When you meet someone new, why is it important to look them in the eye? *(show that you are interested in them, get a good look at them so you'll recognize them later, etc.)*

3. Do you think eye contact is important every time you talk to someone or just the first time you meet someone? *(in general, whenever you are talking to someone; shows interest and attention)*

4. What are some other things that you can do to show the person that you are polite and interested in them? *(smile, say hello, etc.)*

5. Would you want to get to know someone better if he or she acted disinterested in you or snotty? *(probably not)*

6. Why do you think it's important to look friendly and interested in someone when you meet them? *(so they will get a good impression of you, might open up a new friendship, etc.)*

Activity:

Directions: The student is to identify which of the three elements for meeting someone is missing in the situations on the worksheet. Make sure students understand the three parts (looking at the person, smiling, giving a greeting) and that they are to write only the number of the missing element.

Answers: 1. 2   2. 1   3. 3   4. 2   5. 3

Follow-up: Have students role-play the situations on the worksheet, making sure that they are able to meet someone correctly (incorporating all three elements) after they have performed leaving one out. You can also have students make up their own skits, sometimes leaving something out so the others in the class can identify it.

Meeting Other People

These people are meeting other people for the first time, but each is forgetting to do something important. Write the number of what was forgotten:

1 = look at the person   2 = smile   3 = say hello or hi

1. *Jerry, I'd like you to meet my friend Stan.* *Hello there.* _____

2. *This is my father.* *Hi.* _____

3. *I don't think you've met my neighbor, Sally.* _____

4. *This is my brother Bob.* *Hi, Bob.* _____

5. *Come over here, Ann. I want to introduce you to our new classmate. Her name is Kristen.* _____

IV-2 Introducing Your Friends

Objective:

The student will introduce someone by telling the person's name and one item about the person.

Rationale:

Children rarely have to perform formal introductions. When they are playing together, somehow they find out who each other is and a little bit about each other. However, it is not too early to develop the good habit of making sure that everyone in the group knows who everyone else is by name. It also helps people get to know each other by telling something interesting about the person. At this point, introductions do not need to be stiff or formal, as long as the information is given to the other friends.

Thinking Questions:

1. Have you ever been in a situation where you were with two of your friends, but the friends didn't know each other? If so, what was it like? *(ask for anecdotes)*

2. How did the two friends get along and get to know each other? *(probably by playing together, spending time with the mutual friend)*

3. Why is it helpful to introduce the two friends who don't know each other, especially if you're all going to be spending time together? *(so they can talk to each other, find out what they have in common, also it's nice to know who you're talking to!)*

4. What are some things you could tell the friends about each other to help them get to know each other? *(common interests, interesting things they have done, something they are good at, etc.)*

5. When would you introduce your friends to your parents? *(if they came over, if you saw them at a party or in the neighborhood)*

6. Who else might you introduce a new friend to? *(other family members, neighbors)*

7. Why do you think it's important to tell the names of everyone to each other when you're introducing people who don't know each other? *(might be the easiest thing to remember, people like to be called by their own name)*

Activity:

Directions: The students will look at the situations on the worksheet and decide whether or not the characters are doing a good job of introducing a friend to another person. They are to write YES or NO on each line.

   Answers: 1. yes   2. no   3. yes   4. yes   5. no

   Follow-up: Discuss what was wrong or incomplete about numbers 2 and 5. Have students role-play these situations, demonstrating good introductions.

Name _____ Date _____

IV-2

Introducing Your Friends

These people are introducing their friends. Tell if you think they are doing a good job and write YES or NO on the line.

1.   _____

2.   _____

3.  _____

4.   _____

5.   _____

IV-3 Impolite Noises

Objective:

The student will identify proper procedures for handling impolite noises in public, such as minimizing the noise, not calling attention to the problem, or saying "excuse me."

Rationale:

Some noises can't be eliminated entirely, such as coughing or sneezing. However, they can be minimized and certainly should not be used to get attention. Other noises are impolite, such as slurping liquids or burping loudly. Students will first have to decide whether or not the noise can be helped, and if not, then how to handle the noise in public.

Thinking Questions:

1. Have you ever had the hiccups when everyone around you was really quiet? Tell about it. *(you'll probably hear some good anecdotes!)*

2. What did the people around you do when you hiccupped? *(turned and giggled, stared, laughed, etc.)*

3. Some noises can't be helped, such as sneezing or coughing. But can the loudness be controlled? *(somewhat—you can stifle a sneeze and use a handkerchief or tissue)*

4. How could you lessen the noise if you had a sniffle from a cold? *(use a tissue instead of inhaling)*

5. Why do you think people consider burping to be impolite? *(some people overdo it, it calls attention to yourself, etc.)*

6. If someone around you makes an impolite noise to get attention, or he or she is trying to be silly, what could you do? *(ignore it)*

7. If someone makes an impolite noise and really couldn't help it, what should he or she do? *(say "excuse me" and don't make a big deal about it)*

Activity:

Directions: The students are to match the picture portraying an impolite noise with the words by writing the letter on the line next to each picture.

Answers: 1. d   2. a   3. f   4. e   5. c   6. b

Follow-up: Sometimes you just have to scratch! Discuss why the noises pictured may be considered impolite in public. Stress that it is not the noise itself that is the problem (unless it is loud or annoying on purpose), but the context. Again, go over how each noise could be eliminated, reduced, or pardoned.

Impolite Noises

Match the picture of someone making an irritating noise with the words that describe it. Write the letter on the line.

1.

2.

_____   **a.** having the hiccups

_____   **b.** scratching

_____   **c.** whistling

3.

_____   **d.** blowing your nose

4.

_____   **e.** slurping

_____   **f.** sneezing

5.

6.

_____

© 1993 by The Center for Applied Research in Education

IV-4   Excuse Me

Objective:

The student will identify instances in which he or she should say "excuse me."

Rationale:

Saying "excuse me" may not completely make up for the mistake that was made, but at least it is an attempt to acknowledge that something was done inappropriately or bothersome to someone else. Teach students, first of all, to try to avoid the situation, but if it can't be helped, say "excuse me" politely and quietly.

Thinking Questions:

1. Has anyone ever stepped on your foot accidentally? *(probably)*

2. What did the person—if he or she was polite—say to you? *("sorry" or "excuse me")*

3. Does saying those words change anything? Why bother saying it? *(it doesn't undo the situation but shows that you were concerned about your actions and the other person's feelings)*

4. What are some other examples of situations in which people should say "excuse me"? *(bothering someone for something, impolite noises, accidentally knocking into someone, making someone move out of their way, etc.)*

5. How does saying "excuse me" help you break into a conversation between other people? *(shows that you need their attention but are aware that they are busy right now)*

Activity:

Directions: Students are to put a check mark next to each situation on the list for which someone should say "excuse me."

Answers: Check marks by—1, 3, 4, 5, 8, 10

Follow-up: Discuss why each item on the list either did or did not warrant an "excuse me" from a person. Ask students if the behavior could have been prevented or at least minimized by thinking ahead.

Excuse Me

Put a check mark after each item on the list below if you think you should say "Excuse me."

1. interrupting a conversation _____

2. when you answer the telephone _____

3. bumping into someone _____

4. moving past people sitting in a row at the movies _____

5. accidentally burping _____

6. when you give someone a present _____

7. meeting your friend's parents _____

8. asking someone to pass the sugar at dinner _____

9. when you pass a friend in the hall at school _____

10. when you want to talk to the teacher and aren't sure if he is busy or not _____

IV-5 Personal Questions

Objective:

The student will state whether or not questions asked of someone else are appropriate or not.

Rationale:

Children are curious, and sometimes dare to ask questions of others that adults would not. Curiosity can become offensive, however, when the questions are too personal and are not anyone else's business. Young students truly may not know that not all information is fair game for them. This lesson explains that some questions are not appropriate to ask others, depending on how well you know the other person and what the intention is in asking.

Thinking Questions:

1. How would you feel if someone wanted to know when your birthday was and came right up and asked you? *(fine, happy for the attention, etc.)*

2. How would you feel if someone asked you about why your dad got in trouble at work and is it true that he was losing his job? *(not so good, angry, embarrassed, etc.)*

3. What is a personal question? *(something about you)*

4. Why do you think some people would not want to be asked very personal questions? *(might be embarrassing, don't want people to know their business, etc.)*

5. What are some areas that people might be sensitive about or wouldn't want to be asked questions about? *(their age, how much money they make, why they got in trouble, embarrassing home life, etc.)*

6. Is there a difference between asking questions because you are interested and asking questions because you are nosey? *(yes—the motivation is quite different)*

7. If a question makes someone else feel uncomfortable, how could you back off or talk about something else? *(ask different questions, don't ask any questions at all)*

8. If someone asked you a very personal question that you did not want to answer, what could you say to the person? *(sorry, that's not your business; I'm not supposed to talk about that; I don't know the answer; etc.)*

Activity:

Directions: The characters on the worksheet are asking questions. Students are to circle the people who are asking nice, considerate questions. They are to put an X on the questions that are too personal.

Answers: **circle**—1, 3, 4, 7; **X**—2, 5, 6, 8

Follow-up: Discuss the responses. Why were the X'd questions inappropriate to ask someone? Why would they be embarrassing to the character if he or she answered? What are good ways to answer those questions if someone asked them to you?

Personal Questions

Circle the students who are asking nice questions that show they are interested. Put an X on the questions if you think they are too personal.

1. Do you like school?

2. Did you get an F on that?

3. How many people are in your family?

4. Do you live near here?

5. How much money does your dad make?

6. Why do you smell funny?

7. Do you have any pets?

8. Is it true that your family is getting kicked out of your house?

IV-6 Mimicking or Imitating Others

Objective:

The student will identify characters who are imitating others out of flattery or admiration rather than ridicule.

Rationale:

There's a big difference between imitating someone whom you admire greatly and imitating someone with the intention of making fun of him or her. In this lesson, students are given the opportunity to distinguish between the two.

Thinking Questions:

1. When you go to the zoo, what animal is often imitated? Why? *(monkey—it is cute, funny, makes you laugh)*

2. What are some things that people imitate or make fun of about other people? *(movements, voice, things that they say, etc.)*

3. Why is it funny to imitate the voice or movements of other people? *(you can exaggerate what they do that is unusual, etc.)*

4. How could imitating or mimicking others get you into trouble? *(the person might find out, could lead to hurt feelings, anger, etc.)*

5. Is it nice to imitate people who are doing something positive? What are some examples of positive imitating? *(wearing your hair or clothes like someone else, saying the same things they say, playing sports like someone who is good at it, etc.)*

6. What are some things that you would like to imitate about someone else? *(a good athlete's behavior, the way someone famous looks, a good attitude displayed by someone, etc.)*

Activity:

Directions: Students are to write the names of the characters on the worksheet who are imitating others in a nice way. The names should be written in the box at the bottom of the page.

Answers: **Names**—Maria, Anna, Ed and Fred

Follow-up: Discuss what is impolite or silly about the other characters' behaviors on the worksheet. Would those characters imitate the person if that person was aware of them? Is it ever okay to imitate someone else if it was done just for fun and the other person didn't mind?

Name _____ Date _____

IV-6

Mimicking or Imitating Others

Write the names of the characters who are imitating others in a nice way in the box at the bottom.

1. **I want to wear my hair like Kathy does. It's so pretty.**

Maria

2. **That boy walks like this.**

Al

3.

Ricky

4. **And I said . . .**

And I said . . .

Kevin

5. **I wish I could throw a ball like Tim does.**

Anna

6. **We're a rock group. Listen.**

Ed   Fred

7. **This is how Jenny plays basketball.**

Sarah

8. **LAAAA!**

LAAAA!

Kara

Names:

IV-7 Behavior in Public Places

Objective:

The student will identify the problem with the behavior displayed by characters in public places.

Rationale:

There's a big difference between being in public and being in the privacy of your own home. When in public, you are sharing time and space with other people and must be considerate of everyone's needs. Students need to realize that they must be aware of their surroundings and their audience in public.

Thinking Questions:

1. What does it mean if a place or event is "open to the public"? *(anyone can go there or attend the event)*

2. What are some public places in our community? *(zoo, park, library, restaurants, post office, etc.)*

3. What do you have to share with others in a public place? *(the view, tables, time, being waited on, etc.)*

4. Whose needs and interests do you have to consider when you are in a public place? *(everyone else who is there)*

5. Why can't you do whatever you want in a public place? *(it doesn't belong to you, it's not private property, someone might be offended or hurt, etc.)*

6. How does sharing public things benefit you? *(a community can afford to have a zoo or a nice library, the cost of the building is shared, you don't have to do the actual upkeep, etc.)*

7. Why is it important to remember that you are sharing public facilities with a lot of other people? How would it help you be on your best behavior? *(don't want to spoil things for someone else, be careful with things so others can use them, remember to share if people are waiting, etc.)*

Activity:

Directions: After looking at the picture on the left, students are to write on the lines at the right the problem that they have discovered with the behavior.

Answers:

1. graffiti is expensive to erase, often not nice
2. someone is walking on the grass (might be newly planted)
3. a boy is being pushy in line, waiting for tickets
4. a girl is yelling loudly at a game, disturbing others
5. the boy is making shadow pictures on the movie screen, distorting the picture

Follow-up: Discuss alternative behaviors that the characters could engage in and still achieve their goal. How does their inconsiderate behavior affect or hurt anyone else?

Behavior in Public Places

What's wrong with the behavior of the characters in each situation below? Write your answer on the lines.

1. Let's write on the walls of the bathroom!

   _____
   _____

2. KEEP OFF THE GRASS

   _____
   _____

3. Move!

   TICKETS

   _____
   _____

4. Whoooo! Whooo!

   _____
   _____

5. Look - I can make shadow pictures!

   _____
   _____

IV-8 Washing Hands Before Eating

Objective:

The student will identify situations in which a person should wash his or her hands before eating.

Rationale:

If someone learns to automatically wash hands before eating, a very good habit is engrained. Children are busy, often into exciting (dirty) things, and don't even think about washing their hands. Germs seem like a silly joke. If students can learn to wash hands right before eating, it will take care of many related problems such as getting dirt on the tablecloth or clothes, wiping hands across the face, and sharing silverware that has been touched by hands that have been in strange places!

Thinking Questions:

1. Before you eat, what do you usually do before you sit at the table? *(change clothes, wash hands, etc.)*

2. Why do you think you are told to wash your hands? *(they might be dirty, you could get it on your clothes, dirty hands carry germs, etc.)*

3. What are some activities that you do before it is time to eat? *(play outside with friends, do homework, ride bike, etc.)*

4. What could happen at the table if everyone had hands that were really dirty? *(you'd pass around food and plates that had someone's dirt on them, clothes could get dirty, etc.)*

5. How could germs get from your hands to your food or mouth? *(you could touch an apple, touch the silverware, touch your napkin then wipe your mouth)*

6. Why would you want someone who was preparing the food to have clean hands? *(they will be touching the food)*

7. Why is it important to use soap when you wash your hands? *(water alone doesn't get the germs off)*

Activity:

Directions: Students will write YES or NO on the line next to each picture to show whether or not the characters should wash their hands before eating.

> *Answers:*   1. yes   2. yes   3. no   4. yes   5. yes   6. yes

> *Follow-up:* In each case, what type of dirt or grime could be on the person's hands? What things did the boy in #4 probably touch before walking into the restaurant?

Washing Hands Before Eating

Which of these people need to wash their hands before eating? Write YES or NO on the lines.

1. *I've been playing in the mud. But my hands look OK to me!*   _____

2. *I used water, but I didn't see any soap.*   _____

3. *I just took a bath. Where's my dinner?*   _____

4. *This looks like a nice restaurant. Where is the washroom?*   _____

5. *May I help cook?*   _____

6. *What a nice doggie!*   _____

IV-9 Table Manners

Objective:

The student will draw pictures to illustrate several common table manners.

Rationale:

Every family is different and will require different table manners. Families range from very informal eating habits (such as grabbing whatever you can find whenever you happen to get home) to more formal on special occasions (Christmas with the relatives). People who have sit-down dinners on a regular basis are pretty rare, it seems, yet it is important for children to know how to behave if they are in a situation where these manners are expected. Twelve common behaviors are listed for consideration, and not all will be relevant to every family; however, a student who could handle this degree of formality at a meal would be in pretty good shape to face anything!

Thinking Questions:

1. What are some examples of good table manners? *(sit still, pass the food, wait to be excused, don't lick the knife, etc.)*

2. Why is it important to have good table manners? *(so you don't mess up the food, so everyone passes food in the same direction, show that you are considerate of others, etc.)*

3. What might be in front of you when you sit down at the table? *(plate or two, silverware, napkins, glass, bowls of food,* etc.)*

4. What are the different items for? *(*go through the purpose of each item listed above)*

5. Why is it polite to wait until everyone else has food before you start eating? *(shows that you aren't going to rush to beat everyone else, someone might need to have something passed and you'll have your hands free, etc.)*

6. What should you do if you don't like what is being served? *(say "no, thank you" politely, take a small amount, pass the bowl to the next person, etc.)*

7. Why shouldn't you argue or fight about things at the table? *(eating is a time to relax and let your food digest, arguing can make others upset, it's not polite to involve others at the table with your problems, etc.)*

8. After you are done eating, what could you do to help the cook? *(take your dishes to the kitchen, throw napkins away, etc.)*

Activity:

Directions: The student has a choice of drawing pictures to illustrate four of the twelve table manners listed on the worksheet. They are to write the number of their drawing at the top.

Answers: will vary

Follow-up: Have students cover the number at the top and let other students try to guess which manner they drew. Collect examples of all twelve from the class and display them so that they are in order, showing a complete dinner!

Table Manners

Draw a picture to illustrate four of the following good manners.

1. Come when called.

2. Sit quietly in your seat.

3. Wait to say grace.

4. Put your napkin on your lap.

5. Pass food before eating.

6. Ask politely for things you need.

7. Use your silverware.

8. Eat slowly with mouth closed.

9. Say only nice things about the food.

10. Wait for seconds until everyone has had firsts.

11. Ask to be excused.

12. Thank the cook.

Number: _____

Number: _____

Number: _____

Number: _____

IV-10 Eating Out

Objective:

The student will circle the characters who are showing polite behavior in a restaurant.

Rationale:

Waitresses and waiters are not slaves, waiting for the customer's beck and call. When people go out to eat, sometimes expectations change and they are not as considerate to the waitpersons or the customers who will follow them. Showing polite behavior in a public restaurant is something that children can learn at a young age. Even teaching children to order politely for themselves is a helpful social skill involving speaking clearly, looking at someone in the eye, and making decisions.

Thinking Questions:

1. What are some places where you might go to eat out? *(local restaurants)*

2. Why do people sometimes go out to eat? *(may enjoy certain ethnic foods, special occasion, no food at home, etc.)*

3. What is a fast food restaurant? *(a place where you can get your meal in a hurry, have a drive-through, etc.)*

4. How is a sit-down restaurant different from a fast-food place? *(the waitperson takes your order, service is slower, may have more choice of items, etc.)*

5. How is eating at a sit-down restaurant different from eating at someone's house? *(don't have to wash the dishes, food is served by a waitperson, everyone can order something different, etc.)*

6. What table manners would be the same at a restaurant as at home? *(pass food around the table, put your napkin on your lap, sit quietly, etc.)*

7. Since eating out is going to be at a public place, what is going to be shared with others? *(the waiter or waitress, the table—other customers after you, the restrooms, the waiting room before you get in, etc.)*

Activity:

Directions: Students are to circle the characters on the worksheet who are displaying appropriate behavior in the restaurant depicted on the page.

Answers: **Circle**—2, 5, 8, 10

Follow-up: Discuss how the rude characters could change their speech or actions to be more appropriate for the restaurant. What other inappropriate behaviors could have been drawn on this worksheet and why would they be impolite?

Eating Out

Circle the characters below who are showing polite behavior in a restaurant.

IV-11 Opening Doors for Others

Objective:

The student will identify situations for which it is good manners to open the door for another person.

Rationale:

It is courteous to open the door for another person who has his or her hands full, may have difficulty getting the door open, or who is in a hurry. If two people are relatively equal in status or needs, either one could open the door. In some situations, such as getting off a bus or elevator, it is better to get off first and then let someone else on. This lesson goes through several examples of when it is helpful to open a door for someone else.

Thinking Questions:

1. Why is it polite to hold a door open for someone? *(it frees up their hands, lets them go through first, shows you are thoughtful and considerate of their needs, etc.)*

2. What are some situations for which someone might need help with a door? *(if they are carrying something, in a wheelchair, door is stuck, older person, young person who can't reach handle, etc.)*

3. What are some doors that you could open for someone? *(door to a house, restroom door, car door, entrance to public building, etc.)*

4. Why should you let someone go first since it means you get to go second? *(if the person is slow, you'll pass him or her anyhow; it's not always a race to be first; it's better to be polite than first, etc.)*

5. Can you think of any doors that are opened that you should not let someone go through first because it would block the way? *(getting off a bus or elevator)*

6. If you are really in a hurry, how could you hold the door open and still go through first? *(reach behind you and hold it part way open)*

Activity:

Directions: In each picture, there is a person with a star (*) next to him or her and another person. The student is to decide whether or not the person with the star should hold the door open for the other person or not. They should write YES or NO on the line.

>   *Answers:*   1. yes   2. no   3. no   4. yes   5. yes   6. yes

>   *Follow-up:* Discuss why the person in each situation should or should not go through the door first. If you are in a hurry in the type of situations listed, what are some ways that you could be polite and still get through quickly?

Opening Doors for Others

Should the person with the star (☆) next to him or her open the door for the other person in each picture below? Write YES or NO on the line.

IV-12 Giving Up Your Seat

Objective:

The student will identify situations for which it is good manners to give up his or her seat for another person.

Rationale:

It is hard for children to understand why giving up ownership of something, even as simple as a seat, is polite or necessary. If the children are strong and able-bodied, they can learn to give someone less able than themselves a chair, a seat on a bus, or even more room on the couch. In this lesson, several examples are listed for possible times when they may be asked to move or volunteer their seat to someone else.

Thinking Questions:

1. Have you ever been sitting somewhere and then been asked to give up your seat to someone else? When? *(perhaps on a bus, in a crowded waiting room, etc.)*

2. What are reasons why someone else might need your seat more than you do? *(if the person is old, sick, holding something, etc.)*

3. If you give up your seat, what's the worst thing that might happen to you? *(have to stand up, get a worse seat, ride later, etc.)*

4. If you were in a restaurant and were sitting right by the salad bar, and then another family came in and wanted to take your seats, should you move? *(no—the waitress or waiter has already seated you, you were there first, there is no apparent reason why they **need** to sit by the salad bar)*

5. If you stood in line for hours to get the front seat of a roller coaster and someone else wanted it, would it be necessary for you to give up your seat? *(no—again, there is no apparent reason why the other person needs that seat)*

6. What if there was a new person in your class who couldn't hear very well and needed to sit close to the front of the room in order to learn. If you were in the front, would it be polite to give your desk to that person? *(yes—now there is a good reason to give up your seat)*

7. How do you know when you should give up your seat to someone else? *(think about the needs of the other person and if you are willing to give up your seat to help someone out; it may not be necessary or even expected for you to give up your seat on all occasions)*

Activity:

Directions: The student is to match the letter of the reason why it is polite to give up a seat to the person pictured on the left.

Answers: 1. a   2. d   3. c   4. b   5. e

Follow-up: Discuss the specific needs of the people pictured on the worksheet. Why is their need of more importance than the other people in the setting? How great of a sacrifice is involved for any individuals? Under what conditions should your own seat be saved; for example, if you know you get carsick in the back of a car, would it benefit anything if you went to the back seat to let someone else sit in the front? Where does common sense fit into this?

Giving Up Your Seat

Why would it be polite to give up your seat to these people? Write the answer that matches on the line.

1. In a waiting room:

_____

a. so the older person won't have to stand for a long time

2. In a classroom:

May I have a seat near the board?

_____

b. so the person will feel better while the car is moving

c. so the lady will have her arms free

3. Riding a bus:

_____

d. so the boy can see the board

e. so the person can stretch out.

4. In a car:

Oooh - I always get sick in the back.

_____

5. At a ballgame:

Would you mind moving over a little?

_____

IV-13 Public Phones

Objective:

The student will identify appropriate manners for using a public phone.

Rationale:

When using a public phone, people need to be aware that it is a shared machine. Other people might be nearby, waiting to use the phone. If several booths are close together, the noise level should be adjusted so that everyone can hear. Screaming matches or arguments that disturb others in the area are annoying and embarrassing. The phone is there for everyone and should be treated as something that will be left in good working condition for the next user.

Thinking Questions:

1. Where would you find a public or pay phone around here? *(at the mall, gas station, school office, etc.)*

2. How do pay phones help make life a little easier? *(they are found in locations where people may gather, makes it more convenient if you need to call someone while you're away from home, etc.)*

3. What is needed to make a phone call from a public phone? *(a quarter, change, phone card, knowledge of how to reverse the charges through the operator)*

4. What is shared about the phone if it is a public phone? *(anyone can use it, the booth itself as well as the phone are available to the public)*

5. What are some ways to be courteous to others when using a public phone? *(keep your voice down, wait your turn, don't talk too long, don't leave it hanging, etc.)*

Activity:

Directions: Six situations depicting characters using a public phone are on the worksheet. Students are to put a check mark next to those that show the phone user being polite or behaving appropriately.

Answers: check marks by—1, 4

Follow-up: Discuss the problem that the character is having or leaving for someone in each of the unchecked pictures. How did the polite characters show courtesy to other users of the phone or phone booth?

Public Phones

Put a check mark by the pictures that show someone using a public phone in a polite or appropriate manner.

IV-14   Gossip

Objective:

The student will identify whether or not a piece of information or conversation would be considered gossip.

Rationale:

A very basic definition for gossip is simply talk about someone else that is not necessarily based on fact, with a mean-spirited or harmful attitude. Gossip is one of the cruelest, most effective ways to hurt another person. Students should be cautioned to be careful to talk about other people's problems or situations, especially when they do not really know what's going on and when their intention is to stir up trouble or be the first to pass along the news. In this lesson, examples of statements that could be considered gossip are provided for discussion and analysis.

Thinking Questions:

1. What is gossip? *(talking about someone in a mean or unhelpful way, passing along rumors, talking about other people's problems just to pass along information—not to help the person, etc.)*

2. Why do some people like to gossip about other people? *(it makes them feel important to know something bad about someone else, just want to stir up trouble, etc.)*

3. How does spreading gossip about someone hurt them? *(it might not be true, it will affect how other people feel about the person, if it is true it would make the person feel bad that everyone was aware of the problems, etc.)*

4. If someone shares a problem with you and asks you not to tell anyone, what should you do? *(respect their wishes, don't talk about it if the person is not in a life-threatening or serious situation, etc.)*

5. If you are concerned or worried about someone, who would you talk to if you felt that person really needed help? *(someone whom you trusted, who would not repeat gossip; someone who was trained to handle a serious problem such as a counselor or doctor)*

Activity:

Directions: This is a difficult lesson in that the statements and situations given for consideration require some thought and explanation to decide whether or not it would be considered gossip in a typical situation. Students should be instructed to read the statements and think about the spirit in which they are delivered. Are the words factual? If so, could they be harmful to pass along to other people who may continue to do so? Students are to write YES or NO on the lines to indicate their responses.

Answers:

1. no
2. yes (not factual, not helpful)
3. no
4. yes
5. yes
6. yes
7. no
8. yes

Follow-up: Discuss how the statements that sound like gossip could hurt the object of the statement. If we assume that the information is not true, how does that make the situation even worse? How could someone stop the gossip if they were to hear these statements? If the information is true, how could you do something to help the object of the statement.

Gossip

Is this gossip? Write YES or NO on the lines.

1. If someone tells you that her cat died.   _____

2. If someone tells you that he heard Fred's brother is going to prison for killing someone.   _____

3. If someone tells you she likes your art project   _____

4. If someone tells you that Mary was cheating on the test and that she heard Mary cheats on every assignment.   _____

5. If someone tells you that the teacher is a drunk.   _____

6. If someone tells you that Pete has to go to the doctor for diet pills because he is so fat.   _____

7. If someone tells you that John is going to Walt Disney World for vacation.   _____

8. If someone tells you that Amy lied to her father about going over to Jane's house and her father is going to ground her for a year.   _____

IV-15 Answering Questions Appropriately

Objective:

The student will identify characters who are answering questions politely and appropriately.

Rationale:

Smart answers are very annoying, especially when the intent is to avoid answering the question altogether. There is a time to be funny and get laughs and silly answers to possibly obvious questions. When someone, especially an older person or stranger, asks a question, it should be answered directly and politely.

Thinking Questions:

1. What are some questions that you get asked at home? *(where have you been, do you have any homework, where are you going, etc.)*

2. When someone asks you a question, what kind of answer do you think you should give? *(the answer to the question)*

3. If someone asks, "Is this book yours?" and you answer, "Shut up," is that answering the question? *(no)*

4. If you would say, "Yes, now shut up," is that answering the question? *(yes, but not very politely)*

5. What could be changed to make that answer more appropriate? *(leave off the "shut up")*

6. If someone asks you a question while you are busy or thinking about something else, how could you still answer the question or person politely? *(explain that you are busy, ask them to come back later, tell them that you need more time to think about it, etc.)*

Activity:

Directions: Students are to read the cartoons on the worksheet and decide whether or not the person answering the question was polite and appropriate. They are to write YES or NO in the boxes.

   Answers: 1. no   2. yes   3. yes   4. no   5. no   6. yes

   Follow-up: Discuss why the characters who did not respond appropriately were impolite or did not accurately answer the question. Was the girl in number 1 paying attention to the question at all? *(based on the condition of her room, it would seem that she wasn't listening very well!)*

Answering Questions Appropriately

Is the person in the cartoon answering the question appropriately? Write YES or NO in the box.

IV-16 Using Good Language

Objective:

The student will identify or supply appropriate words to convey displeasure or excitement as an alternative to crude or vulgar comments.

Rationale:

It has become sadly commonplace for people to use vulgar words, curses, or swear words without giving them a second thought. In most settings, these words and this type of language would be extremely offensive. Unfortunately, people pick up usage of this type of language easily and often from those at home. In this lesson, students will examine situations in which it may be tempting to use expletives or "bad" language, but for which other words can convey the thoughts and feelings less offensively.

Thinking Questions:

1. Have you ever heard anyone say, "Use good language"? What does that mean? (*choose different words, don't say that, don't swear, etc.*)

2. Some people use words that are vulgar or offensive, or words that are not appropriate for the time and place. Why do you think this would show bad manners? (*other people might not want to hear those words, they would find them offensive, shows disrespect if you know that and use them anyway, etc.*)

3. Why do you think some people swear or curse? (*they are angry, want to get attention, think it makes them sound tough and grown-up, etc.*)

4. Why aren't those words appropriate for being in public? (*they are offensive to other people, impolite*)

5. Some words make fun of racial or ethnic or other groups of people. How could these words hurt someone else? (*makes the other person feel apart from the group, not respected, ridiculed, want to retaliate, etc.*)

6. Sometimes you might be in a situation where you can't help but listen to offensive language, such as at the movies. What are some ways to not make a big deal about the words? (*don't repeat them, don't get silly about it, recognize the words as offensive but don't start using them, etc.*)

Activity:

Directions: Students are to fill in comments that you could say in each situation without using bad or offensive language.

    Answers: (examples)

1. OWWWWW!
2. No, thank you.
3. Bad dog!
4. He has some problems, but he's a good neighbor.

    Follow-up: Have students share their ideas for the worksheet character's comments. What ideas do students have for expressing their anger or frustration besides using words?

Using Good Language

What could you say in each of the following situations to express yourself but still use good language?

1. Hitting your hand with a hammer.

2. Looking at food you don't like.

3. Finding out that your dog ripped up your favorite poster.

4. Talking about a handicapped neighbor.

IV-17 Wearing the Right Clothes

Objective:

The student will draw appropriate clothing for a given occasion or situation.

Rationale:

It would be nice if we could always live in comfortable clothes—whatever that means for the individual! Some occasions call for more formal clothing, and some situations depend on the weather, the time of day, and the intent of the event to help us know how to dress. In this lesson, students are to consider several situations that require thoughtful dressing and decide what would be appropriate.

Thinking Questions:

1. Why do people make a fuss about wearing the right clothes? *(want you to look nice, want to look like everybody else, etc.)*

2. How does your appearance affect what people think of you? *(shows you took time to think about the occasion, shows you want to look your best, know about popular styles, etc.)*

3. Do you ever have to get "dressed up" for something? What? *(going out to eat, to a restaurant, to church, to a wedding, etc.)*

4. Why do you think it's important to look as nice as you can on some occasions? *(everyone else will probably be dressed up, you won't be getting dirty anyhow, it might be fun to dress up, etc.)*

5. What are some occasions when you can wear anything you want? *(playing outside, after school, Saturday, etc.)*

6. Why do you think your parents would care if you went for a walk in the mud wearing your best clothes and shoes? *(it costs money to get them cleaned, it puts wear and tear on expensive items, etc.)*

7. Would you wear a suit (boys) or nice dress (girls) to ride your bike? Why/why not? *(probably not—it wouldn't be comfortable)*

Activity:

Directions: The student is to draw a picture of a person wearing appropriate clothing for the given occasion. Encourage students to add details and to be creative with their drawings.

Answers: (examples)

1. suit or nice dress
2. T-shirt and jeans
3. jeans or skirt
4. pajamas
5. costume
6. nice clothes

Follow-up: Discuss ideas and share drawings with the class. If someone didn't have a lot of money or a lot of clothes, how could they still look nice in most situations?

Wearing the Right Clothes

Draw a picture of what would be appropriate to wear in each of the following situations:

1. a wedding

2. playing ball in the park

3. a normal day at school

4. going to bed

5. going trick-or-treating

6. getting your family picture taken at a studio for holiday cards

---

IV-18 Thank-You Notes

Objective:

The student will identify situations for which a thank-you note would be appropriate.

Rationale:

It isn't necessary to send formal, written thank-you notes for many occasions, but it is a very thoughtful gesture to thank someone who has spent money on you, sent a gift, or taken the time to do something special for you. Children who can be taught to send a thank-you note as a matter of course for such things will be highly esteemed! In this lesson, examples for such occasions are presented for discussion.

Thinking Questions:

1. What is the nicest thing someone has ever done for you or given you? *(ask for examples)*

2. How did you let that person know you appreciated what he or she did for you? *(thanked them, reciprocated, etc.)*

3. What is the purpose of a thank-you note? *(to show your appreciation)*

4. How is writing a thank-you note to someone different from just telling them "thanks" and leaving it at that? *(it's lasting, takes time to write, shows that you made an effort, really appreciated their gift, etc.)*

5. When is it polite to send a written thank-you note to someone? *(if they live far away, if someone gave you a gift, if someone did something very special for you, etc.)*

6. What else could you say in a note besides just "thank you"? *(tell why you appreciated the gift, tell how you will use it, compliment the giver on what good taste they have, pass along any compliments you received on the gift, etc.)*

Activity:

Directions: Students are to examine the situations on the worksheet and to decide which are good reasons to send a thank-you note to the person involved. They are then to write the number of the situation on the thank-you note at the bottom.

Answers: 1, 4, 6, 10

Follow-up: Discuss why the selected answers would warrant a thank-you note. What extra effort was shown in number 10?

Thank-You Notes

For which of these situations would you send a thank-you note to someone? Write the <u>numbers</u> in the thank-you note at the bottom.

1. a birthday gift from Aunt Zelda

2. someone lends you a pencil at school

3. a friend lends you a dollar

4. a friend's family invites you to spend a week at their lake cottage

5. a friend's older brother takes you to the movies

6. your grandmother gives you $50 for Christmas

7. you go to a cookout at your neighbor's house

8. you spend the night at your best friend's house

9. your sister gives you an old sweater that's too small for her

10. a friend's dad takes you to a baseball game, buys you dinner at a very expensive restaurant, and then takes you to meet the players and get their autographs and pictures

IV-19 R.S.V.P.

Objective:

The student will identify the abbreviation R.S.V.P. as a request to call the sender of an invitation if you can attend the event.

Rationale:

The letters R.S.V.P. are from the French—*répondez s'il vous plaît*—which means "please answer." When an invitation is given, it is common courtesy to let the host know if you can attend or not, especially if R.S.V.P. is written on the invitation. In some cases an exact head count is necessary for transporting people to another place, ordering tickets in advance, or getting enough chairs. If the courtesy of a reply is requested, it should be honored.

Thinking Questions:

1. Have you ever gotten an invitation to go to something special? What? *(probably a party, picnic, sleepover, etc.)*

2. What kind of information is usually given on the invitation? *(who is giving the party, where it will be, times, other details)*

3. What does R.S.V.P. mean on an invitation? *(call the host to let them know if you can come or not)*

4. Why do you think the person who sends the invitation wants you to let them know if you can come? *(so they'll know how many people to prepare for)*

5. What could happen if twenty people were invited to a pizza party and nobody called to let the host know they were coming? *(they could order too many pizzas, too few, not have enough drinks, etc.)*

6. When are you supposed to call the host about the invitation? *(when you know you can or cannot make it, or by the time specified on the invitation)*

Activity:

Directions: The student is given a sample invitation with questions about information on the invitation. Answers should be written on the lines at the bottom.

Answers:		
1. Roger and Frank	5. Roger	
2. 1 o'clock	6. 324-5827	
3. birthday	7. by Saturday, July 5	
4. Monday, July 7	8. call to let them know if you can attend	

R.S.V.P.

Answer the questions below about the invitation that you just received.

It's a Birthday Party!

For: Jason Smith

At: Roger's house - 101 W. Third St.

On: Monday, July 7 From: 1:00 to 3:30

Given By: Roger and Frank

R.S.V.P. to: Roger 324-5827

by: Saturday, July 5

1. Who is giving the party? _____

2. What time does it start? _____

3. What kind of party is it? _____

4. When is the party? _____

5. Who are you supposed to call? _____

6. What is the phone number? _____

7. When are you supposed to let him know if you can come or not? _____

8. What does R.S.V.P. mean? _____

IV-20 The Golden Rule

Objective:

The student will state the essence of the Golden Rule and identify examples of how people would appreciate being treated.

Rationale:

No matter what is one's background, religious orientation, or political affiliation, most people would agree that the principle behind what is commonly called the Golden Rule—do unto others as you would have them do unto you—reflects a good social attitude. In this final lesson, students are directed to think about how they would like to be treated by others.

Thinking Questions:

1. What is meant by the Golden Rule? *(it is a famous principle to live by involving how to treat others)*

2. What are the words to the rule? *(do unto others as you would have them do unto you, treat others as you would like to be treated, etc.)*

3. What does it mean? *(just what it says—treat other people the same way you would like to be treated)*

4. Should you only treat others this way who are just like you—the same age, race, nationality? *(no, everyone)*

5. What would things be like if everyone treated everyone else with kindness and respect? *(we'll probably never know, but it would be wonderful!)*

Activity:

Directions: The student is to draw a happy face or a sad face next to the question to indicate whether or not he or she would like to be treated in the manner indicated.

Answers: (probably)

1. happy	3. happy	5. happy	7. happy
2. sad	4. happy	6. sad	8. happy

Follow-up: Have students discuss their own particular "pet peeves" as far as how they would like to be treated by others if it does not appear on the worksheet. What types of problems or disagreements are most predominant in their social circles? Why doesn't everyone follow the Golden Rule if it is such a good idea?

The Golden Rule

Draw a smiling face if you would like someone to treat you this way. Draw a frowning face if you would not like this kind of treatment.

Do unto others as you would have them do unto you!

Would you like . . .

1. someone to smile at you if you were frightened in a new place?

2. someone to laugh when you made a mistake?

3. someone to invite you when everyone else in your class was invited to a party or game?

4. someone to help you if you didn't understand something?

5. someone to listen to you if you had a problem and wanted to talk about it?

6. someone to make fun of the way you walk or talk?

7. someone to forgive and forget if you make a mistake?

8. someone to be your friend at all times, not just when there is no one else around?